"Elegantly written and intensely personal, Japaridze navigates here the nuances and complexities of Georgian and Russian nostalgia, memory, and identity. Far from a typical assessment of Stalin, this book offers a glimpse into current Russian and Georgian societies via their simultaneous adulation and demonization of the former dictator." — **Julie A. George**, City University of New York

"As a Georgian herself, Japaridze presents an experimental, fascinating, and impressionistic view of Stalin's legacy in Soviet and post-Soviet Georgia. In contrast to the traditional academic studies of Stalin's biography and Stalinism in the Soviet Union, Japaridze offers her own interpretation of Stalin's legacy based on her own impressions after her visits to Stalin's birthplace in Georgia. Concentrating on three topics—nostalgia, trauma, and nationalism—Japaridze distinctly explains Stalin's legacy in post-Soviet Georgia, which can help us understand the recent developments in post-Soviet space—especially the rise of Stalin's nostalgia in Putin's Russia today." — **Sergei Zhuk**, Ball State University

"Japaridze's book is a personal tour de force. Although it is her first work, it places her squarely in the courageous intellectual and social tradition of Hannah Arendt, whose groundbreaking work *The Human Condition* is as powerfully emotive as ever. But Japaridze offers a delightful twist—a personal touch. Her book is not just an interpretation of Stalin as viewed in history and by the present generations, but it is also a down-to-earth and psychological deep dive into the yearning and emotional needs of Georgians and Russians, as well as people everywhere. The brilliance of this book is Japaridze's discovery of another Stalin—not the Georgian or Russian Stalin, but a 'Third Stalin,' one not bound by geography, time, or even facts. The 'Third Stalin' is a myth created to make individual Russians and Georgians feel proud through his exploits, be it victory in the Great Patriotic War or through the acclaimed international status accorded to Georgia, a small country. Pride ironically also has the virtue of soothing and justifying the enduring pain of the historic injustices for the survivors and millennials. Japaridze's natural genius is that she demonstrates thorough storytelling—as well as traditional analysis—that we all want to feel good about ourselves, with the consequence that myth creation becomes our opium, our nostalgia, our fantasy. This book is a must-read, and a sequel in keeping with the Arendt tradition is now our demand."
— **Jenik Radon**, Columbia University

"In her distinctly personal yet historically precise journey, Japaridze brings to life the complex personality and cult of 'personality, trauma, nationalism, and nostalgia' that was the multifaceted history and legacy of Josef Stalin. Written with the backdrop of her own Georgian family that lived through and suffered during Stalin's reign, Japaridze's deft handling of history and competing global, Soviet, Russian, and Georgian narratives of the enigma that was Stalin, and his different legacies, is remarkably well-done. For one who himself traveled during Georgia's fateful summer of 1989 to Stalin's birthplace in Gori where Japaridze's meticulously researched story begins and ends, this beautifully written book and personal journey is remarkably authentic. It is a must-read for those interested in this specific period and theme, as well as for those curious, expansive readers simply desirous of a fascinating, colorfully written historical and personal experience." — **Peter Zwack**, Wilson Center

"Vladimir Lenin's body lies disintegrating discreetly in the Mausoleum, but the various avatars of Joseph Stalin haunt both his Georgian birthplace and the triumphant Red Square parades celebrating 'his victory.' In one, the self-appointed dialectician is a local boy who showed the Russians how and what for, while the other is the heir of the tsars and a political ancestor of Vladimir Putin. Japaridze is well-qualified to consider these prismatic reflections of Stalin's posthumous reputation in the former Soviet Union. Born in Georgia and reared in Moscow, she saw her father spend his post-Soviet days back in Tbilisi where her mother nursed the memory of a purged grandparent; she is therefore well-aware of the many shades of grey in Stalin's shadow. But she also shows how the black-and-white caricatures of detractors and defenders alike obscure Koba's genuine history, distorting his retrospective image into a post-revolutionary Rorschach test to evoke their own political psychoses and to advance their contemporary political agendas." — **Ian Williams**, Bard College

Stalin's Millennials

Stalin's Millennials

Nostalgia, Trauma, and Nationalism

Tinatin Japaridze

LEXINGTON BOOKS
Lanham • Boulder • New York • London

Published by Lexington Books
An imprint of The Rowman & Littlefield Publishing Group, Inc.
4501 Forbes Boulevard, Suite 200, Lanham, Maryland 20706
www.rowman.com

86-90 Paul Street, London EC2A 4NE

Copyright © 2022 by The Rowman & Littlefield Publishing Group, Inc.

All rights reserved. No part of this book may be reproduced in any form or by any electronic or mechanical means, including information storage and retrieval systems, without written permission from the publisher, except by a reviewer who may quote passages in a review.

British Library Cataloguing in Publication Information Available

Library of Congress Cataloging-in-Publication Data

Names: Japaridze, Tinatin, author.
Title: Stalin's millennials : nostalgia, trauma, and nationalism / Tinatin Japaridze.
Other titles: Nostalgia, trauma, and nationalism
Description: Lanham : Lexington Books, [2022] | Includes bibliographical references and index. | Summary: "This book examines Stalin's increasing popularity in his native Georgia and in Putin's Russia. Through extensive field research, political commentary, and autobiographical elements from the perspective of the post-Soviet millennial generation, the author analyzes how Stalin's image is manipulated and exploited for political gain"— Provided by publisher.
Identifiers: LCCN 2021053147 (print) | LCCN 2021053148 (ebook) | ISBN 9781793641861 (cloth) | 9781793641885 (paperback) | ISBN 9781793641878 (epub)
Subjects: LCSH: Stalin, Joseph, 1878–1953—Public opinion. | Stalin, Joseph, 1878–1953—Influence. | Public opinion—Georgia (Republic) | Public opinion—Russia (Federation) | Nostalgia—Georgia (Republic) | Nationalism—Georgia (Republic) | Generation Y—Georgia (Republic)—Attitudes. | Georgia (Republic)—History. | Soviet Union—History. | Japaridze, Tinatin.
Classification: LCC DK268.S8 J37 2022 (print) | LCC DK268.S8 (ebook) | DDC 947.084/2092—dc23/eng/20211104
LC record available at https://lccn.loc.gov/2021053147
LC ebook record available at https://lccn.loc.gov/2021053148

Dedicated to Giviko, who refused to take me to the Lenin Mausoleum but never said no to a weekend spree to Gorbushka. We're forever a team—here, there, and everywhere.

Contents

Acknowledgments		xi
Introduction: A Trip to Gori		1
I	Stalin: Nostalgia for the Past, Present, and Future	15
II	Georgian Man of Borderlands	35
III	Soviet Red Tsar	65
IV	Tale of the Third Stalin	85
V	Cult of Personality	97
VI	Trauma and Nationalism	115
VII	Nostalgia	127
Conclusion: Back to Gori		133
Bibliography		137
Index		155
About the Author		159

Acknowledgments

First and foremost, I would like to express my most sincere gratitude to my editor, Eric Kuntzman, who took a chance on a new author without a doctoral degree but with an uncommon idea and a passion for exploring this complex topic. As I was continuously shying away from delving into personal experiences using the prism of Joseph Stalin and his tripartite legacy, Eric tirelessly encouraged me to be brave and daring in following my creative instincts. Alongside my editor, the entire Lexington Books editorial team, especially Jasper Mislak and Kasey Beduhn, were there from the first paragraphs to the very final edits. As a debut author, I could not have asked for a more supportive and caring collaboration, particularly in the midst of a global pandemic when the world had seemingly stopped turning, but this team kept me inspired and motivated every step of the way.

Special thanks to my mentors and reviewers, including but by no means limited to Frank Guridy, Bradley Gorski, Jenik Radon, and Anita Pisch for their continued and undivided support in creating and finalizing this monograph, for their enthusiasm, patience, motivation, compassion, and expertise. My incredible group of advisors at my academic home, the Harriman Institute at Columbia University, particularly my professor, Alexander Cooley, whose class on Soviet Legacies inspired the subject of this book—it all started with a one-page memo, but he encouraged me to pursue this topic further and delve deeper into these themes. My mentor and champion, Victoria Phillips, for all the years of incredible support, true passion for research, and for instilling in her students and mentees the deepest respect for the craft of responsible citation.

The Stalin Museum in Gori, especially Liana Oqropiridze and Ketevan Kukhalashvili for welcoming me on more than one occasion, for sharing their wealth of knowledge, incredible artifacts, and resources that were instrumental in the creation of this work. Moreover, I am highly indebted to the incredibly bright minds I had the privilege of interviewing for this book, and am very grateful for their generosity, insights, and fascinating reflections. All of the amazing scholars, researchers, and journalists whose works were cited and referenced throughout this book and served as the crucial foundation of the research conducted in writing this monograph—thank you from the bottom of my heart.

For supporting the past few years of in-country field trips, countless interviews, and archival research, I am immensely grateful to the CWar Fellowship, the PepsiCo Foundation, the University Consortium, the Carnegie Corporation, the School of General Studies, Columbia's Slavic Department, the European Institute at Columbia University, the University of Illinois Urbana-Champaign, and the Department of State's Program for Research and Training on Eastern Europe and Eurasia (Title VIII).

Last but never the least, I would like to thank my parents for believing in the idea and the motivation behind this book from day one—admittedly, long before I ever did. I love you with all my heart and will forever be grateful for having you in my life. I dedicate this monograph to my late father, Givi Japaridze, who was the creative force that always inspired, encouraged, and kept me motivated no matter what. You are sorely missed every minute of the day, but I am sincerely proud to have had the honor and good fortunate of being your daughter, and I truly hope that as you watch over me, you're smiling at the sight of a finished book that I know I could not have written without the many hours of tireless deliberations and debates about the legacies that we endlessly talked through together at all times of the day and night. Not a day goes by that I don't replay those conversations, savoring every word and every detail, but nevertheless, I am so happy that we were able to put a few of them on paper, including those included in this monograph. This one is for you, Dad.

Introduction

A Trip to Gori

"There are two Stalins," says Simon Sebag Montefiore, the author of *Young Stalin*. "The Russian Stalin and the Georgian Stalin."[1] While in the Russian version the twentieth-century titan's Georgian identity has been Russified, in its original Georgian variant, Ioseb "Koba"[2] Jughashvili is a son of a washerwoman and a cobbler from Gori who turned into a powerful modernizer and a crusader against the evil of fascism, and to this day, continues to be vehemently admired for his absolute power and deeply condemned for his ruthless totalitarianism.

A child of the waning Soviet Empire born at the wake of glasnost' and perestroika and into a society at the brink of change, collapse, and rebirth, I had long harbored deeply ingrained interest in the curious duality of the "Man of Borderlands"[3]—a phenomenon that, at least in the post-Soviet space, is often taken for granted. As a Georgian-born, Russian-bred student at a US institution, the perplexity of my own post-Soviet identity originally compelled me to delve into this topic. Fortunate to receive a grant from my academic home, the Harriman Institute[4] at Columbia University, in January of 2017, in the heat of New Year's celebrations, I embarked on a road trip to Joseph Stalin's birthplace in Gori, a small town of 47,000 people about 60 miles northwest of Tbilisi, where I hoped to dissect my compatriot's "mysterious figure."[5] When I revealed the purpose of my voyage to the taxi driver, Avtandil, who turned out to be a native of Gori, his face with prominent Georgian features gleamed with pride: "You had to go all the way to New York to learn about our Great Stalin? You could have just driven 45 minutes outside of Tbilisi!"

Truth be told, I was not the first traveler from the United States to visit Gori in search of Stalin. In a vivid, albeit subtly crafted report of her journey uncovering the Stalin legend, American documentary photographer, Margaret Bourke-White makes multiple attempts to fill in the many gaps of the

Soviet autocrat's early life by visiting his motherland. She travels to both Didi-Lelo, a tiny village on the outskirts of Tbilisi, and Gori—the two rivaling places that claimed to have single-handedly produced the Great Savior of the Soviet peoples. It was not until 1934 that the "citizens of Gori had won"[6] and were finally able to officially claim the local legend.

In August of 1954, eleven years after Bourke-White's visit, a group of four graduate students from my fellow Columbia University's Russian Institute, which would later become the Harriman Institute—Gay Humphrey, Francis B. Randall, Ted Curran, and Jeri Lindsky—also set off on an eight-week adventure across the Soviet Union to explore the late dictator's birthplace. In his lighthearted diary documenting what is reminiscent of a trip to Disneyland, Randall seems visibly humored by a brightly lit neon sign at the very entrance to the gorge town, proudly proclaiming in Ioseb Jughashvili's mother tongue: "Glory to the Great Stalin."[7] Over six decades later, as Avtandil's 1988 black GAZ-Volga, an unabashed relic and a perfect piece of late-Soviet luxury, rolled into Gori, in lieu of the neon sign I was greeted by a visual incarnation of the "Great Leader" on a glass façade of a local supermarket situated, symbolically, on Stalin Avenue.

The Columbia University students' trip took place one year after the autocrat's death, at which point it had long been established that Gori—not Didi-Lelo—was, in fact, his official place of birth. In his journal, Randall describes the small, "solid brick hut with two rooms" filled with "cute 19th-century furniture reinstated"[8] to recreate the mysterious childhood of one of history's most at once revered and despised figures. During her trip, Bourke-White also notes that compared to the "dozens of other houses"[9] scattered in and around the gorge town, there is nothing remarkable about this wooden house with "board floors, a porch with carved railings, and a roof with a chimney"[10]—except for the iconic hammer and sickle gracing its façade. To this day, the wooden one-story hut (which has since been "upgraded" to brick and timber) where little Soso, a diminutive used by his mother, was allegedly born in 1878, is still standing proud and strong, but its authenticity remains under a constant question mark.

In a paragraph that is quietly buried under the many layers of handwritten pages, Randall briefly mentions visiting a "museum of Stalin's life in the Caucasus."[11] However, it is not entirely clear as to which museum he is referring, as the current—and reportedly the only known—museum of Stalin in Gori opened three years after the Columbia students' visit to the Georgian SSR.[12] While the Stalin Museum was under construction between 1951 and 1954, its doors would remain sealed until 1957 when the aforementioned trip took place. The grand granite and marble shrine described by Randall boasts Koba Jughashvili's old police pictures and photographs of "illegal printing shops."[13] However, in a more revealing sentence, he mentions rather hastily that while the said museum tells numerous stories about the dictator's mother, there is virtually nothing to be seen or heard of his father. This observation, as I would discover firsthand, continues to hold true to this day.

Aside from the bronze statue[14] (removed on former Georgian president Mikheil Saakashvili's order), the Stalin Museum resembles its original décor and content. As the rest of the Soviet Union was busy toppling vestiges of the Soviet Dictator, one year after Khrushchev's 1956 de-Stalinization address and the mass unrest sparked by his "secret speech" across Georgia, the Stalin Museum's building was erected and dedicated to Joseph Stalin as a "conciliatory gesture" on the part of the Soviet leadership to their Georgian brothers and sisters. The current exhibition, which opened in the 1970s under Leonid Brezhnev, still adorns the walls of the impressive edifice a few steps from the dictator's modest home. Although the museum survived another wave of de-Stalinization policies of 1961, which included the removal of Stalin's body from the Lenin Mausoleum in Moscow's Red Square and the renaming of streets and avenues throughout many cities and towns in the USSR, the Gori museum did close in 1989 when the Eastern bloc began to collapse, and anti-Stalin discussions permeated the crumbling Soviet Union's political arena. The cultural establishment was reopened several years after the demise of the Soviet Union, primarily as a potent tourist attraction for foreign visitors.[15]

Inside the museum chronicling and still glorifying the Soviet ruler's life, the same sweeping marble staircase leads upstairs to a second-floor landing with Koba's bust in the heart of the room, accompanied by an imposing oil-on-canvas portrait of the Soviet leader. Books of young Stalin's poetry and his favorite Khvanchkara, a naturally semisweet bottle of Georgian red wine with his iconic visage engraved on the label, are for sale in the gift shop. These souvenirs remain popular among the many visitors of the tourist attraction who, according to the museum's long-time head guide, Ketevan Kukhalashvili, consist predominantly of foreigners.[16]

Ketevan Kukhalashvili highlights the difference in reinterpretation of Stalin and his political and historical legacies under the two opposing leaderships of the United National Movement (UNM), Mikheil Saakashvili's political party, and the currently ruling Georgian Dream founded by oligarch and philanthropist, Bidzina Ivanishvili, noting that during Saakashvili's presidency, the overall image of the museum rested on "the repressions and mass killings that occurred under Stalin's dictatorship."[17] According to Kukhalashvili, the sensitive question of Stalin's repressions was not explicitly tackled in the museum installations until 2009–2010, a decision brought to the fore by the August events of 2008. This would, however, change again under the incoming opposition coalition, the Georgian Dream party when the Stalin Museum underwent yet another reincarnation. Following Bidzina Ivanishvili's ascent to the prime ministerial seat in 2012, Kukhalashvili recalls a meeting organized at the Stalin Museum by Lasha Bakradze, Georgian historian and the director of the Giorgi Leonidze State Museum of Literature in Tbilisi. During this gathering, Bakradze emphasized the importance of studying the Stalin "phenomenon" and his legacy through a historical and not a political lens. In particular, Bakradze recommended creating a focus group consisting of historians to work on assembling and displaying "appropriate" exhibitions at the museum. However, Kukhalashvili laments that the recommendations set forth by the committee are "yet to be implemented."[18]

Most notably, only one "new" room—colloquially referred to as the "gulag cell" was added two years after the Russo-Georgian War of 2008 that now bears a direct, albeit still a reluctant, mention of crimes and purges conducted, by and large, *under* but not *by* Stalin. The dark walls of a modest, dimly lit hallway timidly showcase printouts of Khrushchev's Secret Speech and photographs of a handful of the countless brutally repressed families from Gori. The mass famines and forced collectivization, the infamous Hitler-Stalin Pact, and the partition of Eastern Europe, the Katyn massacre, and other dark pages from Soviet history of that era are hardly mentioned, if at all, but the leadership of the museum agrees that hiding from the past is not their prerogative.[19] "Of course, we cannot escape the truth," Kukhalashvili started, cautiously, "and the truth is that these events did occur, but these were difficult times."[20] Saved for last comes the holiest of holy relics: Stalin's bronze death mask, an eerie site, displayed in a small shrine-like amphitheater submerged in complete darkness. As though it were a mausoleum to a secular saint, visitors are guided through the room in silent, sacral contemplation.

After an entire day spent locked inside a historical capsule, entirely immune to any and all of the distractions of the world outside of the imposing walls and Kremlin-like carpeted corridors, a middle-aged man wearing a black Nike baseball cap casually walked into the marbled, Greco-Italian-style lobby. As though a visitor from an alternative reality, this time traveler from 2017 landed inside the marbled capsule stranded somewhere between 1878 and 1957. "I came back, as instructed, at 5:30 and waited outside, but you never came out," he addressed me, with a smirk. "I thought Koba's ghost had abducted you!" And suddenly it dawned on me that I had, indeed, asked the taxi driver, Avtandil, to pick me up before closing time of the museum. Unsurprisingly, I had spent close to eight hours stranded—at my own will—in a time machine with the meticulous guidance of the museum's staff. They were, of course, enlightening me with their own version of the Soviet "hero's" narrative. As aware as I was of the intricacies of historical interpolations that are generally founded on self-interest[21] and seldom entirely objective, there was something endearing and even contagious about these sweet Soviet *babushkas'*[22] passion and total cult-like dedication to the mission of spreading the tale of the great pride of the Georgian people.

As we were saying goodbye, one of the curators took me aside and whispered, "About that artifact you saw in Comrade Stalin's office downstairs." I nodded, recalling my question about a pair of leather boots that looked brand new, though they were exhibited as a pair worn by Stalin himself in the early 1950s. "Well, let me tell you a secret—and you cannot tell a soul," the lady looked straight into my eyes, as though she were about to share the deepest secret ever confided to another human being. "These boots never belonged to him." She justified this confession by explaining that it was one thing to unveil the story of *batoni Stalini*[23] to foreign tourists but sharing accurate historical facts with no embroidery for the sake of embellishment entailed a different level of responsibility when the visitor was a native child of the Georgian soil.[24] The way she smiled, warmly and ever so timidly, I realized these words were conveyed as a compliment, and I readily accepted it as such. Somehow, by the mere fact of my Georgian heritage, she wanted me to believe that I was entitled to—at least *her version*—of factual information. Meanwhile, foreigners like Randall et al. and Bourke-White were strangers in a strange land, and therefore, their non-Georgianness granted them access to a different version of the Stalin story, but nonetheless, one that was just as compelling.

Leaving Gori and en route back to Tbilisi, comfortably nestled inside Avtandil's time machine—onyx black Volga, I began to ponder whether unlike what Simon Sebag Montefiore argues, there are not *two* but rather *three* Stalins carefully nestled inside a nesting doll or *matryoshka*: the Georgian Koba accessible exclusively to Georgians, the fearless Soviet victor of the Great Patriotic War and a bestselling Russian commodity meant for both domestic and foreign consumption, and the third Stalin—a phenomenon that is seldom touched by historians who focus their attention on the figure of Stalin who belongs to history, archives, and the Soviet past at large, but instead seen through the prism of post-Soviet millennials.

Through the afternoon's perusal of the museum and strolling through the streets of Gori, it had dawned on me that the third Stalin encompasses both Georgian and Soviet variants, as well as another layer that is not spatially tied to any one country or culture. This is Joseph Stalin, the great and ruthless manager who defeated Nazi Germany, a historical, at times even mythologized figure at the heart of a global opus, heavily redacted, frequently leaving out the Great Terror, Siberian labor camps, forced collectivization, and mass starvation that occurred under the leadership of the Soviet Commander in Chief. In this version, the complex figure of Stalin is often not too dissimilar to the one presented, also for foreign consumption, at the Stalin

Museum in Gori, which primarily targets visitors from abroad and less so locals and former Soviets. By the same token, this same Stalin is presented in the same mythological style and format as the source of all evil, the bloody dictator who killed for the sake of killing, ruthlessly eradicated for the sake of eradication.

While Avtandil expertly navigated the backstreets as only a true local can, I pondered about the fog of silence throughout the exhibit and the absence of artifacts that revealed more than even their presence ever could. The subtlest of references to the Great Purges of 1937–1938 in the exposition, save for a small, dark room skillfully tucked away from prying eyes, was the most unexpected aspect of the tour—an approach reminiscent of the intentional policy of national forgetting of the majority of post-Soviet politics. This peculiar detail—or rather lack of it—left me baffled. Momentarily, I wondered if, indeed, like Kukhalashvili asserted in hushed tones as we made our way toward the exit, Comrade Stalin had been deliberately kept in the dark about the Great Terror operations conducted by his cronies, while he led the nation toward socialism and fought for equality for all. The mixed historical narratives and lack of concrete data clad in vagueness and blur pertaining to the Great Purges was the initial source of my interest in the Stalin question and later evolved into absolute terror and fascination with the regime of this period. Alas, as was sadly the case for many born in our part of the world, the darkest pages of this history hit painfully close to home.

In the heart of Tbilisi's historic Art Nouveau neighborhood of Sololaki district, amid the city's architectural eclecticism lies a beautiful mansion, colloquially coined by the locals as the famous "Italian villa." Located on Geronti Kikodze Street #11, the house was built in 1914 by prominent Soviet architect of Armenian descent, Gabriel Ter-Mikelov. The mansion with a majestically crafted stone balcony overlooking a beautiful Italian Renaissance-style garden belonged to two brothers, Arkady and Arshak Milov, at the time prominent figures in the oil-trading sector. Shortly after the 1917 Revolution, the main floor of the mansion was used as a reception area for registering white army officers in the early days of Soviet occupation of the Georgian Democratic Republic, and those who failed to appear and register in person were sent to labor camps. Soon thereafter, the mansion became a famous home to high-ranking communist officials in the Georgian SSR. The residents of this house included Philipe Makharadze,[25] member of the Central Committee Bureau of the Communist Party of Georgian Soviet Socialist Republic, and member of the Soviet Supreme Council, Mamia Orakhelashvili, Old Bolshevik and one of the initiators of Georgia's Sovietization, among other prominent representatives of the Soviet ruling elite and the Communist Party of the Soviet Union at large.[26]

Even at the tail end of the Soviet period, veiled underneath many layers of highly controlled caution and morbid curiosity, clad in a dark, heavy shawl of mystery and taboo, Stalin's violent, bloody purges were seldom discussed around family dinner tables—with the exception of rare kitchen debates on late winter's nights. In this regard, my Georgian family was no exception to this generally accepted and seldom challenged etiquette—be it out of fear, a lingering sense of terror, or perhaps even shame, something I was not aware of until after many years of reflection and analysis of this complicated array of emotions.

As information about the terrifying chapter in our national history began to emerge and spread with the end of the Soviet era, statues of Stalin were toppled, and people began to talk more openly, reopening old but unhealed wounds and reaching for forbidden memories that until now had been shielded from prying eyes. I was first introduced to the tragic story of one of the residents of the beautiful "Italian villa" that later became known as the "Terror House"—my great-aunt, Nina Chichua-Bedia, a victim of Joseph Stalin's political repression campaign, when my maternal grandmother showed me an unscathed photograph of a beautiful woman with curly locks, big brown eyes, and full lips, resting regally in a hammock, that had survived decades of tumultuous Soviet history. Now, in the chaotic mid-1990s, her story was no longer carefully tucked away, buried inside countless pages of volumes of dog-eared books. The vast national and deeply personal traumatic impact of Stalin-era repressions were frequently unaddressed, but its reverberations sustained despite decades of silence and secrecy.

On December 7, 1937, on the basis of a resolution passed by the People's Commissariat for Internal Affairs or NKVD[27] Troika, the Soviet Secret Service run by Lavrenti Beria, the Secretary of the Central Committee of the Georgian SSR, Nina Chichua-Bedia was sentenced to execution with total confiscation of property. Nina Chichua-Bedia (b. 1905) was the wife of an Old Bolshevik, the director of the Georgian Institute of Party History, head of the Cultural Propaganda Department of the Central Committee in Georgian Soviet Socialist Republic, and editor in chief of *The Communist* newspaper, Erik (Ermile) Bedia. Bedia had penned the famed 1935 speech appropriated by Beria, one of Stalin's most trusted leaders during the Great Terror, "On the History of the Bolshevik Organizations in the Transcaucasia," which falsified the history of the revolutionary movement in the region and vastly exaggerated the role of Joseph Stalin.[28] It was this very speech that shaped the image of young Koba in Georgia and created the "cult" of Stalin in his native country and throughout the Soviet Union. The report was well-received by Comrade Stalin and, shortly thereafter, was also published as a separate book for mass circulation and was included into Soviet school curricula as a mandatory reading. According to historian Lasha Bakradze, after Beria's 1935 speech, further studies exploring the path of young Stalin to the throne of the Soviet Union were discontinued, while existing narratives were either banned or carefully recrafted to fit with the revised narrative promoted by the party.[29]

In 1937, Nina Chichua-Bedia exposed Lavrenti Beria and his cronies to the Communist Party, and he, in turn, viciously threatened her: "You talk too much! I shall rip your tongue out!" Before long, Beria would manifest his threat into reality, first arresting and executing Erik Bedia, followed by his wife—my great-aunt, Nina. According to the official narrative pursued by the Party, "The People's Commissariat of Internal Affairs of the Georgian SSR exposed and liquidated large anti-Soviet and right-wing terrorist organization."[30] The Commissariat believed that the organization's mission was to overthrow Soviet authority, separate Georgia from the USSR, and establish an independent state of Georgia. To this end, the Commissariat claimed that the members of the organization were plotting terrorist attacks against officials of Soviet government and the Communist Party of the Soviet Union (CPSU). "They [the alleged right-wing terrorist organization] planned to organize acts of sabotage and terrorist attacks to prevent economic and military development."[31]

The investigation directly pointed the finger at Nina Chichua-Bedia who, the NKVD claimed, was the wife of one of the heads of this "anti-Soviet, right-wing terrorist organization" in Georgia and thus keenly aware of the planned acts of sabotage and terrorism targeting Stalin's most trusted confidant, Beria. Nina, who was allegedly violently beaten (some claim she was even raped) and later shot by Beria himself in his lavish study, was accused of "encouraging her husband's ideology, [and moreover], provoking and motivating him to actively engage in these acts of terrorism."[32]

Following the USSR's glorious victory in the Great Patriotic War, on January 12, 1946, Nina's mother and my mother's paternal grandmother, Ekaterine Chichua wrote a letter to Generalissimo Stalin: "My daughter Nina Chichua-Bedia was born in 1905, and on October 19, 1937, she was arrested by the NKVD's Georgian SSR chapter. Since then, I have received no news of her. Now that our renowned Red Army has gained victory over the [fascist] enemy, please do not decline my request and do inform me if my daughter is alive, and if possible, of her whereabouts."[33]

My great-aunt's ultimate fate was no different from many other members of a tightly knit milieu known at the time as the Soviet aristocracy who openly opposed the Great Terror and its organizers. Some applauded Nina for the courage that she demonstrated in her bravery to stand up to the regime no matter the consequences by shedding light on the Communist Party's criminal activities. But there were also those who condemned her recklessness and naivete. Many argued that the fate of the victims had already been predetermined, and therefore, any opposition to the terror machine was, in and of itself, futile if not foolish. There were also some who dismissed Nina's actions as ill-informed, arguing that had it not been for Comrade Stalin's and his fellow Party members' strength and resilience, the Soviet Union and the rest of the free world would have fallen prey to the Nazi regime. Without Stalin, they still claim, with his countless flaws and imperfections, there would have been no freedom or victory over the enemy. This belief continues to color and actively drive the current Stalin narrative that is as complex and contradictory as ever today—not only in Russia but also in former Soviet Georgia.

Due to the total absence of a legal framework under which those like Nina and her husband were arrested and many repressed, the unspoken attitude of "there must have been a reason if they were repressed" was omnipresent in the silences surrounding the tragic pages in many Soviet families' histories. The silences were often accompanied by traces of shame and guilt. Even after the fear itself began to dissipate with time, as the Great Purges were not only publicly discussed in the media but also condemned by state authorities, these memories remained largely suppressed both on conscious and subconscious levels. Inevitably, in most cases, the unexamined issues and deeply internalized fear and shame ultimately produced trauma often inherited on a transgenerational level.[34]

And yet through all of the pain and tragedy that the Stalin regime had imposed upon my family, like many millions of families throughout the region, as I stared through the blurry window of Avtandil's Volga, I wondered if it was at all conceivable that, after the tragedy my very own family had endured, I was still interested and even fascinated by the figure of Stalin—be it real, historical, or purely metaphysical and mythological—and had traveled from the other side of the world to visit his hometown in a tireless attempt to learn more about the Man of the Borderlands. But was I so unique in this pursuit and the peculiarity of synchronous admiration and hatred of the greatness and terror? Was this something uniquely Georgian of me? Or perhaps more telling of the remnants of Soviet traces that were clearly still alive, albeit partially dormant until now, deep inside of my identity and psyche? It was at that moment, as I took in the picturesque scenery of a native country that for better or worse I had shared with Ioseb Vissarionovich Jughashvili, that I realized that, with a brief trip to Gori, his hometown, I had embarked on a journey to understand this paradox within our society and my own identity that was pining for answers, already suspecting that these answers would likely result in even greater, unanswered questions.

Many a book has been penned in the post-Holocaust literature, with the "third generation" of victims' family members adding their voices to the chorus in a conversation on post-memory and intergenerational transmission of grief and trauma. Although not directly exposed to the "secondhand smoke" of Thane Rosenbaum's novel by the same title, the third generation—in this instance, my generation—is clinging onto the fast-declining number of interlocuters who could serve as direct witnesses of our loved ones' fates. These quests do not deter but instead motivate questions that often result in still more unanswered queries that continue to plague us. Victoria Aarons and Alan Berger coin this compulsion-like condition a frustrated remembrance that transports us back in imagined time in search of moral accountability and ethical reckoning, as a result forming a fraught identity of the third generation.[35]

The more I thought of Montefiore's two Stalins, the more relevant and compelling the idea of the enigmatic third Stalin was beginning to feel in the midst of ongoing political and historical revisionism in the post-Soviet space. This third Stalin explored through the prism of a post-Soviet millennial is, unlike the other two Stalins of Montefiore, not geographically attached to any one country but, instead, temporally most relevant and forever alive, yet, by the same token, intangible, in a fluid state of malleability, and for these very reasons—eternally enigmatic, fascinating and, oddly, ever so relevant. This very Stalin, or rather the phantom of Stalin, is tirelessly manipulated as a cultural trope—less so by historians but increasingly by political leaders in all parts of the world, not solely limited to the Eurasian region, to both criticize and justify, condemn and condone policies and decision-making. But perhaps above all else, the "Third Stalin" has become a source of endless—and, frequently, expertly manipulated—nostalgia, not only in Russia but also in his native Georgia, that continues to grapple with a complex array of emotions vis-à-vis its rebellious son turned Dictator.

Perhaps the most unique feature of the Third Stalin in a matryoshka-like form that encapsulates multiple layers of this polemic figure is the simultaneously ephemeral intangibility, constant malleability and continuity of a legacy on the one hand, and on the other, a direct reflection of a nation, its psyche and fluid identity—or rather, multiple identities at once—as seen through the vestiges of a historical, political, and cultural depiction of a man, and vicariously through him, of an entire epoch. This third Stalin is the temporal and spatially flexible, fluid Stalin that holds the other two parts—Georgian and Soviet Russian Stalins—together and fully intact. As divided and divisive as the other two layers are by their sheer nature of incompatibility and a plethora of contradictions, this construct acts as a connecting thread between Georgian Koba and Soviet Comrade Stalin, and, as an extension, between Georgia and Russia writ large.

As we entered a highway—which Avtandil proudly emphasized had been constructed under Saakashvili's leadership—that, like an artery, connects Tbilisi to the rest of the country, I pondered how this third Stalin may not solely be the depiction of Joseph Stalin in our minds and our own reflections of that complicated era but also a layer in which we find traces of Vladimir Putin, Georgia's first president Zviad Gamsakhurdia, Mikheil Saakashvili—to name but a few of the leaders who, for better or worse, used and at times abused the Stalin narratives and legacies to bend, justify, and rewrite their own modern-day policies that, at first glance, were not at all related to history.

There is a particularly somber, albeit enigmatic attribute of this third Stalin which has less to do with Joseph Vissarionovich Stalin as a historical and political figure, and far more to do with us—or rather, a mythical, often imaginary reflection of us—the post-Soviet generation—with all of our fears, trauma, dreams of greatness, and related morbid curiosity vis-à-vis the atrocities of this period of simultaneous glory and terror. The motivation of this narrative written from the perspective of what is referred to in modern parlance as the Millennial post-Soviet Generation is to demonstrate that it is not only historians, politicians, and policymakers that are guilty of manipulating Stalin legacies but also us, the civilians, who, oftentimes on an entirely subconscious level, dissect these many layers of memory, with all of its inevitable distortions, cracks, traces of crooked and not always justifiable nostalgia, and ultimately view Stalin through this highly subjective and personal prism.

This book is not a biography of one of the most controversial historical figures of the past century. Neither does it pretend to be a historical narrative per se. Rather, through a combination of sociopolitical commentary and autobiographical elements that are uncommon in monographs of this kind, the attempt is to explore how Joseph Stalin's complex legacies and the conflicting cult of his irreconcilable tripartite of personalities still loom over the region as a whole, including Russia and, perhaps to an even deeper extent, Koba's native land—now the independent Republic of Georgia, caught between its unreconciled Soviet past and the potential future within the European Union. Through a constantly evolving lens of the generation of post-Soviet millennials, the aim of this book is to delve into the nuances and intricacies of the proposed "Third Stalin"—the fear, the nostalgia, the fascination—increasingly dominating current debates and decision-making in the modern, post-Soviet sociopolitical arena.

Revisiting history allows us to simultaneously denaturalize the present and the past. The sheer realization that we will never gain a fully detailed, concrete picture of what factually occurred at a given time makes us more amenable to embracing the asymmetrical patterns of bits of colored glass reflecting images of memories, both authentic and imagined. All of these snippets eventually bleed into one another, producing figments that in the end culminate in what we call history, ever changing, malleable but never truly finalized. Gazing through a kaleidoscope of memories, a mosaic of diverse pieces culminating in a legible portrait, we find that there are few definitive answers and even less accurate ones—swirling in perfect harmony, as though casting pebbles upon water, constantly reverberating in additional question marks like never-ending ripples on a blank shore that are meant to remain unresolved.

NOTES

1. Dan Bilefsky, "In Georgia, a Reverence for Stalin," *New York Times*, September 30, 2008. Web. http://www.nytimes.com/2008/10/01/world/europe/01stalin.html.

2. In his early years, Ioseb Jughashvili took the nickname Koba after the famous Georgian outlaw and a protagonist from a classic novella, *Nunu* by celebrated Georgian author Aleqkandre Qazbegi (1848–1893) whose writings young Stalin discovered as a student at the Tiflis seminary. Young Stalin's friend and later political adversary, Ioseb Iremashvili, wrote in 1932 that "Soso's ideal and dream-figure was Koba. . . . Koba had become Soso's god, the sense of his life. He wanted to become another Koba, as famous a fighter and hero as he. The figure of Koba would live again in him. From now on he called himself Koba and would not have us call him by any other name. His face would shine with pride when we called him 'Koba.'" See more: Ioseb Iremashvili, *Stalin and the Tragedy of the Georgians* (Berlin: Selbstverl, 1932.)

3. Alfred J. Rieber, "Stalin, Man of the Borderlands," *American Historical Review* 106, no. 5 (December 2001): 1651–91.

4. The Harriman Institute was formerly known as the Russian Institute at Columbia University. In 1982, the Russian Institute became the W. Averell Harriman Institute for the Advanced Study of the Soviet Union.

5. Ibid.

6. Margaret Bourke-White, *Shooting the Russian War* (New York: Simon & Shuster, 1942), 202.

7. Francis B. Randall, *Diary and Journal of Francis B. Randall*, Guide to the Gay Humphrey Matthaei and Francis B. Randall collection of Photographs, Films, and Clippings, 1954–2010 (1954); The Matthaei/Randall Collection of Photographs, Films, and Clippings, Box 1, Folder 1, Rare Book and Manuscript Library, Columbia University Library.

8. Bourke-White, 203.

9. Ibid.

10. Ibid.

11. Randall, *Diary and Journal of Francis B. Randall*.

12. Meaghan Beatley, "Stalin Museum: The Creepy Attraction in Georgia That Still Worships the Communist Leader Like a God," *Independent*, November 21, 2017. Web. https://www.independent.co.uk/travel/europe/stalin-museum-gori-georgia-open-joseph-communist-leader-dictator-death-mask-a8065256.html.

13. Ibid.

14. For more information about the statue and the city plan, see: *Sak'artvelos istoriisa da kulturis żeglta agceriloba*, vol. 5 (Tbilisi, 1990), 40–45.

15. According to the director of the Stalin Museum in Gori, Liana Oqropiridze, in 2016, the museum had a record year, welcoming over 92,000 visitors—39,000 more than the previous year. Most of the tourists visiting the museum hail from Russia, China, Iran, Israel, Poland, and Germany.

16. Ketevan Kukhalashvili, interview with author, January 8, 2017.

17. Ibid.

18. Ibid.

19. During the author's follow-up research trip to the Stalin Museum in April 2021, the director of the museum, Liana Oqropiridze shared relics from the forthcoming exhibit dedicated to the victims of the repressive regime, slated to open in the "gulag cell" in late 2021.

20. Ibid.

21. Marc Bloch, *The Historian's Craft* (New York: Vintage Books, 1964), 97.

22. In Russian: grandmothers.

23. In Georgian: Mr. Stalin.

24. Bloch, *The Historian's Craft*, p. 97.

25. Philipe (alt. spelling: Filipp) Makharadze lived in the "Italian villa" between 1921 and his death in 1941. The building was often referred to and still remains known in some circles as the "Makharadze's house." In 1923, Kikodze street was renamed after Makharadze before returning to its original name following the collapse of the Soviet Union. For a detailed history of toponyms of Tbilisi streets and the role of street naming in strengthening and cementing Soviet and international identity of citizens of Soviet Tbilisi in the twentieth century, see: Elene Bodaveli, "The Reflection of Communist Ideology in the Street Naming Policy in Soviet Tbilisi (1922–1939)," *Analytical Bulleting* 8 (2015): 156–78.

26. The majority of residents of the "Italian villa" were directly impacted by the Great Purges, with Makharadze as one of the exceptions, and after 1937, the famous Communist Party house became known in Tbilisi as the "Terror House."

27. NKVD acronym stands for Народный Комиссариат Внутренних Дел (in Russian: The People's Commissariat for Internal Affairs.)

28. Oleg Mozokhin, *Delo Lavrentiya Berii. Sbornik Dokumentov* (Kuchkovo Pole, 2015).

29. Lasha Bakradze, interview with author, April 22, 2021.

30. "Letter of Nina Bedia's Mother to Stalin," Soviet Policy, The Archive of the Ministry of Internal Affairs of Georgia. Web. http://archive.security.gov.ge/cerili_stalins_eng.html.

31. Ibid.

32. Ibid.

33. Ibid.

34. Izabella Tabarovsky, "The Price of Silence: Family Memory of Stalin's Repressions," *Wilson Quarterly* (Fall 2016). Web. https://www.wilsonquarterly.com/quarterly/the-lasting-legacy-of-the-cold-war/the-price-of-silence-family-memory-of-stalins-repressions/.

35. Victoria Aarons and Alan L. Berger, *Third-Generation Holocaust Representation: Trauma, History, and Memory* (Evanston, IL: Northwestern University Press, 2017).

Chapter I

Stalin

Nostalgia for the Past, Present, and Future

The ambivalence with which the international community accepts the soaring numbers reflecting Stalin's approval ratings in the post-Soviet space remains paradoxical. Similar sentiments about Hitler in modern-day Germany would undoubtedly not only raise eyebrows in the international arena but, moreover, such tendencies among Germans today would provoke explicit criticism and hinder many countries' ability to view Germany as an ally.

The difference between the two despotic regimes—Hitler's Nazism and Stalin's Great Terror, whereby one was motivated by ethnic cleansing through eradication of an entire race while the other killed more people in the gulag—continues to be greatly debated through the many prisms of the politics of memory. "With Hitler's death, the Nazi movement and all of the atrocities of that regime also died and disappeared in its due time . . . And thus, with the appearance of firsthand witnesses of those atrocities and a very public discourse that followed thereafter began the de-Nazification process,"[1] says Georgian historian and director of the Georgian Museum of Literature, Lasha Bakradze. While in the public discourse, Hitler's motives are driven by a total destruction of the people of an entire race, Stalin's mission is instead often presented as a regime that was guided by a socialist utopia, in turn, justifying the repressions as a necessary condition.[2] Thus, the double standard defining to the Soviet version of communism under the leadership of Stalin that capitalizes on both achievements and brutality of the period, and Hitler's crimes rooted in evil alone persists in the Western narratives of the two tyrannical regimes of the last century. "Aside from the brief flirtation with de-Stalinization under Nikita Khrushchev and later Mikhail Gorbachev, the destruction of the system or *sistema* of Soviet totalitarianism, unlike the Nazi variant of totalitarianism destroyed at its very core, was bypassed in the USSR,"[3] Bakradze adds. Stalin died, but the *sistema* outlived the dictator and survived the criticisms of Stalin and his cronies through the brief debunking of the "Cult of Personality," while the system of Soviet totalitarianism itself remained largely untouched and seldom challenged in those critical years. "By the time the *sistema* was reanalyzed and attempts were made to reboot de-Stalinization under Gorbachev, it was too late."[4] Bakradze notes, explaining that the reason was primarily due to the fact that the witnesses of the Great Terror at the regime's bloody peak were either no longer alive or out of fear, preferred to remain silent. Hence, the public discourse that followed in post-Nazi Germany did not occur in the Soviet Union or even in the post-Soviet space. Both tangible and intangible vestiges of this delusion have not only permeated the historical revisionism in Russia and to an extent in Georgia but, more surprisingly, also the Western sentiments surrounding Soviet atrocities versus German Nazism.[5]

A common moral ground has been achieved in the international arena that downplays the darkest pages of the pre–World War II chapter by the Stalin regime, particularly following the "free world's" brief alliance with Stalin's Soviet Union. Some would even go so far as to argue that between the two evils, Stalin's ideology was still more palatable than that promoted by Hitler's Nazism. But in both cases, human life was ultimately used by both dictators as an instrument for future aims and ambitious goals of their respective regimes. As Joseph Stalin himself allegedly stated in a candid conversation with British field marshal Bernard Law Montgomery in 1947: "A single death is a tragedy, a million deaths—a statistic."[6]

Hitler's attack on the Soviet Union in 1941 drastically changed the Soviet foreign policy, serving as an impetus for the USSR to join the United Nations, an outgrowth of the Second World War's coalition against the Axis powers that be in the newly reordered world order. A global coalition from which the Soviet Union would have been excluded was a notion that was entirely unacceptable for the Red Tsar.[7] Furthermore, he insisted on maintaining his leverage in the arena by gaining veto privileges in the Security Council and additional protection in the General Assembly against the emerging majority of ideologically like-minded, primarily Western countries. Full membership and voting rights were initially requested by Stalin for all fifteen of the Soviet Socialist Republics. However, following the historic negotiation process in Yalta, only three seats were granted: the Belarusian Soviet Socialist Republic, the Ukrainian Soviet Socialist Republic—both of which were seen as having suffered most heavily during the war—and the Soviet Union itself.

Through the admission of Stalin's Soviet Union onto the global arena under the auspices of the world body, the United Nations, the organization's founding members extended an open invitation to Joseph Stalin to join the international community as an ally, casting aside the prewar deeds undertaken by the Stalin regime that were now being downplayed for the sake of the greater benefit of siding with the evil dictator against what was deemed as the greater evil—the Nazi movement.

In 1939, *Time* magazine named Joseph Stalin their "Man of the Year," but contrary to the accolade emphasizing the greatness of a chosen figure, the editorial board elaborated that the decision was prompted by the fact that one year after Hitler appeared on the *Time*'s much-coveted cover, "evil triumphed over good [whereby] Stalin had matched himself with Adolf Hitler as the world's most hated man."[8] The following year, in October of 1941, just four months after Adolf Hitler's Germany invaded the Soviet Union, *Fortune* magazine asked its readers: "Which one of the following statements most nearly describes your present feelings about the Russian and German governments?"[9] Only 4.6% of the respondents reported more negative perceptions of the former over Germany. Meanwhile, 35.1% answered that they were equally evil, and 35% admitted that, given the option to choose between the two evils, the Soviets were "a little better than Germany," and the remaining 8.5% posited the Soviet government was "a lot better than Germany."[10]

As for American sentiments vis-à-vis the Soviet Union and Stalin more specifically in the period between 1939 and the German invasion of the USSR in 1941, we trace little to no variance. According to Ralph Levering, who specializes in US diplomatic history, "The changes that occurred were largely favorable. But even these resulted not from any friendly overtures by either Russia or the United States, but rather from the fact that Russia largely disappeared from the public spotlight as well as for the obvious reason that attitudes could hardly have become more unfavorable than they were at the end of 1939."[11]

American diplomat, historian, and the godfather of the "Soviet Containment" policy, George F. Kennan said during his address at the Special Evening Gatherings series in 1967 on "Aspects of Recent American Foreign Policy" that while the Russian variant of Stalinism has continuously been modified, reflecting the country's political culture and ruling regime's narrative, Stalin's overall image in the United States as that of a "formidable and remorseless enemy"[12] remained largely unchanged after the dictator's death in 1953. The evolution of Stalin's polemic figure and his complicated, ever-changing legacy in Russia and his native Georgia have left the public opinion in the West unshaken. Rather, it is the public perception of the current political regime, be it in Russia or Georgia, which continues to reassess Stalinism, that is affected more than the historical revisionism of the Stalin era in US or Western European narratives.

Kennan noted that even after the Soviet tyrant's death, the lingering trouble for the United States and the Western world as such was that "we could not realize he was dead."[13] Stalinism, to some extent, is still showing twitches of life not only in his native region but also outside of the confines of his former empire. Perhaps this is one of the rare parallels in the Stalin legacy that is shared by both Western and post-Soviet versions of the Stalin myth, whereby the public perceptions on both sides of the former Iron Curtain continue to treat his legacy not as a long-foregone chapter in the history of the twentieth century but rather a phantom that lives on.

To a degree, the lingering fear and quiet, and at times timid and subdued admiration of the enemy has been transferred to another leader—Vladimir Putin—who has acquired some of these familiar undertones in the Western media and popular perception. Active and frequently even nostalgia-driven comparisons to Stalin, albeit often flawed and superficial, and assessments of the leadership styles of the Soviet Dictator and the Russian President have permeated the political rhetoric and foreign media coverage of Russia under Putin. The main gist of these parallels drawn between Stalin and Putin is rooted in establishing and eliciting enthusiasm, adulation, and collective fear as means of social control, but as a later chapter focused on the cult of personalities of these two leaders will aim to show, a closer examination of their leadership and state management styles demonstrates certain cracks in the overgeneralization of these comparisons. The "Cult of Personality"[14] of Joseph Stalin in the West[15] is a costume that today embellishes the political figure of Vladimir Putin.[16] As a result, the autocratic leaders' images for foreign consumption are now combined into one colorful matryoshka doll that nests the different layers of autocracy, authoritarianism, dictatorship, fear, and admiration, layer by layer, in one whole piece—inspired and fueled, above all else, by a creeping, deeply gnawing sense of nostalgia for that, which perhaps never was to begin with. This growing nostalgia with undertones of pride, terror, fascination, and nationalism is not surprising among the older generation that grew up under the Soviet rule. However, it is even more baffling when witnessed as an increasing trend among those who have only heard of the Soviet Union and Stalin through the tales and horrors shared in hushed tones by their parents and grandparents.

Stalin, or rather his omnipresent ghost, continues to fascinate the West no less than in the former Soviet space. His pervasive yet forever-lingering ghost remains at the very heart of the mystery within the riddle inside the enigma that was the Soviet Union and continues to be its successor state, Vladimir Putin's Russia. Fears that prevent open and uncensored discussion of Soviet crimes under Stalin in Putin's Russia will not only strengthen Vladimir Vladimirovich's democratic authoritarianism domestically but will also play straight into his hands abroad, further strengthening his image as the leader who made Russia if not a great power like it once was under Stalin's leadership, at the very least a global player feared and simultaneously quietly respected—a prominent political and historical actor that the rest of the world can no longer overlook or ignore as it did during the tumult and chaos of the 1990s.

In the early 1990s, a tumultuous period of political and economic instability and overall civil unrest in Georgia, my parents decided to immigrate to Moscow—a pragmatic decision criticized by many in our immediate circle in Tbilisi. Russia, after all, was seen in the post-Soviet Georgian context as an occupant whose claws we had finally escaped upon the collapse of the Soviet regime. Thus, seeking shelter in the capital of the direct successor of the USSR, at first glance, appeared to be a counterintuitive decision. Yet, it must be emphasized that we were far from the only Georgian family to buy a one-way ticket to Moscow in the 1990s. Thousands of Georgians, including highly skilled workers who suddenly found themselves unemployed with no prospects of securing jobs and income for their families, flocked to neighboring Russia. Migration was seen not as a choice but rather as an economic necessity. Over the next decade or two, regular remittances from Russia became a stable and resilient financial inflow for Georgia's destructed economy. However, the deep-seated, firmly established guilt of escaping the Motherland in pursuit of a new life in the arms of the big Russian bear was reignited every summer when my parents and I visited our family in Tbilisi.

My path of post-immigration assimilation in Moscow was not a standard one by ordinary Georgian expatriate standards of that period. After much deliberation, my parents made a conscious decision not to send me to either Russian or Georgian schools, instead opting for a newly opened American School of Tomorrow. This further complicated the process of my cultural assimilation, as I was not only a Georgian in a strange and, not so long ago, an adversarial land by some political and historical accounts, but moreover, I was placed in a completely new environment where I was forced to learn a new language—my third, English, which, according to the school's strict curriculum, was the only language that we were permitted to speak from 9 a.m. to 3 p.m. five days a week.[17]

The intricacies of my assimilation as a new "face from Southern Caucasus," a term used widely at the time to describe my compatriots, were undoubtedly complicated by my complete immersion into the American educational and, more generally, cultural system. Already set on pursuing a musical career, when my high school cohosted a national school convention in Moscow in the winter of 1997, instead of choosing a Georgian song that would have been expected of a good South Caucasus girl from Tbilisi, I selected a piece that demonstrated both my rebellious tendencies and, even more so, my already well-formed admiration and fascination for all things American. Standing on stage on Russian soil, clad in a standard schoolgirl's attire—a long, dark blue pencil skirt and a white blouse, I started: "Oh beautiful for spacious skies, for amber waves of grain." To this day, I can vividly recall the radio silence in the concert hall after I finished my a cappella rendition of "America the Beautiful." A million thoughts began to spin through my head, including my mother's cautious comment during one of the rehearsals at home—"Stalin must be turning in his grave!"—until one of the guest judges visiting on special invitation from Chicago burst into applause. Walking away from a Russian-American school competition with a prize for "Best Female Vocal Rendition" after singing a patriotic song about "America the Beautiful" in the dead of a Moscow winter would have been unheard of, if not entirely criminal, just a few years earlier. How far the country and our society had come since the days of Stalin's Cold War was something I would only begin to comprehend and in hindsight appreciate many years later.

Fast-forward two decades, my already complicated national identity was once again challenged with the outbreak of the August War of 2008. A country where I was born was suddenly at war with a neighboring country that had provided my family with shelter, eventually becoming my adopted home. Even in spite of my complex relationship with Russia, a place I had initially struggled to assimilate in, ultimately failing to fully embrace it as my own, over the years Moscow had become home and a place I still look back on with the fondest of childhood memories, not to mention the countless Russian friends who had offered me nothing short of immense hospitality, warmth, and support. Choosing sides in this war was personally challenging, even if politically my allegiance rested with Georgia. The intricacies of this internal conflict intertwined with professional responsibilities were further complicated by the fact that in the heat of the Georgian-Russian war, I was serving as a United Nations Bureau Chief for Eastern European media based at the UN headquarters in New York. In this capacity and under particularly difficult circumstances, what was purely political became deeply personal, and vice versa.

Oddly, my tripartite identity helped me in navigating the conflict, as I tried to report on the war without reverting to either of my Georgian or Russian identities, instead relying on the third pillar—an American reporter observing the events from the outside looking in. It was clear that I was, at the end of the day, a Georgian, but by the same token, it was also undeniable that I strived to separate Russian officialdom from the Russian people and not muddle the two into one single entity—a tendency I have often observed in some US media outlets over the past several years as bilateral relations with Russia continue to deteriorate. As expected, the August War and the many layers of internal and external conflicts stemming from it motivated me to delve deeper into my own identity, and ultimately led me to question national identity from both cultural as well as sociopsychological perspectives rather than as a solely personal endeavor.

And yet again, my complicated mélange of national identities was challenged shortly after the Russo-Georgian War when on the first day of 2010, I received a phone call from the Georgian Public Broadcaster (GPB), the official organizers of Eurovision Song Contest's Georgian chapter. The Eurovision Song Contest (ESC)[18] is an annual event that attracts some 800 million viewers around the globe—an unprecedented platform that most European nations (particularly the smaller ones like my native Republic of Georgia) embrace with open arms. It is an opportunity for a spotlight few countries can refuse.

A year earlier, in 2009, I had cowritten the Icelandic ESC entry, "Is It True?", a runner-up that had received the silver prize at the finals held in Moscow, Russia.[19] This time, however, impressed with the results of the Icelandic entry, GPB officials were inviting me to compose a song for my homeland. I was flattered, to say the least, until I heard their caveat to the attractive offer. The chorus lyrics had to contain the following message, word for word—"We will never give in." This, the GPB representative informed me, was a direct message aimed at the Russian Federation following the August 2008 war between our two neighboring countries. More than write a song which would effectively represent Georgian culture in all of its glory, the GPB wanted me to send a message to the Russia Federation, specifically [then] prime minister Vladimir Putin. And indeed, this would not be the first time Georgia attempted to deliver such a charged message through the ESC.

In 2009, Georgia had made the headlines that quickly spread beyond the song contest by displaying "hard" politics in their pun-tastic 2009 entry, "We Don't Wanna Put In," an anti-Putin message that Georgia hoped to perform at the ESC finals held, ironically, in Moscow. Not surprisingly, the EBU (European Broadcasting Union) immediately banned the entry, urging the composers to either rewrite the lyrics or drop out completely. The Georgian delegation ultimately chose the latter. While the country considered their submission an act of social commentary (acceptable by EBU's standards), it was the undeniable reference to the Russian Prime Minister that resulted in the committee's unanimous decision to ban the entry.

While I faced a choice of publicly mocking Russia—my adopted home for almost a decade—or declining a highly coveted spot in the Eurovision Song Contest, I was, in turn, faced with a larger sociopolitical question: "How could I decline (as I was inclined to do) the invitation on the grounds that overt politics should be excluded from this peaceful event, when this peaceful event is overtly political in its intent?"

After careful consideration, I made a counteroffer to the Georgian Public Broadcaster—a compromise to use a "double entendre" technique to relay the same message but in a form of a love song. Following my submission of "Never Give In," which was included in the preselection concert and performed live on GPB's Channel 1, the officials voiced their verdict: the lyrical content of the song was considered "insufficiently political for the cause." Though undeniably disappointed, deep down, I was also secretly relieved. Had the song reached the finals in its semipolitical form, I, as the guilt-ridden creator, may have found myself on the receiving end of the repercussions from Russia, where my family and I had found shelter during the political upheaval in Georgia, and I had spent my formative years.[20]

An undeniable break of consciousness occurred with the collapse of the Soviet Union, and the world that we—even those opposing communism and late socialism—believed was meant to last forever. Leningrad-born anthropologist and professor at the University of California, Berkeley, Alexei Yurchak writes in his *Everything Was Forever, Until It Was No More*[21] that, in the social interpretation and reinterpretation of that which has been abruptly interrupted, the binary categorizations in describing and retrospectively analyzing the Soviet reality through a post-Soviet microscope is limiting and therefore seldom productive. Yurchak posits that in order to avoid the reduction of descriptions and analyses of various legacies of that which was but has since ended to mere dichotomous adjectives, we must instead try to uncover the in-betweenness of what lies at the heart of the two polar directions of the pendulum that continues to swing from one extreme end to another. Between greatness and terror, fragility and vigor, bleakness and promise, black and white lies a concept that allows us to avoid either of the extremes—a priori negative assessment of past events and a trap of over-romanticization and nostalgia.

At the heart of this over-romanticization and nostalgia—as one of the most iconic symbolisms of an era where everything was forever, until it was no more—lies the metaphysical figure of Joseph Stalin that has not only outlived the Soviet Union and the chaotic 1990s that followed post-collapse but, as a phenomenon, has gradually evolved into an inherent aspect of what it means to be a post-Soviet individual in the new millennium.

A secret symbol of a phenomenon dubbed by Eugenie Ikhlov as *Stalinshchina*,[22] the "Stalin nostalgia" has been immortalized through partial, albeit active, restoration of monuments and the ebbing and flowing of popularity of Stalin memorabilia in the post-Soviet space, especially his homeland.

A boy from Gori, Koba Jughashvili has achieved a national celebrity status, in turn igniting something of a "famous son syndrome" among his fellow countrymen and women. He has evolved into a patriotic commodity, frequently employed by Georgians in their colonial struggle for survival in spite of the mixed ideological connotations that remain omnipresent in and around his polemic figure,[23] while on the other side, modern-day official Moscow continues to rely on legacies of the Stalin era of "national greatness" as an indirect legitimization of the current regime's political course and an effort to solidify the Putin regime's authority.

A complex personality comprised of constant binaries and riddled with severe contradictions, Stalin or "the man of steel" continues to be portrayed simultaneously as a hero and a villain, a poet and a dictator, ultimately ruthless but at times oddly charismatic, at once "neither European nor Asiatic."[24] In a world where villains must *be* and *do* evil not *some* but instead *all* of the time, his lasting legacy in his native Georgia and adopted Russia continues to shatter the prevailing stereotype by stirring perverse and reluctant admiration, sprinkled with twinges of fear and aversion.

Much like his "true" story that "*seems* well known to us,"[25] lamenting the caricature of one of history's most infinitely complicated characters lacks objectivity. Far from harmless in both his actions and intentions, Stalin's legacy[26] is anything but banal. Not unlike the countless volumes of biographies produced over the years, the episodic radio silences surrounding the enigmatic story of Joseph Stalin (including but by no means limited to his birth,[27] his death, and everything else in between) speak louder than words. A sacred symbol of *Stalinshchina* for communists and the surviving Soviet generation, Comrade Stalin continues to embody not only the mass killings and purges of his people but also the power and the glory of the Soviet Union achieved under his tumultuous leadership.

"Stalin is a mysterious figure viewed across oceans," an American documentary photographer, Margaret Bourke-White wrote in 1943, "but he is equally mysterious within the border[s] of his own country."[28] When Bourke-White made this observation exactly one decade before Joseph Stalin's death on March 5, 1953, the supreme ruler's birthplace had just been converted into a shrine. His legacy was yet to be assessed and revised on multiple occasions—not only in his native Georgia and in post-Soviet Russia, both of which continue to grapple with his contrasting legacies, but also in the West.

In 2014, in my pursuit of a dual degree at Columbia University in social psychology and Slavic Studies, I embarked on a journey fueled, above all else, by purely personal motivation of exploring a post-Soviet national identity as a millennial born during the final years of the Soviet era. My goal was twofold: to understand how, if at all, my own triple national identity of a

Georgian-born, Russian-bred, and US-educated citizen was impacted by the collapse of the Soviet Union and the values and traditions that were taught to my generation, only to be dismissed as mere Soviet propaganda; and to explore my newfound fascination with everything Soviet even though just a few years earlier, the very notion of that historical chapter was not only uninteresting to me but, moreover, entirely rejected as something alien that I refused to embrace as my own.

My first assignment as a psychology student at Columbia University was a project on Georgian post-Soviet identity as experienced by and seen through the eyes of the millennial generation born at the tail end of the Soviet Union. The numerous interviews that I conducted over winter and summer breaks were comprised of conversations with Georgian social scientists, political analysts, government officers, both past and present, journalists, artists, and students, to name but a few. The underlying theme remained a constant leitmotif throughout the research: "Is there such a phenomenon as a post-Soviet Georgian identity?"[29]

The two contrasting hypotheses that have been circulating in mainstream Georgian and foreign media and social science literature since the collapse of the USSR suggest that Georgian society is split into two segments. One widely spread hypothesis rejects remnants of Georgia's Soviet past entirely, which may or may not include traces of de-Stalinization as an important attribute, actively evolving from de-Russification toward complete Westernization. This theory argues that the dismantling of the Iron Curtain, followed by the fall of the Soviet Union, resulted in the emergence of a European identity, which in turn served as a fuel driving Georgia's decision to make the membership of the European Union one of its primary goals.[30] This sentiment was vividly depicted in the proud proclamation by then Chairman of the Parliament of Georgia under Eduard Shevardnadze and later Prime Minister under Mikheil Saakashvili's presidency, Zurab Zhvania during his address to the Council of Europe in 1999 when Georgia was welcomed as a member of the Council: "I'm Georgian, and therefore I am European."[31] Cultural psychologists believe that such reforms and the eventual shift toward European beliefs and values may have resulted in the identification deficit or a loss of a stable national identity, resulting in a gradual loss of patriotism among contemporary Georgians in the new millennium.

The second theory suggests that to this day, Georgians born either during or at the tail end of the USSR continue to embrace their Soviet childhood with nostalgia, maintaining a pro-Russian political and cultural course. This school of thought claims that Georgian national identity remains influenced by its Soviet past and a sense of belonging to the Soviet culture, traditions, and ideologies.[32] The seemingly apolitical neutrality of this concept at the offset is not interpreted as neutrally on the receiving end, which posits that any factual acceptance of the Soviet occupation and its declaration equals willingness to accept the occupation as an inevitable and not an entirely negative turn of events. Even if nostalgia and the acceptance of its Soviet past is recalled with both terror as well as fondness, with equal doses of negative and positive aspects of the seven decades that do not automatically cancel out the other perspective, the first theoretical viewpoint immediately dismisses this school of thought as pro-Russian and therefore, anti-Georgian—thus the two attitudes and theories become mutually incompatible, above all else from the perspective of the "pro-European" group.

The purpose of my research was to delve deeper into this paradox, and study how the unexpected shift of the political regime impacted the Georgian national identity of the last generation born amid the Communist Party of the Soviet Union's swan song in the 1980s. While limited sociologically inclined research had been previously conducted by political analysts and, to a lesser extent, sociologists after Georgia regained its independence in 1991, the question of whether Georgian national identity has remained stable or has instead transformed in the aftermath of the two revolutions in 1991 (demise of the USSR) and 2003 (the Rose Revolution) remains unanswered.

Inevitably, the conversations with my pool of respondents, consisting of policymakers, former ministers and diplomats, academics, psychologists and historians, among others, always led to the complex, polyphonic question of Joseph Stalin and his disputed legacy as Georgia's rebellious son and a Soviet Dictator who defined the twentieth century for the Soviet people as a whole, with his compatriots as some of his most severely impacted victims. For better or worse, Stalin remains at the core of Georgia's post-Soviet identity crisis, as both a symptom and the cause, often resulting in a fracture within its divided society, while his omnipresent ghost haunts and continues to permeate and even drive discussions and debates centered around the country's future in the new millennium.

This narrative opens with a line from Simon Sebag Montefiore, who chronicles Ioseb Jughashvili's journey to becoming the most important leader of the twentieth century and emphasizes that there are two Stalins: one, a promising Georgian seminary student turned street Marxist, and another—a Soviet Red Tsar whose Georgian identity[33] has been laundered and entirely Russified.[34] This duality of the Stalin figure is not only spatial and geographical but, as this book will argue, also temporal. The temporal variations of his mythologized, even metaphysical image are all the more apparent to a naked eye when beyond the two Stalins, we also recognize that there is an alternative variant which combines the first two Stalins of Montefiore but, in addition, possess its own unique attributes that chronologically came to life after his physical death and have been routinely created and recreated over time. This monograph is, above all, concerned with this third mythological Stalin whose origins are rooted in memory politics, yet its influence expands beyond policies and politics, impacting our identity formation and perception of the "self" through the prism of Stalin's historical figure. However, prior to turning to the metaphysical and temporal, it is imperative that we first devote attention to the first two—physical and geographical—Stalins, who serve as both heroes and villains of the upcoming two chapters.

The next chapter delves into the complex and at times even conflicting facts and parables surrounding a boy from Gori who became the Georgian "Man of Borderlands." Due to the fact that this book is not a biography of Joseph Stalin but rather a social and cultural narrative exploring the remnants of his legacies that continue to permeate the psyche and politics of the Eurasian region as a whole, including the very country that he was born into at the tail end of the nineteenth century, the chapter will focus primarily on what came of Stalin's legacy in his native Georgia after his death in 1953.

The segment devoted to the "Georgian Man of Borderlands" deals with the complicated relationship of Georgia and the Georgian nation in the second half of the twentieth century and the beginning of the twenty-first with Joseph Stalin's contradictory, deliberately ambiguous, and often mysterious image surrounded by riddles and legends—often of Jughashvili's own creation—in the public perception. The chapter opens with the fall and rise of Stalin under former Georgian president Mikheil Saakashvili's leadership, particularly following the Russo-Georgian War of 2008 and thereafter, the Georgian Dream party founded by Georgian oligarch, Bidzina Ivanishvili. Through exploring the reformation of post-Soviet Georgian identity, we chronicle the identity formation and reformation of Stalin's multiple identities as central to how he constructed his own image in response to both external and internal factors influencing his decision-making and the political environment. In this chapter, we briefly return to the Stalin Museum in his hometown, Gori, and the Museum of Soviet Occupation in Tbilisi—two important places that offer tangible, albeit very contradictory, insights into the aforementioned creation and recreation of Stalin narratives over the past two decades, and also the remaking of the political culture of post-Soviet Georgia under Mikheil Saakashvili and, more recently, the Georgian Dream party.

Historically, the tumultuous relationship between Georgia and Russia has been riddled with complications and contestations, dating back to the annexation of the South Caucasian country by Tsarist Russia in 1801 and, following a brief period of independence between 1918 and 1921, another occupation—this time by the Soviet Red Army, which lasted until the eventual collapse of the Soviet Union in 1991. However, analyzing the bilateral relations between the occupier and the occupied solely through the prism of colonialism fails to grant the complexity of the relationship and its remnants its due justice. Georgia's special status and, to a degree, even entitlement during the Soviet era is perhaps most apparent in the identity negotiation between Georgianness and Georgian Sovietness, which allowed for and often encouraged privileges arguably available to very few if any of the other Soviet states besides the Russian SSR itself. Among other historical factors that have contributed to the formation of difficult relations between then Soviet Russia and Georgia, this chapter looks at identity-related tensions introduced into the bilateral relationship by Nikita Khrushchev's iconic "secret speech" at the Twentieth Party Congress in 1956 and the aftermath of the General Secretary's revelations of his predecessor Joseph Stalin's crimes which resulted in an outbreak of demonstrations in Tbilisi against Khrushchev's perceived denigration of Stalin specifically and the Georgian people more generally.

Thereafter, the narrative turns to the "Russified" Soviet Red Tsar and traces his fall and rise under Gorbachev, Yeltsin, and ultimately Putin, under whose leadership Joseph Stalin's name and his historical legacies have become synonymous with the Great Patriotic War and the victory of the Soviet people on the behalf of the free world against Nazi Germany in World War II. This chapter aims to uncover the interplay between de-Stalinization and the rise of Putinism at the turn of the twenty-first century. De-Stalinization consisted of a series of unfinished political and social reforms in the Soviet Union that were launched following Khrushchev's "secret speech" on exposing and debunking the "Cult of Personality" of Stalin. The multiple revisions of Stalin's legacy and its implications during and, increasingly more so, following the disintegration of the USSR eventually led to the employment of this tactic in revisions of Stalin narratives across the former Soviet space, dictated by the political environment and domestic politics of a given state's ruling regime. But the complete eradication of his military genius following the Secret Speech that was, among other goals, meant to demolish the myth of Stalin, turned out to be largely futile. The chronological boundaries of de-Stalinization as a state policy become blurred after Khrushchev's successor, Leonid Brezhnev's ascension to power, at which point de-Stalinization was largely halted. As already implied in the earlier chapter, the de-Stalinization campaign as such was never truly seen through following these early attempts, and even under Nikita Khrushchev, this policy was ultimately a "silent de-Stalinization" rather than an overt political reform. The policy remained largely dormant until after Vladimir Putin's meteoric rise to power.

Following Putin's ascent to the presidential throne, not only did de-Stalinization remain dormant but, moreover, what occurred was a drastic reversal of any and all remnants of de-Stalinization and more so, a gradual "re-Stalinization" of the nation linked to nation-building that is ultimately rooted in reinstatement of pride in the victory of the Soviet people in the Great Patriotic War. This reintroduction—or rather, reinjection—of national pride in the great power victory and national resilience coincided with the emergence of new museums throughout the country honoring the memory of the Soviet people and reinstating respect and even fear in Russia as a direct successor of the Soviet Empire. Stalinism as a cultural trope tainted with memories of terror and fear and driven by nostalgia for greatness and glory is explored through sociological surveys conducted among members of Soviet and post-Soviet generations. Unlike its Georgian variant, the "Russified" Stalin's legacies are linked less to the person of Stalin and the man behind the Dictator—the Georgian son of a cobbler in the town of Gori—but rather are directly attached to the greatness of the Fatherland's historical past as the "great power" victor against the root of all evil, Nazism.

The third and main section of the book is focused on another Stalin—one that is not tied to a specific spatial concept and is temporally ever present and constantly evolving. This Third Stalin, the primary pillar of this monograph observed through the prism of the post-Soviet era, takes different forms in its Georgian and Russian variants. But unlike these two Stalins, the third Stalin is not attached to geography, nor is it directly linked to the historical figure of the Soviet Dictator. The mythological Stalin is a hybrid of the Georgian and Russian variants, and instead of bearing resemblance to Joseph Stalin of the history books, the perceptions and sentiments of this historical, largely mythologized figure are varied and thus complicated, as are the motivations behind the specific attributes that one sees in this third Stalin.

In the Georgian version of the third Stalin, his image is presented as a "memory project"[35] used as a tool to establish Georgian post-Soviet identity by bringing back the "lost" historical memory of the pre-Russian Imperial and later Soviet Red Army occupations and amplifying the Christian Orthodox faith as the main pillar of Georgianness. In its Russian variant, the mythologized Stalin becomes the symbol of victory and great power politics of the twentieth century, with Russia serving as the historical successor that inherited the Soviet Union's greatness and glory. As noted earlier, this representation—or rather, the individual replica—of the third Stalin is not about Stalin per se but rather a reflection of identities in a constant flux, the unrealized hopes and dreams of the late Soviet era and the rediscovery of our place in the post-Soviet world, an identity that we are still continuously reclaiming and recreating on the ashes of the collapsed empire. The Third Stalin is comprised of legacies of the era—cult of personality, trauma, nationalism, and nostalgia—the remnants of a journey interrupted, and present identities built upon debris of a destructed, ruptured past. In exploring these concepts, this main segment of the book briefly turns to two cultural works that touch upon aspects of the Third Stalin: Tengiz Abuladze's phantasmagoric drama *Repentance*, a classic of glasnost'-era filmography, and Armando Iannucci's satirical comedy, *The Death of Stalin*.

Many members of the post-Soviet generation will resent the notion of being a byproduct or a direct offspring of Stalin's policies—including both the glorious greatness and ruthless terror of the regime. Yet, this proposed third Stalin is inevitably a byproduct of us as much as we are a byproduct of the Stalin era as our own and, even more so, our ancestors' recent historical and deeply personal past. In other words, as this work will aim to demonstrate, revisiting history allows for denaturalizing of the present and the past. Even if we resist the notion that we, the post-Soviet generation, are the offspring of the Stalin era, this third Stalin is, by and large, a product of our politics, beliefs, values, and society seen through the kaleidoscope of our darkest and most intimate perceptions and reflections of ourselves that we are still unable to reconcile, let alone accept. Instead, we can engage with these perceptions through a prism of history—a kaleidoscope that continuously changes patterns of shapes and colors, urging one to constantly question and frequently cast shadows of doubt on every snippet as a mere illusion.

NOTES

1. Lasha Bakradze, interview with author.
2. For more on the comparisons of destruction and mass murders committed by Hitler's Reich versus Stalin's bloody regime, and detailed contrasts between the two tyrants' motivations, see: Timothy Snyder, *Bloodlands: Europe Between Hitler and Stalin* (New York: Basic, 2010); Snyder, "Hitler vs. Stalin: Who Killed More?" *New York Review of Books*, March 10, 2011. Web. https://www.nybooks.com/articles/2011/03/10/hitler-vs-stalin-who-killed-more/; John Mosier, *Deathride: Hitler vs. Stalin. The Eastern Front, 1941–1945* (New York: Simon & Schuster, 2010); R. J. Overy, *The Dictators: Hitler's Germany and Stalin's Russia* (New York: W.W. Norton, 2004); Phillip W. Weiss, *Comparing Hitler and Stalin: Certain Cultural Considerations*, Graduate Center, City University of New York, 2014.
3. Bakradze, interview with author.
4. Ibid.
5. The topics of de-Stalinization and the Cult of Personality are discussed in greater detail in chapter 5.
6. "Report to Washington on Montgomery's Conversation with Stalin," January 17, 1947, History and Public Policy Program Digital Archive, National Archives of the UK. Web. http://digitalarchive.wilsoncenter.org/document/134377.

7. In his widely acclaimed book, *Stalin: The Court of a Red Tsar* (London: Weidenfeld and Nicolson, 2003), Simon Sebag Montefiore chronicles the journey of a cobbler's son who became the last great tsar that shaped the Soviet Empire, whom Montefiore coins "the Red Tsar."

8. Ralph Levering, *American Opinion and the Russian Alliance, 1939–1945* (Chapel Hill: University of North Carolina Press, 1976), 35.

9. Mildred Strunk, *Public Opinion, 1935–1946* (Princeton: Princeton University Press, 1951), 870.

10. Ibid.

11. Levering, *American Opinion and the Russian Alliance, 1939–1945*, 35.

12. George F. Kennan, "The Legacy of Stalinism," *Proceedings of the Massachusetts Historical Society*, Third Series 79 (1967), 130.

13. Ibid., 131.

14. For a comparison of personality cults of Stalin and Putin, please see chapter 5.

15. Under the geographical concept of the "West" from the Soviet and post-Soviet perspectives, the author implies the United States, the United Kingdom, and other parts of Western Europe.

16. For more on comparisons outlining similarities (and differences) between Putin and Stalin, see: Elena Pukareva and Svetlana Pukareva, "Tipy Politicheskikh Liderov: Sravneniye I. V. Stalina i V. V. Putina," *Nauka bez granits* 12, no. 17 (2017): 79–83; Helena Goscilo, *Putin as Celebrity and Cultural Icon* (New York: Routledge, 2013): p. 47; Tornike Metreveli, "The Evolution of Totalitarianism: From Stalin to Putin," *Atlantic Community* (November 2013): 1–5; Vladimir Shlapentokh, "Putin as a Flexible Politician. Does He Imitate Stalin?," *Communist and Post-Communist Studies* 41, no. 2 (June 2008): 205–16; William Zimmerman, *Ruling Russia: Authoritarianism from the Revolution to Putin* (Princeton, NJ: Princeton University Press, 2014); Konrad Putzier, "Putin and Stalin: Mirror Reflections," World Policy, December 23, 2014. Web. http://worldpolicy.org/2014/12/23/putin-and-stalin-mirror-reflections/; Henry Foy, "The Brutal Third Act of Vladimir Putin," *Financial Times*, March 11, 2021. Web. https://www.ft.com/content/59498c92-799f-4c61-ac2e-77e7e302cc32.

17. The author posits that due to this restriction, it was not until she relocated to New York at the age of twenty and began to work as a reporter for a prominent expatriate media outlet, a Russian-American newspaper called *Novoye Russkoye Slovo*, that she began to practice Russian in a more formal setting. She is grateful to the tireless efforts and patience of her editor in chief, Felix Gorodetsky to whom she remains forever indebted for instilling in her the deep appreciation for the beauty and richness of the Russian language.

18. The Eurovision Song Contest (ESC), little known in the United States, is colloquially known as the "Olympics of Songwriting." The ESC encompasses all of Europe and beyond to geographic and cultural outsiders such as Israel, Jordan, Morocco, and the newcomer of 2015—Australia. Inspired by the popular Italian Sanremo Music Festival, the Eurovision Song Contest (originally titled The Eurovision Grand Prix) first started in 1956 in the aftermath of World War II as a cultural move toward European unity and peace. While over the past decades, the contest has acquired a reputation, particularly in the Western music industry, of a kitsch

entertainment show with little musical value, it is worth noting that the ESC has served as a successful platform for international artist debuts, producing the likes of Celine Dion, Julio Iglesias, and ABBA.

19. During a press conference hosted at Moscow's iconic Olimpiyskiy Stadium that once hosted the 1980 Olympic Games and now served as the venue of the 2009 Eurovision semifinals and the contest's grand finale, a journalist from the Russian news agency TASS referred to the author as "a Russian songwriter"—a description syndicated the following day by the majority of Russian-language news outlets, which, in turn, resulted in disapproval in the Georgian media.

20. This excerpt was originally published by *Inquiries Journal*. See: Tinatin Japaridze, "Press Play for Politics: The Weapon of a Eurovision Song," *Inquiries Journal* 7, no. 10 (2015): 1–5.

21. Alexei Yurchak, *Everything Was Forever, Until It Was No More: The Last Soviet Generation* (Princeton, NJ: Princeton University Press, 2005): 13–14.

22. Jaroslaw Anders, "Dead Souls," *New Republic Online*, February 14, 2005. Web.

23. Francisco Martinez, "To Whom Does History Belong? The Theatre of Memory in Post-Soviet Russia, Estonia and Georgia," *Anthropological Journal of European Cultures* 26, no. 1 (Spring 2017): 98–127.

24. Stephen Kotkin, *Stalin: Paradoxes of Power, 1878–1928* (New York: Penguin, 2014), 427.

25. Kotkin, *Stalin*, 7.

26. On examples of how official Moscow continues to rely on the legacies of the Stalin era and a deeper exploration of the phenomenon of "Stalin legacy" in modern Russia, see: Aleksandra Arkhipova, "Stalin bez Stalinizma," *InLiberty*, June 29, 2017. Web. https://old.inliberty.ru/blog/2616-Stalin-bez-stalinizma; Arkhiopova, "Strakh, kontrol' i velikaya pamyat': Komu u zachem nuzhen Stalin?," recording of the oral presentation at the conference *Aktsiya: Anti-Stalin*, Sakharov Center, Moscow, Russia, June 23, 2017. YouTube video, 18:37. Web. https://www.youtube.com/watch?v=x5Dz0mX40Zk. Russian anthropologist Arkhipova argues that in modern Russia under Putin, Stalin is used as a symbol for "anti-positions" against corruption, inertia of political elites, anti-right politics, and as a general symbol functioning in opposition of "the bad of today" and the "good of yesterday," striving for "an idealized sense of order," justice, and a strong, albeit caring, leadership (Arkhipova, "Stalin bez Stalinizma.")

Also from the "Anti-Stalin" conference at the Sakharov Center in Moscow in 2017, see: Ekaterina Shulman, "Navyazannaya Lyubov': Zachem gospropaganda risuyet reiting Stalinu," recording of the oral presentation at the conference *Aktsiya: Anti-Stalin*, Sakharov Center, Moscow, Russia, June 23, 2017. YouTube video, 24:52. Web. https://www.youtube.com/watch?v=O4WKYgWY-CM. Russian political scientist Shulman, on her part, analyzes how the Russian media's heightened attention on the growing popularity of Stalin today allows the Russian political elite to present itself as "the only European" force in Russia against the backdrop of the "ideology-driven, blood-thirsty group under Stalin" (Shulman, "Navyazannaya Lyubov'"). For more scholarly work on how the Russian state uses the legacies and myths of the

Stalinist era, see: Georgiy Pocheptsov, "Ot mifa revolyutsiy k mifu Pobedy, ot mifa Stalina k mifu Putina," Mariupol State University, July 18, 2018; Elena Nakhimova, "Ideologema Stalina v sovremennoy massovoy kommunikatsii," *Politicheskaya Lingvistika* 2, no. 36 (2011): 152–156; Vladimir Efimov, "O Politicheskom Zaveshyanii Stalina," *Journal of Economic Regulation* 11, no. 1 (2020): 6–35.

27. Although official records indicate that Ioseb Jughashvili was born on December 18, 1878, Kotkin writes that Stalin later advanced his birth year from 1878 to 1879. "As late as the end of 1920, he [Stalin] was still giving December 6, 1878 [old style; December new calendar] as his birth date, but in 1922, one of his assistants issues a 'correction' to December 21, 1879, which became the official date." From that point on, December 21, 1879 was celebrated as the Soviet leader's birthday in the USSR. Kotkin notes that it remains unclear to this day as to why Stalin chose a different day as well as a different year. For a more detailed discussion on Stalin's birth year, see: Stephen Kotkin, *Stalin: Paradoxes of Power, 1878–1928* (New York: Penguin, 2015), chapter 1; Miklós Kun, *Stalin: An Unknown Portrait* (Budapest, Hungary: Central European University Press, 2003): 8–10, 60; Edvard Radzinsky, *Stalin* (New York: Doubleday, 1996). According to historian Lasha Bakradze, in his new article on the "Past and Future of the Stalin Museum in Gori," the official birthday of Jughashvili is also forged on the very certificate that is displayed at the Stalin Museum, bearing no mention of the change of dates. See: Lasha Bakradze, "Past and Future of the Stalin Museum in Gori," *De Gruyter Oldenbourg* 103 (December 2020): 9–15.

28. Bourke-White, *Shooting the Russian War*, 197.

29. For more on the "Georgian national identity," see chapter 2.

30. For academic work exploring Georgia's European belonging and political course, please see: Natia Mestvirishvili and Maia Mestvirishvili, "'I am Georgian and Therefore I am European': Re-searching the Europeanness of Georgia," *Central European Journal of International and Security Studies* 8, no. 1 (May 2014): 52–65; Marine Vekua and Ramaz Lominadze, "The Long Way of Georgia to Europe," *Politické Vedy* 4, no. 1 (2017): 134–52; Kakha Gogolashvili, "The EU and Georgia: The Choice Is in the Context," *Europe in Dialogue* 1, no. 1 (2009): 92–129; Lia Tsuladze, "Georgian Dilemma: Concerns for National Identity and Quests for Europeanness," *European Studies* 12, no. 1 (2018): 37–62; Nino Abesadze and Otar Abesadze, "European Values and Georgia: Historical Aspects," *International Journal of Economic Theory and Application* 5, no. 2 (Spring 2018): 33–37. For print and online media outlets on Georgia's European belonging and values, see: "Is Georgia Europe?", *Intermedia Georgia*, August 20, 2019. Web. http://intermedia.ge/სტატია/117737-არის-თუ-არა-საქართველო-ევროპა/21/; "More of Europe in Georgia and More of Georgia in Europe," *Georgian News Agency*, May 5, 2019. Web. https://www.ghn.ge/news/225607-meti-evropa-sakartveloshi-da-meti-sakartvelo-evropashi-salo me-zurabishvili; Gia Nodia, "Georgia and Europe and the Geopolitics of Values," *Forbes Georgia*, January 9, 2014. Web. https://forbes.ge/evropa-da-saqarthvelo-ghir/; Nikoloz Pkhakadze and Eric Livny, "Georgia between Two Fires: Russia or Europe?" ISET Policy Institute, June 6, 2014. Web.

31. The iconic phrase adorns the late Zurab Zhvania's commemorative star plaque in front of the Council of Europe headquarters in Strasbourg. See more: "Welcome to the Council of Europe in Georgia," Council of Europe, accessed on March 23, 2021. Web. https://www.coe.int/en/web/tbilisi/field-office/overview; "Zurab Zhvania addressed the Council of Europe," uploaded on February 10, 2010, YouTube. Web. https://www.youtube.com/watch?v=P4KX1IVvrHg.

32. For academic work on Georgia's nostalgia for its Soviet past and the paradox of Georgia's European aspirations and nostalgia for the USSR, see: Tatsiana Amosava, "Nostalgia for the Soviet Past in the Post-Soviet Countries," Carleton University, Ottawa, Canada, July 10, 2015. Web. https://carleton.ca/jewishstudies/wp-content/uploads/Zelikovitz-Centre-July-10-2015.pdf; Eveline Baumann, "Post-Soviet Georgia: It's a Long, Long Way to 'Modern' Social Protection," *Économies et Sociétés. Série F, Développement, croissance et progrès* 46, no. 1 (February 2012): 259–85; Irakli Chkhaidze, "Post-Soviet Georgia: New Perspectives in Historical Research?" *Civilization Researches* 9, no. 1, UNESCO, 2012. Web. http://www.culturedialogue.com/resources/library/civilresearches/journals/9.pdf#page=45; Katrine Bendtsen Gotfredsen, "Void Pasts and Marginal Presents: On Nostalgia and Obsolete Features in the Republic of Georgia," *Slavic Review* 73, no. 2 (Summer 2014): 246–64; Elisabeth Kovtiak, "A Bridge to the Past: Public Memory and Nostalgia for the Communist Times in Modern Georgia," *Journal of Nationalism, Memory and Language Politics* 12, no. 1 (July 2018): 31–51. For print and online media outlets discussing Georgia's post-Soviet identity and nostalgia for communism, see: "Missing the USSR, Even in Georgia," *Eurasianet*, November 7, 2017. Web. https://eurasianet.org/missing-the-ussr-even-in-georgia; Nino Dalaqishvili, "Georgia's Soviet Nostalgia Proven by NDI Poll," *VOA Georgian Service*, May 12, 2017. Web. https://www.amerikiskhma.com/a/ndi-research-in-georgia/3849689.html; "Why Are Georgians Nostalgic for the Soviet Union?", Ambebi.ge, May 21, 2019. Web. https://www.ambebi.ge/article/234336-ratom-akvt-kartvelebs-sabchota-kavshiris-nostalgia/; Lela Chakhaia, "Who Misses the Soviet Union?", *Netgazeti*, July 3, 2017. Web. https://netgazeti.ge/news/204923/; "Soviet Nostalgia on the Path to Euro-Atlantic Integration through Anti-Western Media Influence," *Qartli.ge*, January 20, 2018. Web. https://www.qartli.ge/ge/akhali-ambebi/article/7447-sabtcothanostalgiaevroatlantikurgzazeantidasavlurimediisgavlenith.

33. See chapter 2 for a more detailed conversation about the concept of Georgian identity, particularly in the post-Soviet context.

34. Bilefsky, "In Georgia, a Reverence for Stalin."

35. For an in-depth discussion of Georgia's post-Soviet "memory project," see: Malkhaz Toria, "The Soviet Occupation of Georgia in 1921 and the Russian-Georgian War of August 2008: Historical Analogy as a Memory Project," in S. F. Jones, ed., *The Making of Modern Georgia, 1918–2012: The First Georgian Republic and its Successors* (London: Routledge, 2014): 316–35.

Chapter II

Georgian Man of Borderlands

All roads of the tale about Stalin inevitably lead us back to his Motherland, Sakartvelo.[1] Koba's complicated, folk-ridden legacy in his native Georgia is partly, if not single-handedly, of his own fabrication—not solely the myths surrounding his historical figure but also the biographical tale of his childhood that remains wrapped in a mystery inside an enigma. Through the prism of Soso's figure and legacy, this chapter briefly examines Georgia's tumultuous relationship with Russia as both a neighbor and an occupier, seldom seen as a friend but more frequently viewed as a threatening foe next door.

Similar to many other former Soviet republics and satellites, displaying Soviet symbols in Georgia became frowned upon after the collapse of the regime and the end of the communist occupation. In commemoration of the Soviet Union's negative legacies and a celebration of an "anti-occupational, national-liberation movement," on May 26, 2006, symbolically marking Georgia's Independence Day, president Mikheil Saakashvili and his party, United National Movement (UNM), founded the national Museum of Soviet Occupation dedicated to the memory of "the victims of the Soviet political repression"[2] between 1921 and 1991. The decidedly anti-Communist exhibition boasts a wall enlisting numerous Georgian public figures that were victims of the regime, as well as one photograph depicting a mass murder and another honoring the "ruthlessly persecuted" members of the Georgian intelligentsia. The collection includes Georgia's declaration of independence, draft constitutions, countless pages of personal diaries attributed to Georgian elites and aristocracy, as well as those coined as "the founding fathers" of the independent republic.

The Museum of Soviet Occupation, sponsored primarily by the Georgian President's Fund, is housed inside the Georgian National Museum as its subsection due to financial limitations at the time of its opening. It is largely driven by the political agenda promoted by its founding fathers— UNM, the ruling party at the time, and to this day, continues to serve as a direct antithesis of another national museum—the Stalin Museum in Gori. The Museum of Soviet Occupation continues to reflect the unresolved dispute over politics and memory vis-à-vis Georgia's complicated Soviet past, its turbulent relations with Russia, and last but not least—the complex relationship with its rebellious son. Not unlike the rest of the country, even in spite of the anti-Communist sentiments that dominate this small space, the artifacts exhibited on its dark, somber walls also remind the visitor that in the Georgian context, Stalin is the simultaneous embodiment of all evil and a brilliant commander who conquered Nazism and ultimately came to rule not only Russia but also half of the rest of the world.

Next to the many rows of photographs, letters, and other personal artifacts that are meant to shed light on the shared trauma endured by the entire Georgian nation is a prominent sign, which reads in bold text: "From 1942 to 1952 more than 5,000 persons were shot in Georgia, and 190,000 were deported." Reconstructed iron-clad doors of NKVD prison cells depict terrifying torture scenes of innocent Georgian victims who fell prey to the Soviet Secret Services, articulating the "temporal and spatial order"[3] of the era, allowing the museum to not merely exist within a context of Soviet occupation but also recreating a cultural context of the period of Georgia's tumultuous history. The museum reflects the UNM's party narrative vis-à-vis Georgia's Soviet question: "mental bridges"[4] between the Soviet era and the post-Soviet Shevardnadze and, thereafter, Saakashvili years are burned, and Soviet occupation of the twentieth century is presented as a central element in the presentation of Georgia's struggle for freedom and independence.

The late Nikoloz (Nika) Rurua, one of the former leaders of the United National Movement, elaborated on the ruling party's mission behind the opening of the museum: "Our aim was to explain that contemporary Russian goals are in essence not any different from the aims of Bolshevik Russia, even though today Georgia is an independent and democratic state. . . . By using historical context, we wanted to explain where today's occupation of our territories originates from, as well as [show] what the effortless concession of freedom can bring [to] the nation."[5] Sprinkled with artifacts and anachronistic photographs of Russia's incursion into Georgia during the August War of 2008, in its very essence, the museum offers a platform for an explicit, unapologetic depiction of historical and fixed memory narratives motivated by an unreservedly anti-Communist policy denouncing the regime and its negative impact on the nation as a whole. In juxtaposition to the Stalin Museum in Gori, the national museum serves as a political symbol of victimhood that aspires to distance Georgia from its Soviet past and toward its European future.

Shortly after the inauguration of the Museum of Soviet Occupation in the center of Tbilisi, a building that faces the former Georgian Parliament headquarters on Rustaveli Avenue, Russian president Vladimir Putin confronted Saakashvili during the two leaders' bilateral meeting in late 2006. Behind closed doors, Putin had allegedly reminded his Georgian counterpart that it was not only Stalin who was of direct Georgian decent, but also his despotic secret police chief, Lavrenti Beria. With a matching degree of skillful sarcasm, Saakashvili "reassured" Vladimir Vladimirovich that should his administration decide to respond by building a Russian museum of Georgian oppression in Moscow, he would be "delighted" to personally assist in securing funding for the project.[6] Little did the young and energetic Georgian President suspect at the time that the two neighboring countries were destined to soon engage in a five-day war that would shake the geopolitical world.

In 2008, during the Russo-Georgian conflict, Stalin's hometown found itself on the frontlines of the war when Russian military forces rolled their tanks into Gori[7] and bombed artillery positions[8] throughout the small town, which housed a major military installation and served as Georgia's transportation hub.[9 10] With the outbreak of the war, as bombs began to fall upon the dictator's hometown, on August 11, then director of the Stalin Museum in Gori, Robert Maghlakelidze loaded his automobile with nearly fifty relics from the shrine, including Koba's iconic pipe, his spectacles, military greatcoat and cap, and his Georgian sword, and, with the Georgian Ministry of Culture's blessing, drove into the capital, where for the next several months, he stored the historic mementoes in a Tbilisi museum.[11] "I had to take this risk in the name of our history,"[12] he told the media in 2008. "Thank God, they [the Russian militants] didn't bomb the [Stalin] museum, but there were no guarantees at all. We said, 'let's preserve these things for future generations.' These personal things cannot be replaced." Today, Maghlakelidze recalls that aside from several windows that were smashed by militants, the majority of the museum remained largely unharmed by the five-day war. The relics were safely returned to Gori by October 24 of that same year.[13]

As one of the consequences of any international conflict, the August War further accelerated the complete eradication of the vestiges of Soviet authoritarianism across post-Soviet Georgia. In 2010, the Georgian Parliament officially passed a law banning public display of Soviet symbolisms.[14] While vocal about what Georgia was *not*, the Georgian state also had to offer an alternative as a way of filling a sudden void and thus solidifying the nation's identity as independent and entirely devoid of remnants of its colonial past. Since Soviet monuments and other tangible memorabilia were now viewed as explicitly negative legacies of Georgia's colonial past, UNM's architectural projects such as the reconstruction of the iconic Bagrati Cathedral located between the two recently lost enclaves, Abkhazia and South Ossetia, were regaining their significance as a "potent symbol for Georgian territorial integrity,"[15] further validating Georgian identity as strictly separate from—if not entirely devoid of—lingering Soviet connotations.

One year after the Russo-Georgian War of 2008 and two days ahead of what would have been Joseph Stalin's 130th birthday, the Military Memorial in Kutaisi,[16] dedicated to the Georgian heroes who died in the Second World War, was destroyed overnight to make way for a new parliamentary building. The memorial, designed and erected in the 1980s—an armed horseman reminiscent of St. George stabbing a Nazi soldier with a spear—was an anti-war composition, according to its late author, legendary Georgian sculptor Merab Berdzenishvili's words. "The Kutaisi memorial is not just a memorial for the fallen. For me, it was also an opportunity to express my thoughts and feelings about the war," the sculptor told RFE/RL's Georgian Service two days later. "It's an antiwar statement. This is a very complex composition, with a lot of interwoven motifs. Every epoch has its dragons. And for the 20th century, it was fascism."[17]

Hundreds of Georgians gathered to protest the destruction of one of the most iconic symbols of Kutaisi, condemning the blast that accidentally killed a local woman and her eight-year-old daughter as an act of "historical vandalism." Then opposition leader and current President of Georgia, Salome Zourabichvili, criticized the leadership's decision to remove the iconic vestige of its era: "This is a memorial to those people who fought for freedom against Nazism. Georgians and non-Georgians, Europeans and Jews who were killed in World War II." Zourabichvili added that "If we want to forget all this, then we are a nation of barbarians, with a barbarian president who can just call up from somewhere and give an order to detonate the explosives, so that no protests can interrupt."[18] The state authorities, on their part, justified the move, stating that the monument's removal symbolized the replacement of old Soviet Georgia with new, pro-European and independent Georgia.[19]

One year later, on June 25, 2010, in the middle of the night and under heavy police protection, following the presidential order, Gori officials toppled the 20-foot-tall bronze statue of Joseph Stalin that had adorned the town's central square since 1952. However, unlike in 1956 when Nikita Khrushchev withdrew the dictator's body from the mausoleum where Lenin's embalmed body continues to rest on display, undisturbed, preserved for eternity and generations to come, against the numerous protests and unresolved debates—almost half a century later, the Georgian leadership moved Stalin's statue a mere few meters away to a garage. Hence, Stalin was not dethroned but instead merely shifted to a different, albeit nearby, location. While thousands of his monuments were abolished in the 1950s as part of the early de-Stalinization process across the USSR and its satellite states, prior to the 2008 war, the bronze statue of Georgia's infamous son had graced his hometown's center, within a walking distance from the museum marking his birthplace. Shortly thereafter, the town residents filed a petition to reerect the monument and the memory of their prodigal son in the same spot but with only partial success. Today, the demolished statue no longer lies on the grounds of a military base in Gori; instead it adorns a small square across from the Stalin Museum—just minutes from the central avenue named after the man himself.

This contradiction, even in his native Gori and Georgia at large, can be partially attributed to Stalin's seemingly deliberate self-construction as a "Man of Borderlands"[20] with a triple mythical identity: a nonnational proletariat, a Georgian on the one hand, and a Russian (or, rather, a Soviet) on the other. Stalin's identity formation and reformation were central to how he constructed his own image, particularly in relation to and, at times, even in direct response to a given political environment or goal. The theory of self-identity formation presented by psychologist Erik H. Erikson posits that "identity formation begins where the usefulness of identification ends."[21] In other words, identity develops from the "rejection and assimilation of childhood identifications,"[22] particularly those characteristics that are admired and thus incorporated into one's own identity.[23] However, as theorist and Stalin biographer Richard C. Tucker observes, Erikson's argument about the "usefulness of identification" ending at the precise point where identity formation begins is less useful vis-à-vis Ioseb Jughashvili's journey to becoming Joseph Stalin. For example, Stalin's identification with Lenin, Tucker writes, persisted as a "permanent keystone" of his identity and was also depicted across numerous Soviet posters of the 1930s proclaiming that "Stalin is Lenin today."[24]

While on the one hand it has been suggested by scholars[25] that Stalin cast aside and, in some cases, even explicitly denied his "Georgianness" as the leader of the Soviet empire, there are also historical records that demonstrate otherwise. Historian Erik Scott in his book, *Familiar Strangers: The Georgian Diaspora and the Evolution of the Soviet Empire* argues that not only did Stalin not abandon his Georgian identity but, moreover, through his extensive correspondence with the network of prominent Georgian Bolsheviks who rose to the echelons of power with him in the 1920s and 1930s, it is clear that his "Georgianness" was important to who he was and, furthermore, connected him to his milieu of compatriots in official positions.[26] Scott posits that while at the helm of the Kremlin, aside from actively corresponding in his native tongue, Stalin also continued to preside over Georgian *supras*[27] and played an active role in the production and promotion of Georgian culture on a pan-Soviet scale. Thus, through what Tucker coins "a case of mistaken identity" between his identities as Jughashvili versus Stalin, this "case" was rooted in a psychological and even a deliberately constructed, absolute, overly "idealized" and thus an altogether "mistaken identity."[28] Furthermore, through the institutionalization of this "mistaken identity" from the 1930s onward, systemic falsification, twisting of truth and facts, or, at the very least, their severe embellishment, was enforced in public by his regime,[29] giving birth to mythologization of the history of Stalinism and its idealization—a phenomenon that continues to persist, to varying degrees, to this very day.

With relative effectiveness, his complex, ambiguous image in the public perception simultaneously appeals to a wide range of devoted communists, Georgia's patriotic nationalists, as well as the more statist segment of the Russian population. And even if his physical vestiges and images are few and far between, his presence is, nonetheless, not only felt but also often revered in many of the Georgian national narratives on a societal level. In order to temper what was seen by the Saakashvili regime as a pro-Soviet and thus a pro-Russian tendency traced not only in the tolerance but also admiration of the Stalin figure, the ruling party established a fact-finding commission on the twenty-first anniversary of the tragic April 9, 1989, event—when Soviet troops, tanks, and other armored vehicles entered central Tbilisi and crushed a peaceful demonstration.[30] The mission of the commission was to investigate and determine the historical truth and facts of the 200-year bilateral relationship between Georgia and Russia. Head of the commission, Vasil Rukhadze stated that most Georgians remain unaware of the "psychological and moral damages" left by tsarist and later communist Russian occupations, and therefore, a lack of a coherent and shared national narrative of the crimes committed by the occupying power continues to present a void in the collective memory of post-Soviet Georgian people. He also added that this void creates space for an immoral sense of nostalgia for friendship with a country responsible for thousands of innocent deaths of Georgians in Abkhazia and South Ossetia during the civil war in the early 1990s.[31] Rukhadze publicly recommended to the Georgian leadership that the government create a fact-finding commission to investigate facts and dispel myths surrounding crimes committed by Russia post-1801, the year that marked the beginning of tsarist occupation of Georgia.[32] Some of the recommendations offered by Rukhadze aimed at strengthening Georgian national identity and creating a common narrative of Georgia's history of struggle included the following: renaming of streets, squares, and other public spaces after victims and heroes of resistance against the Russian and later Soviet occupations; establishing commemoration of Russian annexation (January 8, 1801) and occupation (February 25, 1921) as days of national mourning.

Most of Rukhadze's recommendations were adopted and shortly thereafter implemented by the ruling United National Movement. In addition, as part of the de-Sovietization campaign, the Georgian government initiated the annual "Russian Occupation Week" comprised of public lectures and seminars hosted in high schools and universities nationwide, essay contests, discussions, art exhibitions on enforced colonization and a variety of other cultural activities highlighting the Soviet Union's "imperial activities." In addition, the "Patriots' Camps" established in 2005 by then newly elected UNM and its leader, Mikheil Saakashvili, became increasingly more popular nationwide after the 2008 Georgian-Russian War. The camps were designed to develop the new Georgian youth's patriotism, strengthen their physical and mental health, support their intellectual growth and moral qualities.[33] From 2010 onward, the multi-perspective approach was also reflected in the education system reform. In the newly revised history textbooks, the Democratic Republic of Georgia was presented as a controversial period in the nation's history. The August War further intensified the already conflicting memory politics in the educational system and reemphasized the concept of the "other," making the Russian Imperial and later Soviet Army occupation of Georgia increasingly more topical in the Georgian historiography.[34]

The outgoing leadership, still shaken by the events that transpired in August of 2008, was far from amused by this decision. "Restoring Stalin's monument in the 21st century is an unimaginably barbaric, anti-Georgian, anti-national, anti-state act, because it places Georgia in international isolation," responded soon-to-be former President of Georgia, Mikheil Saakashvili. "Restoring Stalin's statue in Gori, the town which was bombed by Russians [during the August 2008 war], amounts to spitting into the souls of the fallen Georgians."[35] Historian Lasha Bakradze strongly disagreed with Saakashvili's position, arguing that removing Stalin's statue will do nothing to strengthen Georgia's decades-long struggle against the Stalin era and totalitarian rule. "Rather, removing the monument silenced a painful history and shifted the blame onto others,"[36] instead of encouraging society to learn and accept its past and not fear the negative aspects of its recent history. "It might sound outrageous, but I am in favor of keeping the museum as it is, in its original state as the Stalin Museum. I am firmly opposed to getting rid of the traces of the past, as if this would resolve the serious problem of critically coming to terms with the past. This kind of manipulation of history and memory we know from Soviet times just too well,"[37] writes Bakradze in his recently published academic piece about the history and the future of the Stalin Museum in Gori. In the revisionist historical memory, perception of Russia, the successor of the Soviet Union, as a "historical aggressor," and the employment of the overall "optical"[38] vision of the past seventy years was used as a political strategy for strengthening Georgian national identity and its foreign policy vis-à-vis the northern neighbor, dictating what one should and should not remember.

After the opposition party Georgian Dream's meteoric ascent to power in late 2012, the Georgian state embarked on a systematic reevaluation of anti-Stalin and anti-Soviet rhetoric through a mandated revision of the dictator's legacy in the modern, independent country. By 2013, the city officials of Gori and the Georgian Ministry of Culture launched a campaign to restore the monument in Stalin's hometown, causing a split within the National Parliament and, to a degree, even among different generations of ordinary Georgian citizens. The Ministry of Culture convened a commission that same year on the future organization of the museum, and three years later, in 2016, the Georgian Dream made attempts to develop a new concept for the museum, an effort which, according to both member of the committee, Lasha Bakradze, and the head guide of the museum, Ketevan Kukhalashvili, was stalled as other "more pressing political issues"[39] took precedence.

The process of deep reckoning with the darkest pages of Stalinism was never completed—if at all properly initiated—in Georgian school curricula, history manuals, or even the Georgian mass media. "Georgia has yet to analyze its Soviet past, and by ignoring or rejecting our history over the last century and critically assessing our Soviet experience as such, the post-Soviet generation remains entangled amid its unresolved ancestral legacies,"[40] historian Lasha Bakradze notes. Rather than de-Stalinization, these post-Soviet efforts in Georgia resemble a form of a partially failed campaign of de-Sovietization. However, amid this process, the crucial separation between the victims and those responsible for the atrocities of this period was left out of the equation. "This is one of the side-effects of the ongoing lack of critical, in-depth analysis of our history in the Soviet context,"[41] Bakradze adds.

By eliminating, to varying degrees successfully in terms of implementation, crucial pages from Georgia's Soviet history, the state authorities produced an inevitable void. Since the Saakashvili years, this void has evolved into a distinct societal divide—an inherent sense of national pride among the older age group and absolute and utter ignorance of Stalin amid the young generation (aged 18–30) that is either entirely indifferent to or little informed about Georgia's Soviet history and, in particular, the lasting legacy of its rebellious son.[42]

In 2015, the Caucasus Research Resource Centers (CRRC) conducted research on "Passing or Failing the Stalin Test," focused on analyzing the contemporary perceptions of Stalin in Georgia. Based on the polling results, of nearly 1,900 respondents, the nationally representative sample of the Georgian-speaking population in the country selected through random route sampling between the ages of 18 and 90, 23.1% and 26.7% responded that they were told or taught "mostly positive stories" about Stalin in school and by their family members respectively, whereas 35.5% admitted that they were taught "nothing" about Stalin in school and 27.5% of them had also heard "nothing" of him in their homes.[43]

Not only during the United National Movement's rule and Mikheil Saakashvili's presidency but also in the aftermath, following Georgian Dream's ascent to power, Georgian state authorities have been passive in encouraging social scientists to study and analyze the country's Soviet past not only from the prism of an occupied colony but as a lasting phenomenon as such. In Russia, the field of Soviet Studies is still relevant and an area that is well-thought-through and analyzed, according to Bakradze, but in Georgia, not only the Soviet past but also the phenomenon and the figure of Georgia's infamous son, Joseph Stalin, is marginally explored in academia. "When it is explored, it is usually through the lenses of either fanatical pride and admiration or, on the contrary, deep antipathy and total rejection,"[44] Bakradze observes, adding that one of the most valuable angles for studying the legacies of Stalin is his Georgian background, and even more so, his impact on Georgian policymaking in the Soviet years which cannot and should not be minimized, but instead researched and closely analyzed. Instead, through lack of sufficient analysis and limited knowledge of the Stalin question, Georgians' relationship and overall perceptions remain largely "folksy" and frequently mythological.

The extremely subtle manipulation of Stalin's dual image in the political agenda of Georgian Dream, in contrast with an openly critical rhetoric promoted by Saakashvili's pro-Western United National Movement, has been devoid of overtly positive connotations. However, since 2012, Koba's role has been reinstated from that of a faded historical figure buried in Georgia's rejected Soviet past to a vital component of Georgian identity in the present that has successfully outlived the turbulent Soviet history.[45] In 2013, the same year when the new Georgian leadership reerected the monument outside of the Stalin museum, a smaller statue of Soso Jughashvili was approved by the officials and unveiled in the town of Telavi, situated in the eastern region of Kakheti. Within hours, unknown individuals vandalized the monument, coating the infamous son of the nation in orange paint.[46] The same research cited above, which was conducted five years after the demolition of Stalin's monument in Gori found that 48.7% of those surveyed believe the statue of Joseph Stalin "should stand in Gori's central square," whereas 3.9% state that in their opinion, the monument "should be destroyed."[47]

The Museum of Soviet Occupation in Tbilisi was also under serious consideration for a drastic political revision by the incoming ruling party, Georgian Dream, in 2012. Just one month after Georgian Dream party won the parliamentary election with a landslide, the newly appointed Deputy Minister of Culture, celebrated Georgian photographer Yuri Metchitov declared that the museum, established by the prior administration to commemorate the victims of Soviet Russian occupation of Georgian soil, had to change its name in order to convey a different message to the Russian Federation. "While Georgia was not a 'free' country in any sense of the term, we must change the terminology and definitions vis-à-vis a variety of cultural and highly politicized tropes," Metchitov said. "Pursuing these revised policies also presumes changing the name of the Museum of Soviet Occupation, otherwise we will be forced to continuously apologize [to Russia] for using this terminology, which in turn further strains our bilateral relations."[48] The Deputy Minister added that the museum invites what he believes to be "not unfounded irritation"[49] from the Kremlin, and in light of the incoming government's efforts aimed at establishing a much-needed rapprochement with Moscow, the underlying causes of such irritation should be eradicated or at least softened whenever and wherever possible. To this end, Metchitov recommended revising the concept behind the museum of occupation and turning it into a memorial shrine of the Soviet era. Instead of focusing on the atrocities of the epoch, he suggested incorporating some of the positive aspects and attributes of the past century for Georgia and the Georgian nation that should be remembered as vividly as the terrors endured during the last century.[50]

Metchitov's statement coincided with a rally organized by a pro-Russian civil society group, Erekle II funded by the Council of Georgia's Workers, a small pro-Kremlin political party, in front of the Museum of Soviet Occupation on Rustaveli Avenue. The civil society group demanded that the new government change the name of the cultural edifice to the Museum of Soviet Achievements in Georgia.[51] Three days later, another civil rights organization, the House of Tolerance, arranged a demonstration, this time outside of the Ministry of Culture, protesting active rumors of a possible closure of the museum.[52] In response to the renewed interest in preserving Soviet vestiges as part of safeguarding the collective memory, another Deputy Minister of Culture, Alexander Margishvili, reassured the protesters that an actual closure of the museum was not being discussed by state authorities. Over eight years later, the issue remains unresolved, while the museum continues to enjoy the status of a popular tourist attraction in the heart of Tbilisi.

The ultimate "Cult of Personality" of Joseph Stalin denounced by Nikita Khrushchev in 1956 and the duality of his legacy continue to loom over Georgian politics and its feeble post-USSR national identity. How do we interpret the revision of de-Stalinization by the United National Movement after the turbulent August events, followed by a call for the reinterpretation of his legacy, demonstrated by Georgian Dream's cooperation with the Gori officials to reerect Stalin's monument and talks of renaming the Museum of Soviet Occupation? Moreover, what are the effects, if any, of reinterpretation and reevaluation of the Soviet leader's legacy on the national identity of Georgian citizens in the post-Soviet era? These questions remain unanswered, if only for lack of concretely defined sentiments vis-à-vis Stalin in the current Georgian rhetoric, be it political or social. The answer may lie in the very place where Soso Jughashvili originated from and one that continues to house his shrine with pride unmatched by any other part of the former Soviet empire—Gori.

While Georgia, particularly under the leadership of former President Saakashvili, has devoted significant resources and efforts to erasing the symbols of Soviet occupation, it has also managed to separate Georgia's Soviet legacy from the direct legacy of the nation's rebellious son, Soso Jughashvili, in a remarkable manner. To this day, Georgians continue to claim and embrace the positive attributes of Stalin as unique Georgian traits, all the while attributing the atrocities of his regime to Russia and even Russians, arguing that it was the Soviet Union that corrupted a promising and idealistic student at the Georgian religious seminary, not the other way around. Moreover, they claim that the evil of Stalin is a byproduct of Russian tyranny and expansionism that preceded the creation of the Soviet Union. Many believe that the forced centralization of power and the ruthless system of terror of the Stalin regime is not reflective of his Georgian upbringing but rather of a *sistema* or system that he encountered when he found himself at the levers of the Soviet power machine.

Thus, Stalin is quietly revered by his fellow countrymen as a man who "came from a colonized nation, fought against the existing order, and broke the rules by rising to the top of a system led by Russians."[53] Both in admiration of his absolute power and condemnation of his ruthless totalitarianism, amid the battle of a small-country inferiority complex, Georgia continues to take pride in its native son's ability to break all the rules by claiming the Soviet Russian system, thus cultivating fear in the former occupant and, in turn, fostering a sense of "local patriotism"[54] among his compatriots.

The possible correlation between Stalin's legacy and Georgian nationalism is unlikely to be a byproduct of the political propaganda machines of Saakashvili's United National Movement or opposition leader Bidzina Ivanishvili's presently ruling and recently reelected party, Georgian Dream, but instead dates back to Nikita Khrushchev's infamous speech on the "Cult of Personality" at the Twentieth Congress of the Communist Party in February of 1956.

As historian Kevin M. F. Platt notes, the repressions of the general population are not the focal point of the speech. Instead, the core of the defamation of his cult of personality and the attempt to ultimately debunk the myth of Stalin as a great leader, the Savior, is the conflation of victims and perpetrators. The primary attention is paid to the "violence committed both by and against individuals"[55] within and like the party.

In his address to the Communist Party of the Soviet Union, Khrushchev denounced Stalin's leadership, in the process casting aspersions on the Georgian nation as a whole. He asserted that it was under Soviet rule that Georgia developed economically and culturally, whereas prior to the Bolshevik Revolution, Khrushchev claimed, 78% of the pre-Revolutionary Georgian population was entirely illiterate.[56] Furthermore, the General Secretary stated that had it not been for the Soviet rule, Georgia's industrial production would not have grown twenty-seven times as it did after the Bolshevik Revolution. He sarcastically observed that it was under Stalin's "genius leadership" as the "great son of the Georgian nation" that "thousands of innocent people fell victim to willfulness and lawlessness" and 70% of the 139 members of the Central Committee were arrested and shot on Stalin's orders in the early 1930s.[57] A leader who until then had been seen as the towering patriarch of the Soviet nation was accused by his successor as the man who had accorded himself "loathsome adulation" and throughout his rule had sought a "godhead status," but was ultimately a "giddy despot."[58] As Khrushchev recounted various episodes from Stalin's rule of "rampant terror," he reminded the Party Congress: "Comrades, the cult of the individual acquired such monstrous size chiefly because Stalin himself, using all conceivable methods, supported the glorification of his own person[a]."[59]

Nikita Khrushchev urged the delegates to the Twentieth Party Congress to keep his revelations secret as "we should not give ammunition to the enemy[60] and . . . wash our dirty linen before their eyes."[61] Thus, the "secret speech" made on February 25, 1956, was neither printed nor officially broadcasted by the authorities.[62] Although the content of Khrushchev's speech was not publicly known, rumors about insults to Georgian national pride were leaked shortly after the meeting of the Twentieth Congress of the CPSU. Through "shared knowledge and shared silence,"[63] Soviet Georgian and other fellow republics' elites learned that one of the explanations offered by General Secretary Khrushchev for Stalin's flawed personality was his Georgianness, or more specifically a blemish shaped or otherwise influenced by his "Georgian nationality."[64]

This anti-Georgian criticism embedded in Khrushchev's de-Stalinization policy produced an outrage among the socialist republic's citizens; Stalin, who, despite his unjustifiable acts of terror and violence against humanity—not in the least targeting his own compatriots—ultimately hailed from Georgia. Following the leak of Khrushchev's speech, a mass demonstration comprised primarily of high school and university students broke out on March 5, 1956, marking the third anniversary of Stalin's death. The gathering centered around Stalin as the key symbol of Georgian nationalism took place in front of the Stalin monument in the center of Tbilisi. As Irakli Khvadagiani, a researcher at the Soviet Past Research Laboratory (SovLab) in Tbilisi observes, the 1956 demonstrations were among the first—if not the first—protests of their kind to be organized spontaneously, through word of mouth in response to what the citizens perceived as a direct insult aimed at the people of Georgia.[65]

In no way sympathizing with ideologies promoted by communism or the Soviet Union at large, Georgian elites in particular had reached a consolatory consensus that while the Russians continued to "have us where they want[ed] us" as the occupants, "our boy [had] them"[66] wrapped around his Georgian finger. Georgians actively took to the streets, organizing a set of large-scale demonstrations across the republic, including Tbilisi, Gori, Kutaisi, Batumi, and Sukhumi. Initially, the crowds had assembled to celebrate the third anniversary since the passing of Joseph Stalin. However, as rumors about Nikita Khrushchev's "secret speech" at the Twentieth Party Congress denouncing Stalin's "Cult of Personality" began to circulate among those gathered in the streets of Soviet Georgia, the demonstrations began to acquire more pronounced nationalistic undertones and became increasingly more radical both in execution and content.

Four days later, on March 9, 1956, a student riot broke out in the Georgian capital, culminating in a massacre, where several dozen were killed, and hundreds were wounded by Soviet troops that dispersed the demonstrators.[67] Many years later, I would ask my father about this event which he, at the time an architecture student at the Academy of Arts in Tbilisi, attended with fellow classmates, carrying a four-meter-tall portrait of Stalin painted by Armenian painter and twice winner of the Stalin Prize, Dmitriy Nalbandyan. "The sense of euphoria was in the air that day," my father said. "It was less about whether or not you agreed with Stalin's policies, but much more so our collective response to what we perceived as the Kremlin's insult against our nation. We saw Khrushchev's de-Stalinization as an attempt to deprive us of our Georgian identity."[68] He added that it was not until many years later that his peers began to talk more openly about the darkest chapters in our history and the victims of Stalin's Great Terror.

To this day, debates about what motivated these protests stem from two lingering questions: was the underlining reason Georgia's love for its rebellious son whose memory was being marred by his successor or was it, instead, an expression of Georgian national pride and indignation? Timothy Blauvelt, Regional Director for the South Caucasus at American Councils for International Education, believes that denouncing Joseph Stalin equaled "revoking Georgia's favored place in the hierarchy of Soviet nationalities," where Georgia proudly embraced the status of "the most-favored lord republic."[69]

Nodar Notadze, the leader of the Georgian Republic's Popular Front who participated in the events of 1956 in Tbilisi wrote forty-five years later: "In the eyes of Georgians, this [Khrushchev's Secret Speech] was understood as a decisive attack against Georgians,"[70] or more explicitly, a pointed insult against Georgia inflicted by the central apparatus in Moscow. This movement, according to Irakli Khvadagiani, gave rise to self-victimization and even a rebirth of nihilism among Georgians toward the communist regime. "These protests also gave a renewed impetus to a deep-seated sense of nationalism among our people," Khvadagiani notes. "The belief was that if they're shooting us, if they're attacking and punishing us, it is only because we, as Georgians, are different from them, the Russians."[71]

Bearing in mind that Stalin's ruthless regime just decades earlier had destroyed Georgia's intelligentsia and its traditional peasantry, this is particularly paradoxical. Very few who lived under his rule would agree that throughout his tenure, Stalin favored Georgia and Georgians—but oddly, this fact does not seem to impact his approval ratings among a large portion of his compatriots even today. What is all the more paradoxical is that Georgians' collective reaction to the "secret speech" was not to accept that many of the widely accepted facts, values, and beliefs that were taught and promoted by the regime were sources of a political propaganda machine spreading as disinformation. Rather, the collective decision was to defend Stalin's memory and thus our identity and the very core of "Georgianness" as such.[72]

Another interesting fact in this sliver of Georgia's turbulent Soviet chapter lies in the fact that the demonstrations were attended by two active participants who were already at the front line of the Georgian dissident movement—Zviad Gamsakhurdia and Merab Kostava.[73] These two teenagers would eventually lead Soviet Georgia's national independence movement at the tail end of the collapsing empire—the former as the first President of the independent republic of Georgia, and the latter as one of the leaders of the National Liberation Movement in Georgia. Taking into account the active involvement of dissident movements in these demonstrations and their efforts to spread strong anti-Soviet propaganda, it becomes clear that the driving force behind these events was the quest to preserve Georgian identity[74] and its culture even more so than the memory of Joseph Stalin.

In order to understand how, if at all, national identity evolves in different sociopolitical and geopolitical environments, it is necessary to determine what is national identity, and whether it is stable or able to transform over time. On a broad level, national identity is one's identity or sense of belonging to one state or to one nation.[75] The nation from the perspective of one's identity is seen as a cohesive whole and is represented by distinctive traditions, culture, and language.[76] In psychological terms, national identity is "an awareness of difference" and "a feeling and recognition of 'we' and 'they,'"[77] thus recognizing the in-group from the out-group. National identity is not an inborn trait but is instead socially constructed.[78] It stems from and is triggered by the presence of elements from the common points in people's daily lives, including national symbols, language, history, culture, music, cuisine, mass media, etc.[79] Through similar social influences, an individual incorporates national identity into one's own personal identities by accepting the values, beliefs, and assumptions which directly align with national identity.[80]

Like nation building, national identity is not an event but rather a continuous process of transformation. It is dynamic and not stable, whereby a nationality that one is born into can at times vary from that which one acquires over time. In a constant state of flux, nations are in continual contest and subject to reinterpretation.[81] In "The Role of Cultural Paradigms in Georgian Foreign Policy," Stephen Jones argues that the post-Soviet crises following the fall of the USSR have resulted in the newly formed independent states' current institutional weaknesses and the ideological flux of nations seeking new identities, in turn, leading to newly formed ideas, identity and symbols. "The collapse of institutional life, the displacement of universal values by particular identities, the tasks of state-building, the rise of nationalist movements—all of this has made ideas and ideologies singularly visible and important,"[82] he writes. Due to this high visibility, scholars of post-Soviet history have turned to political culture to explain why the relatively newly reformed states, including Georgia, are not like the West, yet, they are not quite like the East either.

In their academic article, "'I am Georgian, and therefore I am European': Re-searching the Europeanness of Georgia," Maia Mestvirishvili and Natia Mestvirishvili note that "despite their remarkable enthusiasm for the European Union, national identity remains more profound for Georgians than a European identity."[83] They further observe that for Georgians, "Return to Europe" entails a less researched aspect—"the symbolic return to the world of European political values: freedom, democracy, justice, solidarity and prosperity."[84] Therefore, this view would suggest that Europeanness is not solely based on obtaining the much-coveted EU membership, but all the more so on "sharing European political values and identity."[85]

Pål Kolstøa and Aleksander Rusetskii's study on "Power Differentials and Identity Formation: Images of Self and Other on the Russian-Georgian Boundary" analyzes how Russia places itself in relation to one of its southern neighbors, Georgia, and vice versa, bearing in mind the geopolitical fact that both Russia and Georgia are "poised between East and West."[86] The researchers believe that in the Georgian-Russian case, the sui generis myth is a strategy of dissociation used by Georgians as an attempt to convince their fellow Europeans (and also themselves) of Russians' non-Europeanness and that they, unlike Georgians, do not belong inside the European gates. "To be sure, some Georgian intellectuals argue that Russian influences have left an indelible mark on Georgian national character. While they identify the Russians as 'the Other,' they find this Other not only without, but also within."[87]

In 2011, during a speech made at Freedom Square in Tbilisi, ironically the site of Stalin's infamous 1907 bank robbery,[88] Mikheil Saakashvili justified Georgia's European roots and its inevitable Western path, in dire opposition to the Soviet occupation. "The Georgian people have always considered themselves as Europeans and they had always made their European decision,"[89] he stated, emphasizing the first social democratic republic's Christian faith, the nation's historical alliance with Byzantine Empire, and the social democratic movement of the early twentieth century in opposition to Bolshevism as examples of Georgia's "European choices." Saakashvili added that the Democratic Republic of Georgia (DRG) had a true European face and it opposed Russia not only because it was an empire, but rather, because it was an "Asian other." The dichotomy of a barbarian Russia and a civilized European Georgia was being highlighted as the United National Movement's vision for the country's post-revolutionary chapter, particularly in the aftermath of the August War. The Georgian President stated: "Our road is taking us to Europe and the Russian road [would take us] to Asia and letting Bolshevism into our space and letting it rule here means burying the free and democratic Georgia forever," in turn, forever tearing Georgia apart from Europe.

We can therefore explore the formation of Georgian national identity after the demise of the Soviet Union with specific focus on two components: a) the birth of a nation's ideology and b) the birth of a nation's identity. "Historically, the birth of a nation as of an ideology precedes the birth of a nation as of an identity. Any ideology, in order to become an identity, should be worked out as an ideology."[90] In this context, we can view the reformation of post-USSR Georgia as a "rebirth" of a nation. This "rebirth" can be directly linked to the "creation of identities and the adoption of an identity by a concrete individual."[91]

During the glasnost' years, Georgian historians began to reevaluate Georgia's national history through a prism that was in dire opposition to the Soviet version, emphasizing independent Georgia's annexation and occupation by the Soviet Red Army and openly listing Soviet crimes against the South Caucasian country and reestablishing Georgia's historical connection to the first social democratic republic.[92] Both Gamsakhurdia and Kostava, the late Soviet period dissidents, alongside their fellow anti-Soviet dissidents, were strong believers that the Georgian culture and its national identity were entirely incompatible with the Soviet power and communist ideology. The paradox herein lies in the seemingly incompatible concepts of Stalinism on the one hand, and Georgian national identity on the other. While Gamsakhurdia was revered as a nationalist leader and a prominent populist who promoted the "Georgia for Georgians" approach and swept 87% of the votes during the first presidential elections in May of 1991, his popularity began to skyrocket and also expanded to those who remained avid supporters of Stalin and his strong leadership at the helm of the USSR.

Many have drawn parallels between Gamsakhurdia's populist style and the overall image of the supreme leader, which Georgian political scientist Ghia Nodia compares to the communist classics of the thirties.[93] However, unlike Stalin, Gamsakhurdia's dictatorial tendencies were manifested, first and foremost, in his rhetoric rather than deeds. Granted, his actions targeting the Georgian radical opposition at the time—the leaders of the Mkhedrioni movement—did bear traces of his dictatorial inclinations domestically. But it was his image outside of Georgia as that of an ultranationalist,[94] particularly in relation to his ethno-religious policies and the presentation of the very concept of "Georgianness" in predominantly ethnic terms, that solidified Gamsakhurdia's dictatorial tendencies as his lasting political legacy. In response to such criticism from abroad, Gamsakhurdia responded:

> Certain mass media outlets define the ongoing processes in Georgia in a peculiar manner. I want to note once again that our attitude towards non-Georgian population was always friendly. We do not plan to deviate from this principle. The Law on Ethnic Minorities, which will soon be issued by the government, will be a good testimony to our disposition. Rumors spread by our enemies about the oppression of ethnic minorities are a crude attempt to create negative public opinion regarding the ongoing political processes, the Supreme Council, and to thwart the development of independence.[95]

By 1989, a renewed wave of anti-Soviet sentiments led by Gamsakhurdia and Kostava mobilized Georgians who, amid the withering Soviet regime, were beginning to pine for restoring independence from the central apparatus in Moscow. On April 9, 1989, Soviet troops, tanks, and other armored vehicles entered central Tbilisi and crushed a peaceful demonstration by ruthlessly attacking the protestors demanding independence from Russia.[96] At least twenty people were killed, and hundreds more injured and poisoned by toxic gas. The brutality of the operation conducted by the Soviet military forces under the direction of General Igor Rodionov further inflamed the existing anti-Soviet sentiments across Georgia and paved the way for Zviad Gamsakhurdia's meteoric ascent to the very pinnacle of power.[97]

Several months later, during a public demonstration in Stalin's native Gori in November of 1989, a crowd of locals chanted, "Long live the new Stalin of Georgia!"[98] Somehow, these seemingly contrasting phenomena of Stalin and Georgian identity could coexist then and continue to coexist to this day. Although Georgia was able attain its independence from Soviet occupation, the nation has not been able to rid itself from the inherent and deep-seated pride to have given birth to a leader of Joseph Stalin's stature, and continues to maintain the shrine to the dictator—the Stalin Museum—as one of its most popular tourist sites.

On the surface, a simplistic explanation for this may lie in Georgia's small geographical size that can, in turn, help one understand the nation's partial sense of inferiority. Due to its size and lack of power on the geopolitical stage, Georgia is unable to claim "greatness" directly, but can do so indirectly by claiming the grand figure of Joseph "Soso" Stalin as the pride of his nation—not as a tyrannical autocrat but as a talented and bright son of an alcoholic and semiliterate cobbler from the small town of Gori. A rebellious offspring of a colonized nation, a child brought up surrounded by the romantic Georgian folklore and anti-Russian traditions, Koba rose to the helm of the Russian-led system and held not only the Soviet Union but also the world across the other side of the Iron Curtain in great fear by fostering respect, terror, and perverse admiration for his brutal rule. This hypothesis reinforces the nation's tendency for nationalism and overly patriotic devotion to the image of Stalin as a Georgian man, first and foremost, and only secondly—a Soviet leader. Furthermore, it brings to the fore the parallel association drawn by many Georgians between the USSR's victory in the Great Patriotic War with Stalin as a Georgian man rather than a Soviet leader and commander.

However, a more nuanced exploration renders a different explanation, albeit not necessarily in contradiction to the one presented above. The deep ambivalence toward and to a degree even an outright rejection of Georgia's participation in the Soviet past is often brought to the surface by the complicated question of Stalin and his rule. Memory becomes a political resource and a source of contestation, which in turn impacts the political rhetoric on the one hand and societal reactions and behaviors on the other. Let us not forget that the likes of Stalin, Lavrenti Beria and Sergo Orjonikidze—who were also at the top of the Soviet political machine and behind some of the darkest deeds of the era—were after all, of Georgian descent, too. Hence, the complication of coming to terms with the Stalin legacy not only as the victims of the regime but also as its active participants—some knowingly, others less so—in the regime's actions, complicit in the processes that either led the participants to repentance or total rejection of these events.

This unvoiced complicity of both the perpetrators and victims, and the constant confusion and even conscious, at times deliberate, conflation[99] of the two in the collective psyche and overall political narratives can also be traced throughout the previously mentioned "secret speech" in 1956. As historian Kevin M. F. Platt notes, this "pregnant silence" signals the lack of options other than "to claim to a shared victimhood and to place blame for collective violence on Stalin alone."[100] Therefore, the speech "On the Cult of Personality and Its Consequences" comes to signify not a defamation of the regime per se but, instead, of the leadership cult at the levers of the apparatus. Thus, the ownership and responsibility are only partial and largely uneven—a tendency that has outlived the Soviet regime and has seen a new reincarnation through the reincorporation of the legacies of the era. The reaction, although specific to the Communist Party elites, may also begin to explain, at least to some extent, the frequently over-romanticized reinterpretation of Stalin and his legacies in his native Georgia.

There is another added, albeit directly related, layer that further complicates the nesting doll—the post-traumatic century's survivor's guilt, as per Shoshana Felman and Dori Laub's *Testimony: Crises of Witnessing in Literature, Psychoanalysis, and History* argument, which is focused more specifically on the treatment of trauma of principally Holocaust survivors and the making and unmaking of the "impossible witness"[101] or, perhaps more appropriate in this context—those "witnessing the impossible" through constructing and reconstructing history. In Felman and Laub's theory, an event as deeply traumatic as the Holocaust is "an event without a witness,"[102] both due to the destruction of most of the evidence of the genocide and, moreover, the lack of a conceptual worldview in which the truth and facts surrounding these events may appear. Therefore, the dehumanized victim becomes the "impossible witness," unable to act as a witness to oneself and to the Holocaust "from the inside" of one's own "Auschwitz self."[103]

In the Soviet and post-Soviet contexts, Platt places this argument in the Soviet context, and takes the notion of the "impossible witness" to the historical trauma to another level. He suggests that following Stalin's death and later the eventual demise of the Soviet empire, a unified collective identity came to be, rooted in both the knowledge and disavowal not only of the "past wounding" but to an extent, if not more severely, the present "rewounding" in political as well as social narratives.[104] Platt argues that in the case of the Holocaust, although the mass suffering and its lingering repercussions have not been laid to rest either historically nor emotionally, this suffering is, nonetheless, in the past. In the Soviet case, however, particularly in dealings with the Great Purges and the mass atrocities and brutal crimes of Stalinism, the processes of reconciliation and reckoning, let alone an actual acceptance of responsibility, were never truly accomplished. The legacies of terror and trauma "permeate our lifeworlds [sic]," all the while continuously "evad[ing] our institutions of justice and public articulation."[105] This concept is equally applicable to inherited trauma passed on through nostalgia, collective memory, and collective violence as such, as well as a newly crafted trauma created and fundamentally based in the present, even if its original roots are tied to the prior generations.

In its very Georgian variant, Stalin is portrayed as a romantic—a Robin Hood of sorts, who, in a perfectly orchestrated crime and a globally notorious operation, raided a national bank in Tiflis in order to fund the Bolshevik Party's cause. He was arrested on seven separate occasions by the Tsarist powers that be, successfully escaping five times, before he ultimately returned to Russia as the leader of the Union of Soviet Socialist Republics. But through it all, in the Georgian narrative, Stalin remained a Georgian, first and foremost, and thus, even his rule of the Soviet people was seen, above all, as a rule of a Georgian presiding over all nationalities under the broad Soviet umbrella.

As Tengiz Buachidze, former Minister of Culture of Soviet Georgia, wrote in the glasnost' and perestroika period: "There was a short period in Stalin's life when he could have chosen the path of a Georgian nationalist. That was his youth, the 'Soselo' [one of his pseudonyms] period, when Soso Jughashvili wrote patriotic poems in the style of Akaky Tsereteli, some published by Ilya Chavchavadze in his journal *Iveria*. What would have happened had he continued on that path, no one can say. But that interest in Georgian poetry, the poetic potential in his following years and subsequent activity disappeared without a trace."[106]

And yet, Soso Jughashvili chose a different path, as Buachidze continues: "Stalin was never a narrowly nationalist player in the 'Georgian little league.' He was a revolutionary of international scope, partner to Lenin . . . who emerged victorious in a merciless ideological battle and through personal vendetta became sole ruler with absolute and unlimited personal power, de facto heir to the Russian autocracy."[107] Whenever Stalin is criticized—particularly by non-Georgians—not as a Soviet leader but rather as a son of Georgia who grew up to become a world-renowned tyrant, many in his native country leap to his immediate defense. As one of my Georgian acquaintances, an elderly pensioner in Tbilisi noted, "He was good while he was in Georgia—he was a remarkable student, a talented young man who wrote beautiful poems dedicated to his mother, robbed a bank to fund political activities to promote socialism, and then he went to Russia and they corrupted him."[108]

Another resident of Gori was even less inhibited in proclaiming his admiration for the great son of a small nation: "My father was persecuted, but I still love Stalin," the Georgian pensioner, sitting in a small boulevard overlooking the Stalin Museum, proudly declared. "Stalin didn't have anything to do with my father's arrest. People were informing on each other at that time. Stalin was a genius, and we live in a genius' town. A man from such a small republic created a huge empire—the Soviet Union!"[109] Does this quote demonstrate genuine and benign historical ignorance, an overwhelming sense of nostalgia for the Soviet past (or, as in the case of this respondent, the Soviet youth), or perhaps a deeply seated reluctance on the part of countless Georgians to admit the nation's acceptance of and even direct participation in the Soviet regime that occupied their country for seventy years? No matter how many decades pass following his death, Stalin's ghost continues to tear the Georgian society apart at its very core.

As this chapter aims to demonstrate, unlike in Russia, where political analysts such as Dmitry Oreshkin[110] and sociologists like Lev Gudkov[111] explain the rise of popularity of the Stalin era as both a reflection of the revised authoritarianism and its renaissance under Vladimir Putin and the rise of longing for authoritarianism in the midst of economic and political stagnation, as well as the overall need for a strong leader to revive Russia's role as a great power, in Georgia's case, admiration for Stalin, on the one hand, and support of authoritarianism, on the other, do not overlap. In the Russian variant, the hero of the next chapter, the Stalin legacy and the resurgence of support for the Soviet Dictator carries strong political undertones; the Georgian version is practically devoid of any traces of explicit political content, instead relying on national identity and the notion of Georgianness as its main foundation.

Although Stalin's image in modern-day Georgia hardly ever exhibits clearly pronounced political messages or related content, his legacy, albeit indirectly, has permeated and even influenced the political culture of this independent post-Soviet and self-reportedly European country. According to American political scientist, Lincoln Mitchell, over six decades after the tyrant's death, Georgia's domestic political culture has yet to shed Stalin's brutal influence. Time and again, the nation finds itself in pursuit of messianic leaders such as former Prime Minister Ivanishvili who, despite leaving Georgian politics and, in his own words, "letting go of the reins of power . . . for good,"[112] remains the "prime political mover"[113] in the country. These sentiments and other legacies of the Stalinist era—including what Mitchell describes as the "lingering distrust among citizens and between citizens and the state,"[114] as well as political structures where informal politics and actual proximity to the leader are frequently viewed as more significant than holding any formal political position—continue to "weigh down Georgia's political evolution."[115]

Irrespective of the political leadership and a pro- or anti-Stalin rhetoric employed and promoted by a given ruling party in the new millennium, it is ultimately the reigning image of Joseph Stalin as a "wise leader"[116] of a superpower and the great victor of the Great Patriotic War that drives the legacy of the dictator in the post-Soviet era. In Georgia's case, unlike that of Russia, this is seldom a consequence of nostalgia and longing for the Soviet Union per se, and to an even lesser extent, the remnants of a longing for a firm hand to govern the nation. Despite—or perhaps *in spite of*—the strong anti-Soviet ideology and political rhetoric employed in the aftermath of the five-day Russo-Georgian war in 2008, a lingering trend of nationalism with Soviet undertones continues to prevail in Georgian society.

A direct byproduct of its recent history, a post-Soviet Georgian national identity has yet to shed its characteristics and overall mentality reminiscent of its pre-Soviet self that is often recalled with fondness and nostalgia by the older Soviet Georgian generation that witnessed both negative as well as positive aspects of life under the communist rule. While society is far from nostalgic for an imminent return to communism and much less so to the Russian Imperial and later Soviet occupations, Georgia continues to harbor complex and at times conflicting feelings about its seventy-year history spent under occupation as one of the "wealthiest" and "most privileged"[117] republics within the Soviet space.

Over a quarter of a century after the fall of the Soviet regime, Georgia continues to grapple with its complicated, severely divided, and at times even self-contradictory relationship with the polemic figure of Georgian Koba and the "Russified" Stalin. In Georgia, Stalin remains at the intersection of greatness and terror—with the balance constantly shifting over time, through the different political and social periods in the country's post-Soviet existence. As greatness gains traction, terror loses ground and the historical image of the myth of Stalin gets farther and farther away from the collective memory actively distancing itself from the past. In this process, the mythological figure gains more traction and becomes increasingly more vivid in the mind's eye of the beholder. While in Russia's case the glory of the Great Patriotic War demonstrates the specific direction of the valence of greatness, which outweighs the terror, in his native Georgia, the debates regarding the specificities of the valence of Stalin's greatness in contrast with the terror and atrocities of his rule continue to ebb and flow. Yet, they appear to be ultimately rooted in the ethnocentric idea and ideals of Georgianness as a national identity, with the Stalin kaleidoscope used as a prism through which the nation views itself within as well as without, in relation to the "other."

Paradoxically, for the majority of Georgians, as demonstrated in 2013 by the previously discussed Carnegie Endowment and the Caucasus Research Resource Centers poll, the ambivalent legacy of Stalin in independent Georgia—both under the leaderships of Mikheil Saakashvili's UNM and Ivanishvili's Georgian Dream—continues to bear traces of national symbolism. As demonstrated in this chapter, while it is undeniably influenced by politics, Stalin's legacy in Georgia is driven increasingly less and less by strong political content, instead resting comfortably upon the pillars of national identity and national pride.[118] In the next layer of the Stalin figure—the tale of the Russified Koba turned Soviet Red Tsar—we delve into a different facet of this complex creature viewed through the prism of a briefly de-Stalinized and increasingly re-Stalinized climate in post-Soviet Russia.

NOTES

1. In Georgian: Georgia.
2. Official website of the Museum of Soviet Occupation in Tbilisi, Georgia, accessed April 20, 2017, and July 5, 2021. Web.
3. Sharon Macdonald and Gordon Fyfe, eds., *Theorizing Museums: Representing Identity and Diversity in a Changing World* (Cambridge, MA: Wiley-Blackwell, 1996), 5.
4. Toria, "The Soviet Occupation of Georgia in 1921 and the Russian-Georgian War of August 2008: Historical Analogy as a Memory Project," 330.
5. Nutsa Batiashvili, "Sites of Memory, Sites of Contestation: the Tbilisi Museum of Soviet Occupation and Visions of the Past in Georgia," *Cultures of History Forum*, June 1, 2017. Web. https://www.cultures-of-history.uni-jena.de/exhibitions/georgia/sites-of-memory-sites-of-contestation-the-tbilisi-museum-of-soviet-occupation-and-visions-of-the-past-in-georgia/#fn-text8.
6. James Kirchick, "Statute of Limitations," *New Republic*, August 12, 2010. Web. https://newrepublic.com/article/76970/russia-georgia-conflict-putin-stalin.
7. "Russian Jets Attack Georgian Town," BBC, August 9, 2008. Web. http://news.bbc.co.uk/2/hi/europe/7550804.stm.
8. "Rossiiskiye BBC razbombili pozitsii gruzinskoy artillerii bliz Gori," Lenta.ru, August 9, 2008. Web. https://lenta.ru/news/2008/08/09/gori/.
9. Ibid.
10. Anne Barnard, "Georgia and Russia Nearing All-Out War," *New York Times*, August 9, 2008. Web. https://www.nytimes.com/2008/08/10/world/europe/10georgia.html.
11. The article does not specify the name of the museum in Tbilisi, but it was likely the National Museum of Georgia.
12. Mark Trevelyan, "Curator Hides Stalin Mementoes from Russian Bombs," Reuters, August 31, 2008. Web. https://www.reuters.com/article/idINIndia-35253120080831.

13. "Rogor gaarides stalinis muzeumis eqsponatebi rusebs," Kvira.ge, August 7, 2020. Web. http://kvira.ge/586780.

14. "The Plenary Sitting of the Parliament of Georgia," Parliament of Georgia, December 10, 2010. Web. http://www.parliament.ge/en/media/axali-ambebi/the-plenary-sitting-of-the-parliament-to-of-georgia-26511.page.

15. Angela Wheeler, "Restored: Architectural and Territorial Integrity in the Republic of Georgia," *Aesthetics of Decay*, unpublished (April 4, 2015), 1.

16. Kutaisi is the third most-populous city in Georgia and fifth among the oldest cities in Europe.

17. Nana Gachava, "Georgian President Blasted over Monument's Demolition," Radio Free Europe/Radio Liberty, December 21, 2009. Web. https://www.rferl.org/a/Georgian_President_Blasted_Over_Monuments_Demolition/1910056.html.

18. Ibid.

19. "V Kutaisi vzorvan Memorial slavy: pogibli dva cheloveka," RBC, December 19, 2009. Web. https://www.rbc.ru/society/19/12/2009/5703d8729a7947733180d544.

20. Stalin's heavily accented Russian betrayed his image as the "Man of Borderlands," a fact that produced a number of sinister puns from his enemies, including Leon Trotsky who stated that "Russian always remained for him not only a language half-foreign and makeshift, but far worse for his consciousness, conventional and strained." See: Leon Trotsky, *Stalin: An Appraisal of the Man and His Influence* (New York: Harper & Brothers, 1941), 20. For more on Stalin as the man of borderlands, see: Alfred J. Rieber, "Stalin, Man of the Borderlands."

21. Erik H. Erikson, *Identity: Youth and Crisis* (New York: W. W. Norton, 1968), 159–63.

22. Erikson, *Identity and the Life Cycle* (New York: W. W. Norton, 1980), 122.

23. The roots of "identification" and "identity" both stem from "idem," meaning "the same," and it is therefore imputed that "identification" means "to become the same as" and "identity" means "to remain the same." See more on this topic: Carol Maurine Sutcliffe, "The Role of Teachers in the Identity Formation of Adolescents Restrained in Their Becoming," University of South Africa, November 1996. Web. https://core.ac.uk/download/pdf/43175455.pdf.

24. Robert C. Tucker, "A Case of Mistaken Identity: Djughashvili-Stalin," *Biography* 5, no. 1 (Winter 1982): 18.

25. As Stalin biographer and theorist of Soviet politics Robert C. Tucker writes, in his metamorphosis from Jughashvili into Joseph Stalin, the son of the Georgian cobbler in Gori shed his Georgian ethnic identity and accepted a Russian national identity, primarily through Bolshevism, and thus "joined the Russian nation." In doing so, Tucker argues, Stalin abandoned "a losing for a winning side in history." See: Robert C. Tucker, *Stalin as Revolutionary, 1879–1929: A Study in History and Personality* (New York: Norton, 1973), 81, 82, 115, 120, 137, 140–142. In his trilogy on Stalin, historian Stephen Kotkin recounts instances where Jughashvili sought to deliberately downplay and at times outright abandoned his full "Georgianness" in order to blend into his Russian environment and later as Joseph Stalin navigated between his Georgian, Russian, and Soviet identities to fit his policies and politics. See: Stephen Kotkin, *Stalin: Paradoxes of Power, 1878–1928* (New York: Penguin, 2015).

26. Erik Scott, *Familiar Strangers: The Georgian Diaspora and the Evolution of the Soviet Empire* (London: Oxford University Press, 2016).
27. In Georgian: a traditional feast as part of the Georgian social culture and identity.
28. Tucker, "A Case of Mistaken Identity," 21.
29. Ibid., 23.
30. This event and its significance in Georgia's modern history is further discussed later in this chapter.
31. Vasili Rukhadze, "Kolektiuri Mekhsiereba" ("Collective Memory"), Pirvelebi, n.d. 2010. Web. https://iberiana.wordpress.com/iberiana/rukhadze2/.
32. On January 8, 1801, Russian Tsar Paul I signed a decree on the incorporation of the Kingdom of Kartli-Kakheti into the Russian Empire. The decree was confirmed thereafter by Tsar Alexander I on September 12, 1801. For more on the incorporation of Georgia within the Russian Empire, see: Nikolas K. Gvosdev, *Imperial Policies and Perspectives towards Georgia: 1760–1819* (Basingstoke: Macmillan, 2000), and David M. Lang, *The Last Years of the Georgian Monarchy: 1658–1832* (New York: Columbia University Press, 1957).
33. For more about the "Patriots' Camps," see: "Information about the Patriotic Camps," Official Portal of Ministry of Diasporan Affairs of Georgia, 2008. Web. http://civiclab.narod.ru/civic/c1_info/2008inf/patricamps08.htm; Eka Chitanava, "Salome Jashi Shows and Talks about Young Generation Raised in Patriotic Camps," *Georgia Today*, February 12, 2010. Web. www.georgiatoday.ge/print_version.php?id=7720&version=497.
34. For an in-depth exploration of Georgian historical narratives in the education system in the late Soviet and post-Soviet periods, see: Nino Chikovani, "The Georgian Historical Narrative: From Pre-Soviet to Post-Soviet Nationalism," *Dynamics of Asymmetric Conflict* 5, no. 2 (July 2012): 107–15; Salome Mekhuzla and Aideen Roche, "National Minorities and Educational Reform in Georgia," European Centre for Minority Issues (ECMI), September 2009. Web. https://www.files.ethz.ch/isn/106681/working_paper_46_en.pdf.
35. "Culture Ministry: Stalin Statue, Removed Three Years Ago, Planned to Be Put in His Museum," Civil.ge, July 30, 2013. Web. https://civil.ge/archives/123060.
36. Lasha Bakradze and Giga Zedania, "Stalinis muzeumshi," *Liberali*, no. 7 (August 11, 2009): 8–9; Bakradze, interview with author.
37. Lasha Bakradze, "Past and Future of the Stalin Museum in Gori," *De Gruyter Oldenbourg* 103 (December 2020): 11.
38. Eviatar Zerubavel, *Time Maps, Collective Memory and the Social Shape of the Past* (Chicago: University of Chicago Press, 2003): 26–27.
39. Kukhalashvili, interview with author.
40. Bakradze, interview with author.
41. Ibid.
42. Based on the findings of the joint Carnegie Endowment and Caucasian Research Resource Centers (CRRC) survey conducted in late 2012, 22% of young Georgians aged 18 to 30 described their attitude toward Stalin as "indifferent," while over a quarter of the young respondents entirely refused to answer any questions

pertaining to their attitudes toward the Soviet leader (3%), "do not know" how to answer the question (16%), or otherwise admitted that they "do not know" who Stalin is (10%). Carnegie Endowment and the CRRC interpreted all of the answers that contained "I don't know" as a sign of indifference or lack of knowledge. See more: "The Stalin Puzzle," Carnegie Endowment for International Peace, March 1, 2013. Web. https://carnegieendowment.org/files/stalin_puzzle.pdf.

43. Alexi Gugushvili, Giorgi Babunashvili, Peter Kabanchik, Ana Kirvalidze, and Nino Rcheulishvili, "Collective Memory, National Identity, and Contemporary Georgian Perspectives on Stalin and the Soviet Past," Caucasus Research Resource Centers, Tbilisi, Georgia, September 2015. Web. https://www.researchgate.net/profile/Peter-Kabachnik/publication/282072355_Collective_Memory_National_Identity_and_Contemporary_Georgian_Perspectives_on_Stalin_and_the_Soviet_Past/links/56022e8d08ae42bbd541f78a/Collective-Memory-National-Identity-and-Contemporary-Georgian-Perspectives-on-Stalin-and-the-Soviet-Past.pdf.

44. Bakradze, interview with author.

45. Alexi Gugushvili and Peter Kabachnik, "Stalin Is Dead, Long Live Stalin? Testing Socialization, Structural, Ideological, Nationalist, and Gender Hypotheses," *Post-Soviet Affairs* 31, no. 1 (September 2015): 1–36.

46. The symbolic choice of color, which may have carried undertones hinting at Ukraine's Orange Revolution, was never confirmed.

47. Gugushvili et al., "Collective Memory, National Identity, and Contemporary Georgian Perspectives on Stalin and the Soviet Past."

48. "Gauqmdeba tu ara sabtchota okupatsiis muzeumi?" *Netgazeti*, November 12, 2012. Web. https://netgazeti.ge/news/17425/.

49. Ibid.

50. "Iuri mechitovi: okupatsiis muzeumis dasakheleba da arsi absurdia," *Tabula*, November 23, 2012. Web. http://www.tabula.ge/ge/story/62773-iuri-mechitovi-okupaciis-muzeumis-dasaxeleba-da-arsi-absurdia.

51. "Saprotesto aqcia muzeumis gauqmebis cinaaghmdeg," Palitratv.ge, November 15, 2012. Web. https://www.palitravideo.ge/yvela-video/akhali-ambebi/23513-saprotesto-aqcia-okupaciis-muzeumis-gauqmebis-tsinaaghmdeg.html.

52. "Aqcia kulturis saministrostan," Ministry of Culture's Myvideo.ge page, November 16, 2012. Web. https://www.myvideo.ge/?video_id=1852094.

53. Caitlin Hu, "Why Georgians Fight to Keep Statues of Stalin, as the Rest of the Former USSR Tears Them Down," *Quartz*, November 7, 2014. Web. https://qz.com/292901/historical-statues-illegal-stalin-statues-keep-popping-up-in-gori-georgia/.

54. Thomas de Waal, ed., "The Stalin Puzzle: Deciphering Post-Soviet Public Opinion," 49.

55. Kevin M. F. Platt, "Secret Speech: Wounding, Disavowal, and Social Belonging in the USSR," *Critical Inquiry* 42, no. 3 (Spring 2016): 660.

56. "Khrushchev's Secret Speech, 'On the Cult of Personality and Its Consequences,' Delivered at the Twentieth Party Congress of the Communist Party of the Soviet Union," February 25, 1956, Russian State Archive of Contemporary History, stock 1, inventory 2, document 3, Russian Federal Archives, Moscow, Russia.

57. Ibid.

58. Ibid.

59. Ibid.

60. This comment likely refers to the capitalist world and, more specifically, the Cold War rival of the Soviet Union—the United States of America.

61. "Khrushchev's Secret Speech, 'On the Cult of Personality and Its Consequences,' Delivered at the Twentieth Party Congress of the Communist Party of the Soviet Union," February 25, 1956, History and Public Policy Program Digital Archive, From the Congressional Record: Proceedings and Debates of the 84th Congress, 2nd Session (May 22, 1956–June 11, 1956), C11, Part 7 (June 4, 1956), 9389–9403. Web. http://digitalarchive.wilsoncenter.org/document/115995.

62. Following a number of bootleg versions, the "secret speech" officially appeared in print for the first time thirty-three years later, during Mikhail Gorbachev's glasnost' campaign. It was published in the *News of the Central Committee of the Communist Party of the Soviet Union*'s April 6, 1989 edition.

63. Platt, "Secret Speech: Wounding, Disavowal, and Social Belonging in the USSR," 651.

64. Lasha Bakradze, "Georgia and Stalin: Still Living with the Great Son of the Nation" (Washington, DC: Carnegie Endowment for International Peace, 2013), 47.

65. Irakli Khvadagiani, interview with author, December 6, 2020.

66. Bakradze, "Georgia and Stalin," 48.

67. "March Riot Dead in Tiflis Set at 100," *New York Times*, April 22, 1956, 1.

68. Givi Japaridze, interview with author, January 11, 2021.

69. Timothy Blauvelt, "Status Shift and Ethnic Mobilisation in the March 1956 Events in Georgia," *Europe-Asia Studies* 61, no. 4 (June 2009): 653.

70. Nodar Notadze, "Siskhliani paraskevi," in G. Vepkhvadze, ed., *9 marti, 1956: kadrshi da kadrgaret* (Tbilisi: Garchi, n.d.), 94–104.

71. Khvadagiani, interview with author.

72. The previously cited research conducted by the CRRC in 2015 showed that an overwhelming 37.6% of those surveyed have "not heard" about the demonstrations in Georgia in 1956. See: Gugushvili et al., "Collective Memory, National Identity, and Contemporary Georgian Perspectives on Stalin and the Soviet Past," p. 41.

73. Both Gamsakhurdia and Kostava were detained for participating in the 1956 protests—the first of several arrests as a result of their dissident activities.

74. For more on Georgian national identity and its formation and evolution in the pre-Soviet, Soviet, and post-Soviet periods, see: Tatia Kekelia, "Building Georgian National Identity: A Comparison of Two Turning Points," in Alexander Agadjanian, Ansgar Jodicke, and Evert var der Zweerde, eds., *Religion, Nation and Democracy in the South Caucasus* (London and New York: Routledge, 2015), 120–34; Lali Surmanidze and Lia Tsuladze, "The Formation of Nation-State and Cultural Identity: A Georgian Perspective," *IBSU Scientific Journal* 2, no. 2 (2008): 87–102; Gigi Tevzadze, "The Birth of the Georgian Nation: Identity and Ideology, Political and Societal Identities, Nationality and Religiosity," *Identity Studies* 1, no. 1 (January 2009): 5–21; Oliver Reisner, *Die Schule der Georgischen Nation: Eine Sozialhistorische Untersuchung der Nationalen Bewegung in Georgien am Beispiel der 'Gesellschaft zur Vorbereitung der Lese-und Scheibkunde unter den Georgiern' (1850–1917)*,

Wiesbaden, 2004; Reisner, "Georgia: The Making of a National Culture," International Conference at the University of Michigan, Ann Arbor, May 18, 2008.

75. Richard Ashmore, Lee Jussim, and David Wilder, eds., *Social Identity, Intergroup Conflict, and Conflict Reduction*, Rutgers Series on Self and Social Identity, vol. 3 (Oxford University Press, 2001).

76. "Definition of National Identity in English," *Oxford Dictionaries*.

77. Yoonmi Lee, *Modern Education, Textbooks, and the Image of the Nation: Politics and Modernization and Nationalism in Korean Education* (New York: Routledge, 2012).

78. Benedict Anderson, *Imagined Communities: Reflections on the Origin and Spread of Nationalism* (London: Verso, 1991).

79. János László, *Historical Tales and National Identity: An Introduction to Narrative Social Psychology* (New York: Routledge, 2013).

80. Ervin Staub, "Blind versus Constructive Patriotism: Moving from Embeddedness in the Group to Critical Loyalty and Action," in Daniel Bar-Tal and Ervin Staub, eds., *Patriotism: In the Lives of Individuals and Nations* (Nelson-Hall, 1997), 213–28.

81. Ronald Suny, "Rethinking Social Identities: Class and Nationality," in *The Revenge of the Past: Nationalism, Revolution and the Collapse of the Former Soviet Union* (Stanford, CA: Stanford University Press, 1993).

82. Stephen Jones, "The Role of Cultural Paradigms in Georgian Foreign Policy," in Rick Fawn, ed., *Ideology and National Identity in Post-communist Foreign Policy* (New York: Routledge, 2003).

83. Natia Mestvirishvili and Maia Mestvirishvili, "'I am Georgian and Therefore I am European': Re-searching the Europeanness of Georgia," *Central European Journal of International and Security Studies* 8, no. 1 (May 2014): 52–65.

84. Ibid.

85. Ibid.

86. Pål Kolstø and Aleksander Rusetskii, "Power Differentials and Identity Formation: Images of Self and Other on the Russian-Georgian Boundary," *National Identities* 14, no. 2 (2012): 139–55.

87. Ibid.

88. An armed bank robbery organized by top-level Bolsheviks, including Vladimir Lenin, Joseph Stalin, and fellow Russian revolutionary Maxim Litvinov, took place on June 26, 1907, and funded the revolutionary movement. More on the "Tiflis bank robbery," see Simon Sebag Montefiore's *Young Stalin* (Vintage, 2009).

89. "The President of Georgia Met the Representatives of EU Countries," Official Website of President of Georgia, Mikheil Saakashvili, May 12, 2008. Web. www.president.gov.ge/en/PressOffice/News/SpeechesAndStatements?p=2337&i=1.

90. Gigi Tevzadze, speech at the symposium on "Georgia at the Crossroads of European and Asian Cultures," the Harriman Institute at Columbia University, May 4, 2009.

91. Ibid.

92. Iakob Putkaradze, "Ar unda dagvrches 'tetri lakebi': sakartvelos gasabchoebis samartlebrivi shepaseba" ("We have to Fill 'Blank Spots': On the Legal Justification of the Sovietization of Georgia"), *Komunisti*, August 25, 1989; Levan Toidze,

Interventsiats, okupatsiats, dzaldatanebiti gasabchoebats, paktobrivi anektsiats (*Intervention, Occupation, Forcible Sovietization, Actual Annexation: It's All of This*) (Tbilisi, Georgia: Metsniereba, 1991), 143–44.

93. Ghia Nodia, "Political Turmoil in Georgia and the Ethnic Policies of Zviad Gamsakhurdia," in Bruno Coppieters, ed., *Contested Borders in the Caucasus* (Brussels: VUB University Press, 1996).

94. When asked if he would describe himself as a nationalist, Gamsakhurdia responded that it would be more accurate to use the term "patriot." See: Interview with Zviad Gamsakhurdia, *Sakartvelos Respublika* 36:56, February 22, 1991, 1.

95. Interview with Zviad Gamsakhurdia, *Sakartvelos Respublika* 39:59, February 27, 1991, 1–2.

96. Esther B. Fein, "At Least 16 Killed as Protesters Battle the Police in Soviet Georgia," *New York Times*, April 10, 1989. Web. https://www.nytimes.com/1989/04/10/world/at-least-16-killed-as-protesters-battle-the-police-in-soviet-georgia.html; "27 Years On from April 9 Tragedy: Georgia Remembers Heroes Who Died for the Country's Independence," Agenda.ge, April 9, 2016. Web. https://agenda.ge/en/news/2016/843.

97. Kirk Bennett, "Georgia's Dilemma," *American Interest*, July 10, 2017. Web. https://www.the-american-interest.com/2017/07/10/georgias-dilemma/.

98. Inga Kochieva and Alexi Margiev, *Georgia: Ethnic Cleansing of Ossetians 1989–1992* (Moscow, Russia: Europe Publishing House, 2005).

99. Alexander Etkind, *Warped Mourning: Stories of the Undead in the Land of the Unburied* (Stanford, CA: Stanford University Press, 2013), 7–11, 170.

100. Platt, "Secret Speech: Wounding, Disavowal, and Social Belonging in the USSR," 662–63.

101. Shoshana Felman and Dori Laub, *Testimony: Crises of Witnessing in Literature, Psychoanalysis, and History* (New York: Routledge, 1991).

102. Ibid., xvii.

103. Marianne Hirsch and Leo Spitzer, "The Witness in the Archive: Holocaust Studies/Memory Studies," *Memory Studies* 2, no. 2 (2009): 151–70.

104. Platt, "Secret Speech: Wounding, Disavowal, and Social Belonging in the USSR," 652.

105. Ibid.

106. Tengiz Buachidze, "Martovskaya tragediia 1956 goda v Tbilisi," *Literaturnaia Gazeta* 7 (1988): 111.

107. Ibid., 111–12.

108. Anonymous, interview with author, December 27, 2019.

109. Salome Asatiani, "The Great Terror: In Stalin's Birthplace, Forgiving and Forgetting," Radio Free Europe, August 14, 2007. Web. https://www.rferl.org/a/1078153.html.

110. Dmitry Oreshkin, *Jughaphilia and the Soviet Statistical Epic Poetry* (Moscow, Russia: Mysl', 2019); Sergei Medvedev, "Jughaphilia," Radio Svoboda, March 29, 2020. Web. https://www.svoboda.org/a/30511648.html.

111. Lev Gudkov, "Stalin—eto mif," Lenta.ru, June 12, 2019. Web. https://lenta.ru/articles/2019/06/12/stalin/.

112. "Bidzina Ivanishvili politikidan 'sabolood' midis," Civil.ge, January 11, 2021. Web. https://civil.ge/ka/archives/390513.

113. Lincoln Mitchell, "In Stalin's Hometown, Absent Statues and Lingering Legacies," *Observer,* July 31, 2015. Web. http://observer.com/2015/07/in-stalins-hometown-absent-statues-and-lingering-legacies.

114. Mitchell, interview with author, November 10, 2016.

115. Mitchell, "In Stalin's Hometown, Absent Statues and Lingering Legacies."

116. Lev Gudkov, "The Archetype of the Leader: Analyzing a Totalitarian Symbol" (Washington, DC: Carnegie Endowment for International Peace, 2013), 34.

117. *Georgia Mineral & Mining Sector Investment and Business Guide: Strategic Information and Regulations* (Washington, D.C.: International Business Publications, 2013), 23.

118. Bakradze, "Georgia and Stalin," Carnegie Endowment for International Peace, 53.

Chapter III

Soviet Red Tsar

While the tale of the Georgian Stalin is primarily focused on what lies beneath the Dictator's multilayered mask, in its Russian variant, the Soviet Red Tsar serves, above all, as a model of ruthless leadership that defeated the global evil of the twentieth century—Nazism. This chapter explores (Soviet) Russia's brief flirtations with de-Stalinization and its eventual path toward re-Stalinization under the leadership of Vladimir Putin in the new century.

In the early 1990s, with the taste of freedom and democracy, which many equated with complete chaos where "anything goes," came a sense of romanticization of the not-so-distant past where everything had seemed predetermined, forever, and comfortably stagnant. The change was sudden, abrupt, and, contrary to what many expected in the West, deeply disturbing and uncomfortable. Those who until now had spent (and, to a degree, continued to do so well into the mid-1990s) hours in mile-long lines for a loaf of bread or a pair of shoes from "the near abroad" were now queuing up in front of the notorious symbol of the capitalist world—the golden arches of American fast-food empire. Burger-starved throngs of consumers anxiously waited in endless lines undoubtedly longer than the queues outside Lenin's mausoleum had been in years.[1] In the average Soviet citizen's mind's eye, the alien capitalist America had finally landed on socialist soil. With Gorbachev's glasnost' and perestroika underway, the Soviet Union was parting the Iron Curtain and shifting its gaze toward the West. While the Soviet Union continued to actively strengthen its ties with the Western world, with the winds of change came the former "Evil Empire's" very first McDonald's in Moscow. Thus began the mass-*McDonaldization* of the late Soviet society, which peaked in popularity and reach under the new dawn of Boris Yeltsin's post-Soviet democratic Russia.

The term *McDonaldization*, coined by American sociologist George Ritzer, describes the international phenomenon by which "the principles of the fast-food restaurant are coming to dominate more and more sectors of American society as well as of the rest of the world . . . sweeping through seemingly impervious institutions and regions of the world."[2] Referring to the McDonald's chain as an institution that has come to "occupy a central place in American popular culture,"[3] Ritzer labels the fast-food franchise as the "ultimate icon of Americana" that successfully permeated the Soviet marketplace against the ramifications posed by the rigid system of communist bureaucracy. Some even joked that reminiscent of Peter the Great's St. Petersburg that offered Russia its window to Europe, Gorbachev's introduction of McDonald's onto the Soviet scene had granted the previously isolated communist society a window to the capitalist-consumerist world and, with that, a taste of America in the shape of a double-cheeseburger with an optional side of "freedom fries."

Like other nine-year-old children in Russia, I would look forward to a weekend spree with my parents to the golden arches in Moscow's iconic Old Arbat Street, which housed my favorite McDonald's in town. I would sit at one of the faux marble tables in the heart of the city's historical district, devouring a box of an all-American Happy Meal and sharing a large order of French fries with my father. At a nearby table, frequent McDonald's goers, impersonators of Lenin and Stalin clad in Red Army military uniforms and carrying miniature Soviet flags, were also sharing freedom fries and two small paper cups of Coca-Cola. "We never thought this day would come," my father would tell me, chuckling at the amusing sight of Stalin and Lenin unreservedly devouring the taste of capitalism. "Eating American food in Russia—out in the open without hiding behind closed kitchen doors—would have been unheard of just a few years ago." His words meant little to me at the time. But as history would demonstrate, the symbolic importance of Big Macs and milkshakes would take on a new meaning—as would the Soviet public's perception of America no longer depicted by the authorities in their active anti-American propaganda as "a frightening place of the homeless, jobless, drug-addicted victims of ruthless capitalists."[4]

Alas, the initial embrace of the cholesterol-infused American soft power by former communists would not last forever. The "happily ever after" of Russia's love affair with the West would eventually come to an abrupt end and, with the rise in tensions and sanctions, the relationship between Russia and the West would, once again, sour. As the metaphysical Stalin was preparing to make a comeback in the early 2000s, McDonald's, on its part, was slowly going out of favor with the Russian state authorities under Vladimir Putin. Shortly after the United States and the European Union announced their sanctions in 2014 (primarily targeting the Kremlin) in response to Russia's annexation of Crimea and the eruption of war in Eastern Ukraine, the Russian authorities, in turn, responded by placing embargoes on a variety of food product imports from the West. Although the state officials insisted the timing was an unfortunate coincidence, Russian authorities would simultaneously close ten outlets of the American eatery, placing the fast-food giant under extensive investigation with allegations of malpractice of food safety.[5] Only days later, nationwide protests erupted in several Russian regions, urging for a mass-closure of all McDonald's restaurants across the country. "Down with American Fast Food,"[6] chanted the anti-McDonald's activists in Bryansk, near the Russia-Belarus border, as the golden days of American "golden arches" reached their lowest point yet. In a nostalgic blog piece on the Soviet days gone by, Russian photographer Mitya Kushelevich laments the partial closure of the American restaurant in Putin's Russia, interpreting it as "the writing on the wall for a lot of Russians." He further elaborates that this is not a bullet targeting the United States in response to the Western sanctions but rather a message aimed at the Russian people as a warning that "the window to the world is closing."[7]

Back in 1991, as the first flagship restaurant promoting American freedom opened in downtown Moscow on Pushkin Square with "a splash of brilliant color in the middle of a gray city," the Soviet TV channels actively advertised the unprecedented slogan, wooing toward Americanization of society: "If you can't go to America, come to McDonald's in Moscow."[8] The days of pro-American propaganda seem to have left nothing but an aftertaste—at least for the foreseeable future, as Russia embraces patriotism and an overt anti-American propaganda rhetoric that no soft-power "burger diplomacy" is likely to combat. Today, as *McDonaldization* is going out of style, *re-Stalinization* is making a comeback—in fact, he is already back and, many would argue, stronger and more popular than ever since his death.[9]

More baffling than the older generation's affinity with and loyalty to Stalin is the growing popularity of this historical figure among the Russian youth, many of whom were born after the collapse of the USSR. But unlike our ancestors, for whom the greatness and terror of the Stalin years are deeply ingrained in our living memory, for the new generation, Stalinism itself has become a cultural trope from which we are removed both temporally and spatially—yet not sufficiently and entirely detached to leave us devoid of its lingering side effects. As American journalist Mac McCall hailing from another Georgia—the US state—writes, over the past decades, the figure of Stalin has evolved into a Rorschach test of Soviet and post-Soviet generations, whereby the subjects' inkblots depicting memories of terror, fear, nostalgia, and greatness all offer psychological interpretations on a canvas that projects their "diagnoses of the country's ailments and prescriptions for its successes."[10] Although McCall uses this analogy for the Republic of Georgia, one could very easily expand the same diagnosis to the Soviet and post-Soviet Russian subjects as well.

Many if not all of the Russian millennials, otherwise referred to more colloquially as the post-Soviet generation, have known no leader but the present ruler as of the past two decades—Vladimir Putin. Less and less, Russian schools educate the young about the Red Tsar's reign in the midst of terror and mass purges, instead focusing on presenting Stalin as the Soviet modernizer.[11] For example, in 2007, a state-mandated educational initiative designed a national curriculum which posited that Stalin's plans and courses of action did not stem from despotic spurs of madness, and neither were they motivated by repressions of the Soviet people. Rather, the curriculum claimed, they were "well-thought-out, understandable, and sound."[12] Perhaps as a direct result of this, 47% of Russian youngsters between the ages of 18 and 24 surveyed in late 2018[13] were unaware of the Stalin-era repressions that killed millions of Soviet citizens according to official state-published numbers and well into the millions according to non-state-affiliated scholars.[14]

As is frequently the case with any form of cognitive dissonance following an unexpected rupture in a collective memory and identity, the drastic shifts in the geopolitical and social environments (granted, the two do not always go hand in hand or even occur at the same time) drive societal adaptation through a forced, collective modernization of a myth. In this particular instance, the myth of history and the collective past undergoes changes not in spite of but rather in support of a disruption of a past that, at least in its current form, apparently never occurred to begin with. In other words, we are facing a past that never was, much like nostalgia for that which also never was, except as a figment of our colorful imagination. A monolithic version of a Soviet past suddenly invites an array of interpretations, forcing one to lose track of the different versions and the numerous grey spots between truth and untruth—if such concepts do, indeed, stand the test of time and a wide plethora of changes and reinterpretations.

Therefore, it is due to the avoidance of a cognitive dissonance at best or a post-traumatic syndrome at worst that a given society embraces the revisions to its historical past as it has been known thus far in a futile attempt to "find a feasible explanation to the changes in reality that seldom make sense," which, according to Russian social scientist and political analyst Dmitry Oreshkin, is "what ultimately allows every one of us to find something suitable to us and acceptable to our being."[15] To this end, if we take Oreshkin's thought one step further, having lost that one single tangible image—a master version—of the

Motherland (or, in prior tsarist times, also referred to as the Fatherland[16]) and its history, the post-Soviet psyche has no choice but to dismember itself from the monolithic Soviet faith and look for other historical interpretations of a past that are more polyphonic and thus more malleable, flexible, and fluid.

State-funded and thus approved modern Russian history textbooks, including Alexander Filippov's controversial *Modern History of Russia, 1945–2006: A Teacher's Manual*, promote the prevailing rhetoric that the Stalin era was an inevitable consequence of the "hard international environment,"[17] leaving no viable alternative to Soviet Russia under the dire circumstances of that period. Such narratives that capitalize on historical factors and threats, emanating first from Nazi Germany during World War II and later from the collective West during the Cold War, allow Stalinism and the regime's bloody, ruthless policies to shed the primary responsibility in the name of "tragic inevitability,"[18] indirectly transferring the responsibility to the "other" as the ultimate root of all evil.

Meanwhile, history books on the Soviet Union and the Cold War that condemn Stalinism and explicitly denounce Joseph Stalin's rule are explicitly condemned by Russian state-operated media and other government affiliates. Andrei Suslov is a Perm State University professor of history who authored *Single Concept of History in Russia*, a chronicle on the creation and recreation of unified narratives of Russian national history in high school textbooks nationwide. In 2017, his latest book, *A Teachers' Guide to Studying, Understanding and Examining the Stalin Repressions* was explicitly criticized by Roskomnadzor, the Russian state information watchdog that supervises communications, information technology, and mass media, classifying the textbook as "dangerous to the health of children."[19] Instead, Roskomnadzor, in tandem with the Russian state writ large, insists that textbooks, particularly on history of the great Russian nation, should promote a "patriotic education" rather than sow discord in the country's youth vis-à-vis their history and the nation as a whole.

Suslov's work, according to the Russian civil society and human rights organizations, fails to coincide with the narrative promoted by the Russian state authorities that often "whitewashes Stalin's history," an act that is far more "dangerous" than teaching the young about the dark pages in the nation's history "given the risk it poses to rationalizing violence against people."[20] Thus, any overtly critical assessment of the Stalin era or Soviet history more broadly is immediately interpreted by Russian state authorities as bluntly anti-Russian. The faintest opposition to or critical assessment of the USSR's foreign policy (i.e., the Molotov-Ribbentrop Pact, which has since been interpreted as the Soviet Union's shared responsibility for the outbreak of World War II; the Soviet attack on Finland and Poland; annexation of the Baltic states; the Katyn massacre; mass arrests and execution of Soviet citizens across the USSR, etc.) is immediately protested by the Russian state apparatus as a direct attack on its history and presented as a distortion of historical truth by its neighbors in the near abroad who ungratefully refuse to accept the triumphalist rhetoric of "Soviet liberation" of Europe and the world.[21]

Although initially the Putin administration appeared to encourage openness about the Stalin years and the reconceptualization of this period's meaning and significance in Russia's Soviet chapter, these efforts have since been curbed. This is especially true now, as the once-soaring popularity of Vladimir Putin continues to decline, as though mirroring the contracting oil prices and Russia's overall economy that has plummeted since its peak years. Today, in the heat of a gradually creeping rehabilitation of Stalin in Putin's Russia, the Soviet dictator's image as that of "the father of the nation" is challenged less and less.

As the past decades have faded the more vivid memories of the Stalin years of terror and purges under his reign, what has instead resurfaced, especially among the young, is the legacy of Joseph Stalin as a leader who, against all odds, brought victory to the Fatherland in the Great Patriotic War. This page in the Soviet history is portrayed, time and again, as an epic victory that not only brought fear and respect to Russia on the geopolitical stage but also became a pillar upon which the contemporary Russian national identity continues to rest in the time of its weakening economy, contracting oil prices, and, lest we forget, the ongoing global pandemic that among other countries has also severely impacted the Russian Federation and, as a direct consequence, also the Putin regime.

The Great Patriotic War and Russia's Soviet-era "great power" narrative has a trifold, mostly politically charged goal with three segments of targeted audience members on its receiving end. The first segment is domestic—the Russian public, which comprises the majority of the Putin regime's electorate. Through this prism, if not for Russia's economic successes, at least for its historical greatness that commands both fear and respect, the memory of the Great Patriotic War continues to remain a source of pride for the citizenry. The Victory Day parades that are traditionally celebrated with great fanfare, particularly under Vladimir Putin's leadership over the past twenty years, further emphasize Russia's political and historical grandeur as a victor and a savior of the world from the evil of Nazism. In the midst of its waning economic prowess, the Kremlin is capitalizing on this narrative through tireless state-endorsed and often government-operated propaganda legitimizing the ruling regime and its policies that are not always entirely popular with country's majority. Although it is difficult to quantify the emotional legacy of the Great Patriotic War vis-à-vis promoting patriotism as a national idea (if not ideology) of Russia today, honoring veterans of World War II has been skillfully manipulated by the Kremlin in recent years as an instrument for glorifying the Great Patriotic War in the name of Russian national pride and unity.

What complicates this rhetoric for domestic consumption is the ultimate figure and heroic depiction of Joseph Stalin as the commander of the Soviet Red Army and its victorious leader whose complexity continues to divide societies. There is little consistency in how the Russian leadership today assesses Stalin's role and credits the Soviet dictator for the great victory, particularly when the same leader was also denounced by the Putin administration in 2010 for a series of mass executions of 22,000 Polish military officers and members of intelligentsia in 1940, known as the Katyn massacre.[22] The end product is a sanitized version of Soviet history with an uncertain reassessment of the legacy of its polemic leader and his complicated contribution to an otherwise grand chapter in Russia's Soviet past.[23]

The second group is comprised of post-Soviet elites—the layer of society that in the Soviet days would have been referred to as its "intelligentsia" in the near abroad, or as Russia sees these countries—its immediate backyard. The "great power" policies and politics in this iteration posit that, as demonstrated by history, the greatness of Russia and the region as a whole can only be achieved through the "brotherhood of arms," which united the *Russkiy mir* or the Russian world beyond Russia's immediate territory through the suffering, martyrdom, and the eventual victory over the evil Nazi regime. The post-Soviet states, particularly those that the Kremlin still considers to be within its sphere of interest (i.e., Ukraine, Belarus, etc.), are encouraged to unite forces with Russia and agree to political, economic, and even military integration with their big brother for the greater unity in a quest of "us" versus "them." The parable of the peoples of the USSR coming together and fighting for collective survival through the great hardships of the war proclaims that it is through unity rather than division that the Union was able to achieve the insurmountable.

Thus, the historical revision of the myth of the Great Patriotic War serves as a driving element in the Kremlin's growing expansionism in its near abroad, including in Ukraine and Georgia. At the same time, the narratives about the battle against Nazism during World War II continue to be mirrored to this day in Russia's alleged struggle against "neofascism" in Ukraine.[24] The near-religious symbolism of the Great Patriotic War as an inherent and inseparable segment of Russia's post-Soviet identity remains a driving force and a legitimizing factor of Russia's frequently aggressive policies in its "backyard," allowing the leadership to present these actions as Russia's fight against the evil—a moral mission whose roots date back to the Second World War.

The third group is seen by the Russian authorities as the "West" in a collective sense of the geopolitical concept, which places the United States and Western Europe under the same umbrella. These societies have inherited their own legacies pertaining to World War II and its legacies, which do not always (if ever) correspond to the messages promoted by Russia in its Great Patriotic War narrative. In this version, the part played by the United States in World War II is not only minimized to a secondary role but at times entirely absent from purview. In the "collective West,"[25] the moral victory over Nazi Germany is often seen as synonymous with the liberal world's battle against authoritarianism. As demonstrated in the aftermath of the Second World War and, particularly, the Yalta Conference, the Soviet Union was no stranger to totalitarianism as a core attribute of its political culture throughout a large portion of the last century.

Yet, per Vladimir Putin's approach to the revision of the Great Patriotic War narrative and political exploitation of wartime historical legacies, it is clear that as far as the Kremlin is concerned, as George Orwell once wrote, "who controls the past controls the future; who controls the present controls the past."[26] By mobilizing and often molding the myths pertaining to World War II in the public discourse, the state authorities are able to shape perceptions of the present regime and thus cultivate public support. Revising the Second World War legacy and the specific legacy of the war's supreme victor, Stalin, allows the Russian leadership today to mythologize and manipulate social perceptions not only of its history but, perhaps even more so, its current centralized reality and the vertical of power that continues to govern the nation as a whole. Instead of directly glorifying the Stalin years or the great tyrant himself, the Kremlin cautiously reverts to instead emphasizing positive aspects of his rule. This, in turn, indirectly encourages the rebirth of the Stalin cult of personality and the country's present political direction of authoritarianism as one that has been successfully tested by time and experience, particularly in juxtaposition with the chaotic 1990s when official Moscow and the rest of the Russian Federation flirted, albeit unsuccessfully, with democracy—an experiment that is deemed by both Russian liberals and, increasingly so, those in the current administration's apparatus as an absolute fiasco.

In early 1991, 70% of Russian SSR citizens in what was then a barely breathing Soviet Union believed that the name of Joseph Stalin would only be uttered from that point on within the context of the Great Purges and the mass terror under his leadership. Only 10% of those surveyed at the time believed that Stalin would be remembered in positive light, while the remaining 20% were largely indifferent to the very notion of this historical figure. Throughout the next decade, Stalin's popularity continued to ebb and flow. The decisive point occurred with Vladimir Putin's ascent to power in 2000. Some view this phenomenon as a direct reflection of Russia's readoption of a more authoritarian style of governance, while others believe that the increased popularity of the Soviet autocrat is instead a reflection of the general population's disappointment with the last three decades of post-Soviet reality that has left many disenchanted. Ultimately, both viewpoints have the legitimate right and reason to coexist as two sides of the same coin that explains Stalin's resurgent and lasting popularity in Russia—the topic of this chapter.

The rehabilitation of the Stalin figure continues to remain a constant leitmotif in Putin's Russia. The Kremlin's highly capable and experienced spin doctors employ cautious but at times overt reminders of the many merits of Joseph Stalin as a military supreme commander who led the USSR through its most challenging years and allowed the country to reemerge as a superpower in a largely bipolar world. For many, the very image of Joseph Stalin in Russia today has come to be equated with a symbol of law and order after the lawlessness and chaos of the nineties, evoking simultaneous admiration and fear of the iron discipline practiced under his rule. Stalin's name is becoming increasingly synonymous with the military heroism of the Soviet Union and its successor state, the Russian Federation, and is directly linked with the numerous economic achievements that the USSR boasted under his management. As a result, the complex legacy of the Stalinist period gives birth to an enduring sense of patriotism, especially for those who fought and died on the battlefield. To this end, patriotism is undeniably strongest among the veterans of the Second World War, as serving in the Great Patriotic War at the time was indeed seen as a patriotic duty of the Soviet citizenry writ large.

One of Vladimir Putin's earliest policies upon assuming the role of the second President of the post-Soviet Russian Federation was the restoration of the original national anthem handpicked by Joseph Stalin in 1943, but with revised lyrics. The Soviet-era anthem was first unveiled and presented to the public on January 1, 1944, and officially adopted as the national anthem of the Soviet Union by March 15, 1944. The lyrics of the original version emphasized Stalin's wartime heroism, "inspir[ing] us to keep faith with the people," the greatness of the Soviet nation and the "the victory of Communism's immortal ideal." The lyrics—that had once praised Stalin, Lenin, and the Communist Party—were rewritten, as per the Kremlin's official request, by Sergei Mikhalkov, a famed children's poet and the author of the hymn's original version; they now glorify the "Russian eagle . . . hovering high" and the "Fatherland's tricolor symbol" leading the Russian people to victory. The new version proudly exhibits the previously unpalatable references to God, while the original reference to "an unbreakable union" of "peoples in brotherhood strong"[27] has been replaced by an "eternal union of fraternal peoples," still hinting at nostalgia for the once unified republics under the Soviet umbrella.

This was not the first time that Mikhalkov had offered to rework the words of the national anthem. Following Stalin's death in 1953 and the impending de-Stalinization, Mikhalkov's lyrics to the anthem were entirely discarded, and the hymn was played without any lyrics until, in 1977, post-de-Stalinization efforts of Khrushchev and now under the leadership of Brezhnev, the poet proposed a new verse that carried a direct reference to Stalin and on May 27, 1977, the new version was approved by the Presidium of the Supreme Soviet.

Although the first President of post-Soviet Russia, Boris Yeltsin, swiftly swapped the Soviet anthem for nineteenth-century composer Mikhail Glinka's piece, "Patriotic Song" (albeit without lyrics, as the Yeltsin administration failed to agree on a unanimously acceptable text), which never fully caught on with Russian citizens,[28] the incoming Vladimir Putin signed the State Duma's resolution to return to the iconic Soviet anthem as a way of paying tribute to Russia's military, cultural, and scientific victories during the twentieth century.

Honoring Russia's Soviet roots in this manner became a central point of heated debates among Russian politicians, in turn, underscoring the existing ideological divide between the Communists and Putin's United Russia supporters on one side, and the more Western-leaning liberals on the other. Russia's "cultural intelligentsia" consisting of artists, musicians, actors, and the like protested the return to the Soviet anthem with utmost vehemence. Their passionate criticism, they posited, was rooted in fear of an inevitable return to authoritarianism, instead of seeking Russia's post-Soviet identity by breaking with the patterns of Stalinism once and for all. And yet, an overwhelming majority of Russia's then 146 million citizens supported Putin's decision to adopt the State Duma's resolution into law. Many would argue that this approval, in and of itself, demonstrated an already brewing tendency for nostalgia for the Soviet Union and its prior greatness through a national anthem as a soft-power weapon.[29]

On what would have been Stalin's 125th birthday in December of 2004, then leader of the United Russia party and the speaker of the State Duma, Boris Gryzlov, urged the nation to reassess the statesman's legacy. He noted that Stalin's negative "excesses" should by no means devalue the "extraordinary"[30] qualities of a commander in chief to whom the country ought to be greatly indebted for the victory in the Great Patriotic War. Meanwhile, Alexander Kuvayev, who at the time led the Russian Communist Party of the Future, described the Soviet dictator as "the most successful state leader" and lamented that, in these times of great uncertainty, it is the political figure in the vein of Joseph Stalin that "Russia needs today."[31]

Such rhetoric would have been unheard of under the leadership of Mikhail Gorbachev, who in the late 1980s launched a brief de-Stalinization movement under the broader umbrella of perestroika, exposing the Communist Party's lies and historical distortions. Instead of focusing on the greatness of Stalin, he began to capitalize on the historical greatness of the father of the Soviet Union, Vladimir Lenin.[32] Under his successor, Boris Yeltsin, the Soviet model was entirely rejected and, although no state-level de-Stalinization was undertaken, Stalin's deeds were no longer kept secret nor embellished to hide the blemishes of a regime that many began to openly refer to as "criminal." One of the explanations to Yeltsin's caution to entirely debunk the Stalin myths and distortions and issue an official mandate to begin the de-Stalinization processes is rooted in the fierce opposition that he faced from the Communist Party and its leader, Gennady Zyuganov, by the mid-nineties. While Russia's weakening economy and the many hardships of the decade weighed heavily on Yeltsin's shoulders, the Communists in post-Soviet Russia continued to view the Stalin years as glorious for the entire nation. By further alienating a major part of the population that, at the time, remained avid supporters of the Communist Party and were already exhibiting vivid symptoms of nostalgia for the Soviet Union, Yeltsin was aware that he would have strengthened the opponent's position by criticizing the Soviet rule and its dictator much too severely.[33]

This has since changed, and rather drastically. In 2013, during a ceremony marking the sixtieth anniversary since the autocrat's death, Russian Communist Party leader Gennady Zyuganov openly praised Joseph Stalin, noting that it was this very man who "raised Russia from its feet . . . and stood at the helm of the Soviet government for 30 years, raising it to the heights of its greatest victories."[34] It is worth noting that a similar phrase but with a twist—"raising Russia from its knees"[35]—has become a common staple when praising the Putin years and how, over the past two decades, Russia's status and image has been elevated in the global arena largely thanks to the leadership of Vladimir Vladimirovich Putin.

While Stalin's native Georgia is demolishing his monuments and other relics associated with seven decades of Soviet occupation, Russia is witnessing a growing resurgence of Soviet vestiges, including a new statue that was recently unveiled in Novosibirsk, the third-largest city in Russia. Alexei Denisyuk, the leader of the All-Union Communist Party who had originally pitched the idea to city hall in 2008, posits that the unveiling of the bust in 2019 when Stalin's popularity is soaring with a groundbreaking 70%

approval, "is not about honoring Joseph Stalin [but instead it is] about resurrecting and furthering his cause and mission."[36]

Since the seventieth anniversary of the Soviet victory in the Great Patriotic War, museums honoring Comrade Stalin have been opening across Russia, including one located three hours out from central Moscow in Khoroshevo under the direction of the Ministry of Culture of the Russian Federation led by its long-time minister and Putin appointee, Vladimir Medinsky. The museum, launched by the Military Historical Society, primarily focuses on Stalin's triumphs in the military and economic domains. Whether or not through sheer coincidence, the Russian Military History Society was directly mandated[37] by the Putin administration in 2012—the year of mass demonstrations in Moscow organized by the opposition forces challenging his regime, and also the year when Vladimir Putin was, yet again, elected to preside over the Russian Federation. The organization and its operations are funded by the Ministry of Culture, receiving millions of dollars in state funding every year for a variety of projects, including a state-sponsored bust of Stalin that was erected near the Russo-Estonian border, in the town of Pskov.

A tour guide who works for the Military Historical Society, Sergei Zaborovsky, admits that this museum, much like the narrative itself surrounding the Soviet ruler, has shifted rather dramatically over the past decade. "We have started to look at Stalin in a more favorable light," he says. "Maybe it's because the situation in the world is not the best—we need strength, [and, above all], we need something to unite us."[38] A schoolteacher in Khoroshevo, Irina Mikhailova, praises the work of the museum and its very existence, noting that "the Stalin Museum is very important to us [in Khoroshevo]." Mikhailova adds that "It is important not to forget those who helped create the peaceful environment we live in today,"[39] clearly referring to the Red Army's victory over Nazism.

That same year, Perm, a city located on the European side of the Ural Mountains, which back in the 1990s was coined as "the capital of Russian civil society," began to modify the existing references to Joseph Stalin, particularly those carrying negative connotations. In October of 2012, then prime minister Dmitry Medvedev made a speech in Perm on the Day of Memory for Victims of Political Repression, noting that "we must remember what took place . . . Incidentally, these words perhaps ring more emphatically here in the Perm region than they do in other places, where people have by now forgotten about what happened in the 1930s and the 1940s."[40] Medvedev reiterated the need to hold Stalin and the rest of his cabinet accountable for the massacres that took place under his leadership. But in addition, the Russian Prime Minister emphasized that it is important to also remember the brighter pages in the tumultuous Soviet history of that period—particularly the Great Patriotic War.

Even despite Medvedev's call to assess the events of that entire era with "sober objectivity,"[41] shortly thereafter, the Perm-36 museum removed explicit reference to Stalin's crimes, along with references to Soviet dissidents who were held and some who died in the camp.[42] The monument under its original management was forced to close in 2015 after the Russian Justice Ministry labeled it a "foreign agent"[43] based on what the Perm department of the Ministry claimed were "political activities" undertaken by the NGO that ran the Perm-36 memorial museum, as well as evidence of foreign funding operations.[44] "Now it's a museum about the camp system, but not about political prisoners. They do not talk about the repressions or about Stalin,"[45] former director of the museum, Viktor Shmyrov observes.

The museum known colloquially as the "Gulag Museum" and, more formally, the Museum of the History of Political Repression Perm-36, was unveiled in the original location that once housed part of the enormous prison camp system of the USSR. Several years ago, the Russian government took over the site and, since then, the focus of Perm-36 and the museum's exhibits has shifted from labor camp atrocities and its victims to the Soviet Union's victory in World War II. According to the museum's brochure in English, "gulag was an absolutely necessary element of the system. Without the gulag's cheap slave labor, Stalin's socialist modernization program of the country's economy would have been impossible."[46] Perm-36 covers 150,000 sq. ft. and boasts over twenty buildings. To date, this is the only surviving Stalin-era labor camp in Russia.

Yet another edifice with a twofold educational and cultural mission was opened with a fanfare in December of 2015 in Penza by the Communist Party of the Russian Federation—the Stalin Center, launched by a thirty-year-old deputy in the regional parliament and local Communist Party leader, Georgy Kamnev. To mark the eightieth anniversary of the Soviet constitution, Russian communists across the region of Penza officially declared 2016 to be the "Year of Stalin." The versatile and multidisciplinary program was comprised of roundtable discussions, Stalin-themed literary soirées and debates, as well as tours of the region's Stalin-era architectural sites. In addition, special "Stalinist scholarships" were designed for schoolchildren who were encouraged to write about Joseph Stalin and of his great legacy for various communist journals throughout Russia.

The cultural center is made up of several small rooms with old photographs and newspaper clippings dating back to the historic period, collages comprised of several thematic angles all ultimately leading to the unifying legend of Comrade Stalin, including a seasonal New Year's poster with a painting of Stalin raising a glass of champagne and proudly proclaiming: "Life has become better, comrades!", a lecture hall that adorns a giant portrait of the

Soviet leader, and a golden bust of the man himself decorating an otherwise modest entrance to the building. According to the center's director, its main goal is "to popularize and implement the practices that were in use during Stalin times and are still relevant today."[47]

Unlike a variety of the other museums and shrines honoring the Soviet dictator throughout Russia, the Penza Stalin Center is not funded by the Russian state but is instead sponsored by current Communist Party supporters and constituents throughout the region. Yet, similar to the political narratives on the topic circulating across Russia, Kamnev also ponders the complexities of the Stalin question through the prism of his era: "The historical conditions have to be taken into account. Some things which were then morally permissible are now impermissible. After all, human rights didn't appear all of a sudden—it was a long process."[48] He goes so far as to encourage normalizing the actions undertaken by the Stalin regime in today's political rhetoric and historical assessments: "There were times when Tsar Peter decapitated his enemies in the [city] square, and it was considered normal. It was the same under Stalin. Human rights as we understand them now were not observed. At that time, repressions were the norm. There was nothing reprehensible about them."[49]

On March 5, 2019, the sixty-sixth anniversary of Stalin's death, over 500 people gathered on Red Square, the location of Stalin's tomb under the Kremlin wall. In 2019 alone, 8,600 red carnations, seen as symbols of victory, were laid on Comrade Stalin's grave. Ahead of the May 9 celebrations, commemorating the surrender of Nazi Germany in 1945, a banner carrying Stalin's image was flown in downtown Surgut, a city in western Siberia, proudly proclaiming in bold white print on a bright red background next to his photograph: "He saved the Jews of Europe from genocide: Poland, Germany, Romania."[50] Two days later, a bust of Joseph Stalin was unveiled with great fanfare in southwestern Siberia, Novosibirsk, one of the cities where hundreds of thousands of Soviet citizens declared as "enemies of the Soviet Union" were forced to relocate and later brutally executed during the Great Purges of the Stalin era. The mayor of Novosibirsk, Anatoly Lokot, an active member of Russia's Communist Party, attended the ceremony in commemoration of the seventy-fourth anniversary of the Allied victory over Nazism, and as he unveiled the Soviet Dictator's bust, he proudly stated: "By unveiling this monument, we honor the generalissimo of the Great Victory, and we will not allow the so-called liberals to distort our history."[51]

As seen in this chapter, in the eyes of many in Russia today, Stalin continues to be seen as the savior and the necessary evil against the perils of Nazism. Moreover, he is not only glorified and deeply revered as a political and historical figure but, over the past years, he has become an intrinsic part of the modern Russian national identity and a revised symbol of Russian patriotism through continued mythologization of the Soviet Union's glorious past as a great power. In response to the liberal West that disrespected, humiliated, and even tried to destroy Russia in the 1990s, the revised patriotic agenda finds new meaning in the history and myth of Stalin and Stalinism and seeks to reinstate the prior greatness of the nation and continues to defend Russian national interests no matter the consequences.

The general social attitudes among Russians toward erecting monuments to the Red Tsar have evolved dramatically over the past two decades under Vladimir Putin. In 2005, 55% of Russians surveyed by the independent polling and sociological research organization Levada Center were against any construction of new monuments to Stalin, while over 35% admitted that they regard these initiatives positively. By 2017, those against the idea of resurrecting the memory of Stalin through statues, portraits, and other memorabilia dropped to under 40%, directly mirroring the waning criticism of Generalissimo Stalin and his growing popularity among Russians today.[52] It must be noted that by no means do these numbers suggest that all of the respondents who approve of Joseph Stalin's rule, policies, and legacies are, in fact, Stalinists. What is more concerning is the fact that under closer inspection, we find that the majority of the general population's "factual" knowledge about Stalin and the era as a whole are rooted in a mythologized version of Stalin and illusions about the great leader whose image has been tirelessly and meticulously airbrushed to fit a specific political rhetoric or environment at a given time—the main topic of the forthcoming chapter on the mythologized, metaphysical Stalin.

Unlike the two Stalins presented thus far—Georgian Koba and Russified Soviet Red Tsar—the tale of the Third Stalin is not rooted in the past alone but, rather, it belongs equally to the present and the future. Devoid of concrete, static spatial and temporal elements like the other two Stalins, the hero of the next and the main segment of this narrative is a hybrid—an invisible thread between space and time, a bridge connecting him to us and vice versa.

NOTES

1. Francis X. Clines, "Upheaval in the East; Moscow McDonald's Opens: Milkshakes and Human Kindness," *New York Times*, February 1, 1990. Web. https://www.nytimes.com/1990/02/01/world/upheaval-east-moscow-mcdonald-s-opens-milkshakes-human-kindness-reuters.html.

2. George Ritzer, *The McDonaldization of Society*, 3rd ed. (Thousand Oaks, CA: Pine Forge, 2000), 1–19.

3. Ibid., 7.

4. Elizabeth Shogren, "Soviets Pursue an American Dream: Trends: Once Cursed in the Soviet Union, U.S. Pop Culture—from 'Tarzan' to Rap—Is Where It's At," *Los Angeles Times*, August 1, 1991. Web. https://www.newspapers.com/newspage/175295533/.

5. Aside from the façade of failure to meet sanitary requirements, the Russian authorities' decision to close several branches of the American fast-food restaurant was seen as an anti-American propaganda aimed to divert the Russian citizens from consumerism toward nationalism. In place of the American burger haven, Vladimir Putin proudly inaugurated a Russian domestic alternative to the American prototype—"a patriotic Russian restaurant chain to rival foreign fast-food joints," patriotically called Let's Eat at Home. See: Tom Parfitt, "Vladimir Putin Backs Russian Fast-Food Rival to McDonald's," *Daily Telegraph*, April 9, 2015. Web. https://www.telegraph.co.uk/news/worldnews/europe/russia/11524817/Vladimir-Putin-backs-Russian-fast-food-rival-to-McDonalds.html.

6. Adam Taylor, "How McDonald's Went from Hero to Zero in Russia," *Washington Post*, April 16, 2014. Web. https://www.washingtonpost.com/news/worldviews/wp/2014/04/16/how-mcdonalds-went-from-hero-to-zero-in-russia/.

7. Mitya Kushelevich, "Taste of Freedom: What the Closure of the First Moscow McDonald's Means for Russia Today," *Calvert Journal*, September 1, 2014. Web. https://www.calvertjournal.com/articles/show/3046/mcdonalds-moscow-closure-russia-martin-parr.

8. Michael Dobbs, "Moscow Plays Ketch-Up; Fast Food Comes to Slow Food Capital," *Washington Post*, February 1, 1990. Web. https://www.washingtonpost.com/archive/politics/1990/02/01/moscow-plays-ketch-up/2addbab1-da1c-4101-a2f3-3131a3a97035/.

9. Ahead of Russia's observance of Victory Day in 2019, Moscow-based Levada Center conducted a poll surveying over 1,600 respondents nationwide on perceptions and attitudes toward Joseph Stalin. Of those surveyed, 70% of respondents stated that they view the late Soviet Dictator and his role in Russia's history in favorable light, in comparison with the previous record approval rating of 54% in 2016. Furthermore, the 2019 poll showed that 51% of those surveyed by Levada view Stalin as a person in a positive light—the highest recorded percentage since 2001. A record low of 19%—down from 32% in 2016—posited that they view Stalin's role in Russian history negatively. See more: "Dynamics of Attitudes towards Stalin," Levada Center, April 16, 2019. Web. https://www.levada.ru/2019/04/16/dinamika-otnosheniya-k-stalinu/.

10. Mac McCall, "Georgia's Love-Hate Relationship with Joseph Stalin," *Atlas Obscura*, November 19, 2020. Web. https://www.atlasobscura.com/articles/gori-georgia-joseph-stalin.

11. Elina Ibragimowa, "Why Stalin is Causing a Classroom Storm in Russia," *Deutsche Welle*, July 29, 2017. Web. https://www.dw.com/en/why-stalin-is-causing-a-classroom-storm-in-russia/a-39866244.

12. Martyn Conterio, "Perm 36: The Soviet-era Gulag Museum Where Putin is Rewriting History," *History Answers*, March 7, 2017. Web. https://www.historyanswers.co.uk/people-politics/perm-36-the-soviet-era-gulag-museum-where-putin-is-rewriting-history/.

13. For more on Russian youth perceptions and attitudes toward Stalinist repressions, see 32-year-old Russian YouTube sensation, Yury Dud's documentary about Kolyma and the legacy of Stalinist repressions told through the stories of residents among the ruins of labor camps. "Kolyma: Birthplace of Our Fear," vDud', April 23, 2019. YouTube video, 2h17m. Web. https://www.youtube.com/watch?v=oo1Woul38rQ&t=1s.

14. "Represii XX veka: pamyat' o blizkikh," VTsIOM, October 5, 2018. Web. https://wciom.ru/index.php?id=236&uid=9344.

15. Oreshkin, *Jughaphilia and the Soviet Statistical Epic Poetry*, 17.

16. Anita Pisch writes that while pre-Soviet Imperial Russia largely regarded itself and was perceived as a "fatherland," under Stalin's leadership, it was being increasingly referred to and seen as "motherland" (232). See: Anita Pisch, *The Personality Cult of Stalin in Soviet Posters, 1929–1953: Archetypes, Inventions and Fabrications* (Canberra, Australia: ANU Press, 2016).

17. Thomas Sherlock, "Confronting the Stalinist Past: The Politics of Memory in Russia," *Washington Quarterly* 34, no. 2 (October 2009): 96.

18. Ibid., 97.

19. Elina Ibragimowa, "Kak Rozkomnadzor vmeshalsya v pedagogicheskiy konflikt," *Deutsche Welle*, July 26, 2017. Web. https://www.dw.com/ru/как-роскомнадзор-вмешался-в-педагогический-конфликт/a-39825535.

20. Ibid.

21. Mariya Golubkova, "Obyavit' vsemirnym naslediyem," *Rossiyskaya Gazeta*, November 21, 2019. Web. https://rg.ru/2019/11/21/rossiia-potrebuet-priniatiia-specialnoj-rezoliucii-oon-ko-dniu-pobedy.html.

22. In 2010, the State Duma, the lower house of the Russian Parliament, officially declared that Joseph Stalin and his cronies were responsible for ordering the execution of thousands of Polish officers and intelligentsia in the Katyn Forest near Smolensk, one of the "hero cities" in the Soviet Union. See more: "Gosduma obvinila Stalina," Interfax, November 26, 2010. Web. https://www.interfax.ru/russia/166628.

23. For more on the "third wave of de-Stalinization," see chapter 4.

24. "Great Patriotic War, Again," *Economist*, May 2, 2015. Web. https://www.economist.com/europe/2015/05/02/great-patriotic-war-again.

25. Maria Domanska, "The Myth of the Great Patriotic War as a Tool of the Kremlin's Great Power Policy," Ośrodek Studiów Wschodnich/Centre for Eastern Studies, December 31, 2019. Web. https://www.osw.waw.pl/en/publikacje/osw-commentary/2019-12-31/myth-great-patriotic-war-a-tool-kremlins-great-power-policy#_ftn25.

26. George Orwell, *1984*, (New York: New American Library, 1983), 204.

27. "Russia Unveils New National Anthem Joining the Old Soviet Tune to the Older, Unsoviet God," *New York Times,* December 31, 2000. Web. https://www.nytimes.com/2000/12/31/world/russia-unveils-new-national-anthem-joining-old-soviet-tune-older-unsoviet-god.html.

28. A nationwide poll conducted in November of 2000 showed that only 15% of the Russian population supported the Glinka anthem. See: J. Martin Daughtry,

"Russia's New Anthem and the Negotiation of National Identity," *Ethnomusicology* 47, no. 1 (Winter 2003): 51.

29. Ibid., 62.

30. "Boris Gryzlov schitayet Stalina 'nezauryadnym chelovekom,'" RIA Novosti, June 6, 2008. Web. https://ria.ru/20041221/766724.html

31. "Stalina mogila ispravila: 125-letiye vozhdya otmetili u Kremlyovskoy steny," *Kommersant*, December 22, 2004. Web. https://www.kommersant.ru/doc/535369.

32. Richard Sakwa, *Gorbachev and His Reforms, 1985–1990* (Deddington, Oxon: Philip Allan, 1990).

33. Maria Lipman, "Stalin Is Not Dead: A Legacy that Holds Back Russia" (Washington, DC: Carnegie Endowment for International Peace, 2013), 17–18.

34. Alexander Winning, "Communists Mark Anniversary of Stalin's Death," *Moscow Times*, March 5, 2013. Web. https://www.themoscowtimes.com/2013/03/05/communists-mark-anniversary-of-stalins-death-a22089.

35. Andrew Osborn and Polina Ivanova, "Sixteen More Years? Russian Parliament Backs Move to Keep Putin in Power," Reuters, March 11, 2020. Web. https://www.reuters.com/article/us-russia-putin/sixteen-more-years-russian-parliament-backs-move-to-keep-putin-in-power-idUSKBN20Y0VC.

36. Eva Hartog, "Is Stalin Making a Comeback in Russia?" *Atlantic*, May 28, 2019. Web. https://www.theatlantic.com/international/archive/2019/05/russia-stalin-statue/590140/.

37. Russian Federation, "Ukaz Prezidenta Rossiyskoy Federatsii ot 29.12.2012 g. № 1710," Kremlin.ru, December 29, 2012. Web. http://www.kremlin.ru/acts/bank/36611.

38. Katherine Jacobsen, "Russia Opens New Stalin Museums, Grapples with His Legacy," *Times of Israel*, December 19, 2015. Web. https://www.timesofisrael.com/russia-opens-new-stalin-museums-grapples-with-his-legacy/.

39. Katherine Jacobsen, "New Museums in Russia are Airbrushing Stalin's Legacy," *Business Insider*, December 18, 2015. Web. https://www.businessinsider.com/new-museums-in-russia-are-airbrushing-stalins-legacy-2015-12.

40. "Dmitry Medvedev: Stalin vyol voynu s sobstvennym narodom," Interfax, October 30, 2012. Web. https://www.interfax.ru/russia/273531.

41. Ibid.

42. Georgiy Ivanushkin, "Iz muzeya istorii politicheskikh repressiy ubrali upominaniya o Staline," Agency of Social Information, March 3, 2015. Web. https://www.asi.org.ru/news/2015/03/05/iz-muzeya-istorii-politicheskih-repressij-ubrali-upominaniya-o-staline/; Laurence Peter, "Stalin Wiped from Soviet Gulag Museum," BBC, March 3, 2015. Web. https://www.bbc.com/news/world-europe-31711287; "Gulag Museum to Reopen But Proof of Stalin Crimes Removed, Director Says," *Moscow Times*, March 5, 2015. Web. https://www.themoscowtimes.com/2015/03/05/gulag-museum-to-reopen-but-proof-of-stalin-crimes-removed-director-says-a44496. By 2018, the Perm-36 Museum had partially reintroduced direct references to Stalin's crimes and the Great Purges, including archival lists of those who were to be executed signed by the Dictator himself. [Photos, with permission granted by Bradley Gorski from his personal collection, are available upon request.]

43. The Foreign Agent Law in Russia requires nongovernmental organizations that receive foreign funding and are engaged in political activities on Russian territory to register and declare themselves as "foreign agents." See more at: Russian Federation, "Zakonoproekt № 102766-6 O vnesenii izmeneniy v otdel'nye zakonodatel'niye akty Rossiyskoy Federatsii v chasti regulirovaniya deyatel'nosti nekommercheskikh organizatsiy, vypolnyayush'ikh funktsii inostrannogo agenta," State Duma of the Russian Federation, 2013. Web. http://asozd2.duma.gov.ru/main.nsf/%28SpravkaNew%29?OpenAgent&RN=102766-6&02.

44. Halya Coynash, "'Perm-36' Labelled 'Foreign Agent' as Moscow Seeks to Expunge Memory of the Gulag," *Kharkiv Human Rights Protection Group*, May 8, 2015. Web. http://khpg.org/en/index.php?id=1430909081.

45. "Gulag Museum to Reopen But Proof of Stalin Crimes Removed, Director Says."

46. "Perm-36 Soviet Political Repression Camp (GULAG) & Chusovaya History Museum Excursion," Travel Agency Krasnov, 2014. Web. http://www.uraltourism.com/perm36.php.

47. "Stalin Center Opens in Central Russia," *Moscow Times*, December 22, 2015. Web. https://www.themoscowtimes.com/2015/12/22/stalin-center-opens-in-central-russia-a51301.

48. Daniil Turovsky, "Russian City Opens Cultural Centre Celebrating Stalin," *Guardian*, January 11, 2016. Web. https://www.theguardian.com/world/2016/jan/11/stalin-russia-penza-cultural-centre-meduza.

49. Ibid.

50. "V Surgute aktivisty ustanovili banner s blagodarnost'yu Stalinu," Znak, May 8, 2019. Web. https://www.znak.com/2019-05-07/v_surgute_aktivisty_ustanovili_banner_s_blagodarnostyu_stalinu.

51. "V Novosibirske ustanovili pamyatnik Stalinu," RIA Novosti, May 8, 2019. Web. https://ria.ru/20190508/1553341814.html.

52. Adam Balcer, "Long Live Stalin! Putin's Politics of Memory," *Heinrich Böll Stiftung*, July 2, 2018. Web. https://eu.boell.org/en/2018/07/02/long-live-stalin-putins-politics-memory.

Chapter IV
Tale of the Third Stalin

Separate from the first two Stalins of Montefiore—Georgian and Russian Stalins who are above all geographically bound to the two countries, the "Third Stalin" introduced in this work is not geographical as much as he is temporal and constantly evolving in a permanent state of chaos—much like the fluid society it represents at any given point in time. This third metaphysical Stalin shares faint, barely recognizable traits with the once living and breathing Great Dictator. A reflection, be it authentic or entirely imaginary, of a traumatized, abruptly interrupted psyche and identity in the post-Soviet space portrays the late dictator as a reconstructed strongman figure encompassing and representing the national identities of both his native Georgia and Soviet Russia. The nostalgia, terror, pride, and nationalism entrenched in the Third Stalin, although traced among a variety of populations as a growing trend, is above all paradoxical amongst the post-Soviet generation of millennials.

This chapter explores Stalin as a "memory project" that rests upon four main pillars: cult of personality, trauma, nationalism, and nostalgia—elements that are less connected to Joseph Stalin's biographical and historical figure per se, but instead representative of the generations borne of Dictator's rule and, as some would argue, as a direct consequence of his regime. Each of the individual subthemes of the tale of the Third Stalin are an integral part of the Stalin figure seen and lived through the perspective of the late and post-Soviet generations—in turn, also becoming an integral part of us, this very generation.

To a degree, this third temporal layer encapsulates the other two Stalins of Simon Sebag Montefiore, holding the geographical figures together, and thus serving as a common, unifying thread between them. To this end, this third Stalin is not only the reflection of Russia's and Georgia's current political policies and politics but, increasingly, also a direct reflection of the post-Soviet self—with all of its fears, nostalgia, trauma, dreams, and ultimately unrealized hopes of greatness, shattered by the collapse of the empire, and morbid curiosity ignited by scars left by years of ancestral terror, discussed until recently only in hushed whispers behind closed doors. At its very core, the eternal attribute of this third Stalin is the undying, ever-present memory of an era, encompassing an array of distortions, inaccuracies, embellishments, cracks, and constant longing. It is precisely through this prism—a kaleidoscope of countless memories, many of them frequently and even directly contracting themselves—that we explore the Third Stalin.

In Russia, the successor state of the Soviet Union, the depiction of this proposed third Stalin narrative continues to evolve, reflecting the current domestic political environment, and is frequently used as a formal justification of modern-day policies. This is especially pronounced now, at the time of the writing of this book, shortly after Russia marked the seventy-fifth anniversary of the victory in World War II, or as Russians prefer to refer to this historic event as the Great Patriotic War.

Amid the renewed interest in uncovering Soviet history through archival material, Russia's dual role persists as that of a willing prisoner and an unapologetic participant in the not-so-distant dark pages of its historical past. Yet, more actively than ever before, the regime of Vladimir Putin is strengthening its grip in response to the requests voiced by civil society to open secret archives dating back to the "Great Terror" and the Stalin-era purges of 1937–1938. This growing revisionism has been interpreted by many Russian scholars as Putin's direct defense of the Stalin regime and a loosely camouflaged justification of the Soviet Dictator's actions and deeds.[1] Furthermore, Stalin's purges and the prewar era as a whole are viewed in modern-day Russia through the prism of the Great Patriotic War as a "necessary evil," rather than as a historical tragedy separate from the victory in the Second World War. This argument has been set forth by Vladimir Putin himself, most explicitly during one of his annual "Direct Lines" with the nation televised in December of 2009. During the live broadcast, Putin was asked to elaborate on his attitudes toward Stalin. In answering this question from the audience, the then Prime Minister of the Russian Federation noted that while one should refrain from portraying Stalin's rule between 1924 and 1953 with a single stroke without focusing on the numerous changes, challenges, and countless upheavals experienced by the Soviet Union during those decades, he nonetheless urged Russians to evaluate Stalin's rule through the prism of the victory of the Soviet nation against Nazism, a global evil. Putin emphasized, however, that this victory came at "a very high price," including the repressions that "undeniably occurred" and should be condemned as an "unacceptable form of state management."[2]

This theme resurfaced once again two years after Putin returned to the presidential seat. During the Seliger National Youth Forum in 2014, the Russian leader addressed the subtle thread connecting public opinion and official sentiment: "We can of course criticize the commanders and Stalin himself, but can anyone say with certainty that a different approach would have enabled us to win [the Great Patriotic War]?"[3] In Putin's statements, as though echoing the public sentiment demonstrated through the sociological polls, the ambiguous link between Stalin's tyrannical rule and the brutality of his decision-making paired with the greatness of his leadership are traced as a constant leitmotif. The official assessment of the flaws of Stalinism is justified in the name of heroism and the ultimate victory of his regime. Furthermore, Putin argues that disrespecting Stalin today by labeling him as a mere tyrant also "insults the Soviet Union and modern Russia."[4] By equating honor and respect of the Stalin figure with that of the nation as a whole, Putin and the modern-day Kremlin apparatus signal to the outside world, particularly the collective West frequently criticizing the atrocities of that era, that Stalin's historical figure, his legacies, and the greatness of his role in the history of the Soviet Union are intrinsically linked with the Russian national identity and the nation as a whole that places great pride in its strong leader.

When asked by journalists in 2013 if Stalin's monument should be restored in Lubyanka Square in central Moscow that once housed the old KGB headquarters, Putin compared Stalin to Oliver Cromwell as a fellow "tyrant" whose statues in England have not been removed by the British government, unlike the monuments of Stalin that have been toppled across the former Soviet space. "It is not about the symbols, you see. It is about respect for every period of our history,"[5] Vladimir Putin responded. "Why destroy the monuments?" he asked rhetorically, noting that it is essential for a healthy society that social harmony remain preserved, and it is through statues and memorials honoring the nation's past leaders that a nation can remember and respect its history.

Rarely will the masses in Russia today dispute the Stalin regime's atrocities and crimes, particularly those committed prior to the Great Patriotic War, but attempts to salvage his reputation and legacy persist and have visibly increased over the past several years. Moreover, upon closer inspection, it becomes apparent that the Russian President's refusal to create a publicly available database of open-source information on the mass killings under Stalin's rule and further avoidance of de-Stalinization are largely driven by his own political interests of maintaining a tight, albeit gradually weakening, grip on political power.[6] Thus, any efforts or lack thereof toward de-Stalinization are presented by the more right-wing, Kremlin-aligned Russian politicians as an open "provocation aimed at splitting Russian society"[7] at its core.

In the midst of the Soviet renaissance and the rebirth of forgotten illusions of social equality and justice, Ilya Udovenko, senior researcher at the Gulag[8] History Museum in Moscow, believes that so long as Russia continues to perceive itself as a direct successor who inherited the glory and power of the Soviet state, any true or pseudo efforts aimed at de-Stalinization will inevitably fail. "Today, there is hardly a living person in Russia who would willingly agree to find themselves in a Stalinist regime of the 1930s or even the 'glorious' 1940s, but the sense of nostalgia and countless illusions persist to this day, no matter what,"[9] Udovenko observes. How then, if at all, could de-Stalinization and Putinism coexist? Or are the two phenomena entirely unrelated?

The shift in the Stalin narrative is not only visible in the strictly political rhetoric of Russia's current leadership but also on a broader societal level. The number of those who condemn Stalin's crimes, stating that they were "absolutely unjustified" decreased from 60% back in 2008 down to 45% in 2014.[10] According to the latest Russian polls conducted by the independent polling center, Levada, even in the midst of current debates about the historical revisionism of the Stalin era and half-hearted talks of de-Stalinization (or lack thereof), Comrade Stalin, as he continues to be referred to in colloquial post-Soviet parlance, is more popular in Russia today than even Vladimir Putin. In 2019, a record 70% of Levada respondents publicly stated that the late dictator, Georgian-born Joseph Jughashvili, played a highly positive role for Russia. All the more striking is that a staggering 51% of respondents admit that they view Stalin "as a person" in a largely "favorable" light—the highest percentage of approval since 2001.

As discussed in the earlier chapters, both in Russia and Georgia, the process of de-Stalinization was never fully undertaken, let alone completed—with the only limited albeit controlled attempts in the early phases of de-Stalinization pursued by and under Nikita Khrushchev in 1956, 1961,[11] and 1964.[12] With Mikhail Gorbachev's glasnost' in the 1980s, a myriad of questions surrounding Stalinism and de-Stalinization reemerged as one of the central issues in the late Soviet period's reevaluation of its history.[13] Although in the midst of glasnost', more open and revelatory conversations and debates were beginning to take place not only about Stalin's legacy but also of his crimes and the Great Purges, many were still reluctant to confront the guilt, the reckoning, and responsibility still vibrant in the living memory.

De-Stalinization even in the waning days of the Soviet Union was limited to tackling and confronting cultural memory more so than the political dimensions of the policy that remained carefully orchestrated and tightly controlled by the vertical of power. While the crimes of Stalin's era and his complicated, in many ways traumatic legacy were addressed, the passivity and in some instances the complicity of the population and the legacy of the generational guilt, albeit seldom admitted, continued to persist. One of the few areas where significant strides toward de-Stalinization were made in the late Soviet period was in satire.[14] The trauma of Stalinism and uncensored revelations about that era flooded every medium, including literary works, memoirs and exposés, films and theatrical productions, exhibitions, and public debates on Stalinism and the victims of his bloody rule. After decades of silence preceding the advent of glasnost', satire raised troubling questions on previously taboo topics, explored the deep roots and the complex legacy of Stalinism, compelling and even encouraging people to "look deep into the past and face the very worst, in order to become healed."[15]

In discussing the varieties of de-Stalinization under different post-Stalinist regimes, American political scientist Jeremy Azrael stresses that "a great many measures of de-Stalinization were the result of deliberate decisions made by incumbent leaders and elites under conditions that permitted real choice, not only the choice of sponsoring more limited reforms or different reforms from those that were actually introduced but even the choice of maintaining Stalinism more or less intact."[16] While Azrael observes that the majority of leading political forces in the Kremlin after 1953 did favor the de-Stalinization policy as a way of regaining lost prerogatives and privileges as political elites, as soon as this objective was met, most of these apparatchiks became opposed to further reform. This was likely also due to the fact that many of the surviving apparatchiks who succeeded Stalin were, in fact, not only morally complicit but also responsible first-hand for many of the crimes and deeds that the Soviet Dictator was now being held solely responsible for executing.

Although de-Stalinization in the Russian context is frequently viewed as a mid-to-late Soviet concept and phenomenon, in 2010, the admission of the Katyn massacre by then president Dmitry Medvedev was cautiously coined as the "third wave of de-Stalinization."[17] A formal statement issued by the Russian State Duma on November 26, 2010, stated that "the Katyn crime was committed on direct order by Stalin and other Soviet leaders"—the first time that the Russian state had officially recognized that Stalin and his milieu were directly responsible for the massacre. Three years earlier, in 2007, while visiting one of the sites of mass executions conducted during the Great Purges of 1937–1938, Vladimir Putin uttered, "It is incredible. Why [were they killed]? Those who were executed, sent to camps, shot and tortured number in the thousands and millions of people. We need to do a great deal to ensure that this [tragedy] is never forgotten."[18] It was not until 2008 when Dmitry Medvedev replaced Putin in the presidential seat that renewed talks of de-Stalinization began to permeate the media and political circles in Moscow.

The following year, the new leader of the Russian Federation shared a video blog on the Kremlin's official website in which he explicitly condemned "Stalin's crimes."[19] But subsequent to Medvedev's comments and the State Duma statement on the Katyn massacre and Stalin's role in the crimes of the era, very little movement on the third wave of de-Stalinization followed these half-hearted attempts.

According to the Academy of Sciences sociologist, Leonty Byzov, in the present-day Russian narrative, Stalin is portrayed as a symbol of justice and, at times, even a viable alternative to the current Russian government which, in turn, is perceived by many respondents as "unfair, cruel and not caring about people."[20] Byzov further posits than it is "purely a mythological image of Stalin, very far from the real historical figure."[21] This mythological image of Joseph Stalin is not merely rooted in mythology, however; rather, it is one of numerous facets of the overall Stalin legacy that, similar to a Russian nesting doll, matryoshka, remains clad in thick, colorful layers that seldom match and constantly contradict themselves.

Alexander Dugin—controversial Russian political analyst, strategist, and philosopher who was once revered but ultimately disowned by the Kremlin as an unofficial ideologist of the Putin administration and at times described colorfully as "Putin's brain"[22]—also sees Stalin as a mythological image that in its current form hardly resembles the historical Stalin who now belongs to a distant and actively fading past.[23] It can also be argued, in contradiction with Dugin's theory, that historical Stalin as the victor of the Great Patriotic War was also the mythological Stalin who, as a byproduct of the propaganda machine and history books, was presented to the nation as an ever-archetypal and mythological figure whose image was manipulated to fit various circumstances and political goals as necessary.

The present-day Stalin—be it mythological or metaphysical—is as alive or perhaps even more alive in the modern narratives and the collective societal mind than ever before. General interest in the Stalin question had died down under Leonid Brezhnev's rule in the 1970s and made a brief reappearance in the form of an "anti-interest" in the 1980s, as Dugin recalls. "We witnessed his image and relevance fade into the imaginary rather than temporal past until his significance was once again reintroduced and reinstated in the public psyche of the nation,"[24] the Russian philosopher notes.

While in the late 1980s, in the post-glasnost' and perestroika climate, Stalin as a relevant historical figure began to disappear from political and social narratives of the late Soviet era, by the 1990s, he made another—stronger and more striking—comeback onto the modern stage. "The more we distance ourselves from the historical aspects of the figure of Stalin, the more we notice how his mythical image gains increased interest and traction in the sociopolitical conversations of the present day, and in turn, as if by default, the more we distance ourselves as society from any possibility of reaching a consensus vis-à-vis the Stalin question,"[25] Dugin observes. By the early 1990s and to a degree even the early 2000s, the faintest hints of criticism of Joseph Stalin in Russia were perceived as "outright anti-Stalinist," Dugin reminisces. "The consensus on anti-Stalinism is also shifting these days,"[26] he adds, noting that the collective society is actively contradicting Stalin with the present era and anticipating or hoping to see the future through his historical prisms.

Along with further distancing themselves from reaching a collective consensus on how to interpret and accept the political and historical aspects of the figure of Stalin, as well as the assessment of his legacies, both good and evil, Dugin believes that Georgia and Russia have encountered different truths, with neither of the truths necessarily more or less authentic than the other. "History, like any myth of another kind, is an interpretation of the past," Dugin says. "This process also implies finding multiple new truths that do not automatically cancel out other truths. These different interpretations and perceptions all deserve their place in the historical narratives and modern-day assessments—and seldom, if ever, do they go hand in hand."[27] While the mythological perceptions and contrasting versions of "different truths" may deserve their place under the sun, this approach is further complicated if not outright impossible to abide by when dealing with political facts that seldom lend themselves to the coexistence of contrasting and irreconcilable truths on the same stage—particularly when dealing with the assessment and reassessment of a recent past that is still vivid in the living memory.

In the global political culture and not merely in the post-Soviet space, today, we are witnessing growing tendencies leaning toward increased populism and authoritarianism, whereby these foreign concepts are no longer foreign even in the "liberal West." As Richard Ned Lebow writes, most if not all government policies—be it domestic or foreign—are either inspired by or entirely rooted in memories, and their controlled politicization is, to a large degree, also a source of active political contestation. "The ability to influence these [collective and institutional] memories and, thus, their putative behavioral and policy implications, is one means of achieving influence in the present over the future,"[28] he writes.

This mechanism of policy- and decision-making is at the heart of a number of present-day authoritarian and antidemocratic regimes, no longer strictly limited to the East of the Atlantic Ocean. Moreover, as this book strives to demonstrate, what often fuels and drives these systems and allows the regimes to successfully cultivate social and political followings that frequently evolve into mass movements is, indeed, a meticulous manipulation of the curious interplay between memory politics of the past and the imagined wishful memory of the future. Whether it is about Confederate vestiges[29] and memorials being toppled in the United States, most recently during the civil unrest following the killing of George Floyd in May 2020, vandalizing of national monuments in the United Kingdom linked to racism[30] and slavery,[31] or the renewed wave of toppling Lenin sculptures and statues throughout Ukraine in a movement poetically coined as "Leninopad" ("Leninfall") in the midst of the Euromaidan events of 2013[32] and 2014,[33] the very act of destruction of historical monuments evokes complex feelings, resulting in controversial debates. The debates, on the one hand, are entrenched in effacing of monuments as a rebuke to the ancestral memory, while on the other hand, opposition of their removal is interpreted as passive tolerance if not outright support of racism and slavery as acceptable and accepted chapters in our collective history.

Prior to returning to the third thread in this debate, it is worth pausing for a moment to note that when discussing events that have transpired, we must separate between the terms "past" and "history," as the two should not be used interchangeably. While the past is comprised of verified factual information, history is, in turn, a process whereby the event or a set of events are contextualized and interpreted, and at times, a number of simultaneous interpretations are being offered for the same event in order to produce an informed historical argument in retrospect.

Inevitably, history is the act of building, rebuilding, or reconstructing narratives of the past in the present day. Due to the very fact that any creation of a narrative process allows the narrator to edit and amend any one detail of the content in order to serve his or her purpose, history ought not to be viewed through a prism of truths and facts but instead as an interpretation of sorts, with a highlighted caveat that there is seldom one master version of the interpretation. And yet, even the flexibility of interpretation has limitations. History as a social science field cannot be counterfactual or hypothetical, while the past as a construct in our mind's eye is more malleable, and less restricted to "factual" interpretations.

In this equation, we cannot ignore the crucial role played by memory in interpreting the past and creating a historical narrative through expressions of personal reflections. Frequently, the separation between memory and history when interpreting events of the past is blurry, and the distinctions between the two are almost irreparably omitted. With time, the personal truth of a given individual overrides the other "truths" within the broader historical narrative, but through this process, both variants continue to inform and muddle the process of recollection. According to the International Coalition of Sites of Conscience, a US-based nonprofit global network of historical sites, museums, and memorials, there are four varieties of "truth": forensic truth, rooted in factual, verifiable past; personal truth, comprised of personal memories; social truth that is also seen as the collectively held truth, which is expressed through reflections in art, political speeches, etc.; and a healing truth, the version of truth that is contextually closest to the topic at hand, collectively concerned with historical reckoning of the past.[34]

At this point, we can return to the third and final thread of the debate that is largely separate from the other two threads—the slippery slope of removing vestiges of our past that, in turn, serves as an impetus to revise, rewrite, and even erase history in its entirety. Historian Annette Gordon-Reed explicitly separates the eradication of historical monuments in response to the Black Lives Matter movement from the likes of "Leninfall" in Ukraine and the toppling of Stalin statues in Georgia, and even more so, the eradication of disgraced figures from Kremlin photographs. "You are not going to have American history without [Thomas] Jefferson," Gordon-Reed said, adding: "It's not the Soviet Union."[35] One could contradict Gordon-Reed, and pose the following question: who is to say that if Thomas Jefferson and George Washington are perceived as the Founding Fathers of the United States, that Vladimir Lenin and Joseph Stalin were not, on their part, also the Founding Fathers of the Soviet Union—a country no longer present on the world map that continues to be seen as both an occupying force and a great global power? How do we function in a society without an ephemeral past that even history textbooks dismissed, overnight, as mythology on the one hand, and on the other, have elevated and turned into a sacral text that cannot be touched by a human but only retold like a book of Gospel? Inevitably, we end up with a man-made, constructed text or a series of texts that are ultimately nothing less than historical myths concocted about the past—and, in their most extreme form—historical propaganda, be it state-controlled or otherwise conveniently serving another higher power at the helm of the sociopolitical or religious vertical.

This brings us back to the other end of the spectrum—a phenomenon rooted in the preservation of heritage and national identity or a plethora of identities entrenched in the concept introduced by political psychiatrist Vamık D. Volkan's notion of "chosen trauma,"[36] and further adapted to the discipline of history by historian Kevin M. F. Platt as "chosen but disavowed trauma."[37] A collective memory that finds comfort in and often subconsciously feeds off of self-inflicted wounds is all the more amplified and even irritated by the abruptness of a "radical rupture"[38] as occurred at the demise of the Soviet Union, which was not a mere collapse of a political and socioeconomic system but an abrupt, forced rejection of values and belief systems, identities, and even memories.

The importance and relevance of memory—a highly malleable construct that undergoes multiple reconstructions and renegotiations, for identity formation—is, of course, not only unique for post-Soviet identities per se. However, it is this precise interplay and cognitive dissonance between memory, rupture, rejection, nostalgia, greatness and terror, admiration and humiliation that is, as this work argues, at the core of the post-Soviet legacy of the Stalinist period and, more specifically, of the complex cult of personality of Joseph Stalin in his native Georgia and Soviet Russia.

As was noted earlier, the Third Stalin is not a historical construct, nor is he the direct replica of an actual man—the son of a cobbler father and a washerwoman mother—who became one of the most feared and most revered political and later historical figures. The Third Stalin provides a self-reflection, a mirror image of ourselves composed of themes that all bear some resemblance to Stalin's mythological figure as a leitmotif: cult of personality, chosen trauma, reemergence of nationalism, and the creeping ailment-like sentiment that we call nostalgia, which takes different forms and is motivated by contrasting sentiments and goals in the Georgian and Russian variants.

NOTES

1. On the revisionism of Stalin's Great Terror and Stalinism more broadly, and how these events are analyzed through the prism of the Second World War in modern Russian academic works pertaining to the era, see: Sergey Shokarev, "Prezident V. V. Putin ob 'izvrasheniyakh' nashey istorii," *Istoricheskaya Ekspertiza* 4, no. 1 (2017): 142–44; Konstantin Morev, "Stalin i Stalinizm v Replikakh Vladimira Putina," *Istoricheskaya Ekspertiza* 4, no. 1 (2017): 134–41; Todd H. Nelson, "History As Ideology: The Portrayal of Stalinism and the Great Patriotic War in Contemporary Russian High School Textbooks," *Post-Soviet Affairs* 31, no. 1 (Summer 2014): 37–65.

2. "Conversation with Vladimir Putin: Full Transcript," RBC, December 3, 2009. Web. https://www.rbc.ru/politics/03/12/2009/5703d80a9a7947733180cf19.

3. "Vladimir Putin at Seliger 2014 National Youth Forum," Kremlin.ru, August 29, 2014. Web. http://en.kremlin.ru/events/president/news/46507.

4. Oliver Stone, *The Full Transcripts of the Putin Interviews: Oliver Stone Interviews Vladimir Putin* (New York: Hot Books, an Imprint of Skyhorse Publishing, 2017), 25.

5. "News Conference of Vladimir Putin," Kremlin.ru, December 19, 2013. Web. http://en.kremlin.ru/events/president/news/19859.

6. "Putin Keeps Stalin's Crimes Under Wraps in WWII Battle with West," *Moscow Times*, February 13, 2020. Web. https://www.themoscowtimes.com/2020/02/13/putin-keeps-stalins-crimes-under-wraps-in-wwii-battle-with-west-a69274.

7. "Kaluga Expert: De-Stalinization is a Provocation Aimed at Splitting Society," Regnum News Agency, April 11, 2011. Web. www.regnum.ru/news/1392889.html.

8. Gulag acronym stands for Glavnoye Upravleniye Ispravitelno-Trudovyvh Lagerey (in Russian: Chief Administration of Corrective Labor Camps.)

9. S. Medvedev, "Jughaphilia."

10. Prior to 2008, pro- and anti-Stalin sentiments among the Russian population were balanced and largely comparable across respondents. Based on the results of a survey conducted in 2001, 38% of those polled described their feelings toward Joseph Stalin as "admiration," "respect," and "sympathy," whereas 43% of the respondents admitted that in the same context, they feel "hostility," "disgust," and "fear." For a sociological analysis of how general sentiments and dynamics in public narratives toward Stalin have evolved throughout the 2000s, including the public opinion's neutralization vis-à-vis the Soviet Dictator between 2008 and 2014, and a growing divide between positive and negative perceptions of his historical figure and political legacies since 2014 until now, see: "Figura Stalina v obshestvennom mnenii Rossii," Levada Center, March 3, 2016. Web. https://www.levada.ru/2016/03/25/figura-stalina-v-obshhestvennom-mnenii-rossii/.

11. The Twenty-Second Party Congress in 1961 presented detailed accounts of Stalin's crimes, and was followed by the removal of his body from the mausoleum later that same year—a symbolic step toward rejection of the Stalin figure and his legacy.

12. Despite his efforts following the "secret speech" nine years earlier, even after General-Secretary Nikita Khrushchev fell from power in 1964, a decisive policy pertaining to de-Stalinization failed to emerge.

13. Under Mikhail Gorbachev, de-Stalinization swiftly evolved into re-Leninization, as the Soviet system and the apparatus under Gorbachev's leadership attempted to create a new model of socialism and communism in order to preserve the weakening Union. For more on the Gorbachev years, with particular attention paid to the "Cult of Personality" of Stalin in the glasnost' years, see chapter 5.

14. On the efforts of Soviet and, in particular, Russian satirists aimed at exorcizing the ghost of Joseph Stalin throughout the twentieth century, see Karen L. Ryan, *Stalin: In Russian Satire, 1917–1991* (Madison, WI: University of Wisconsin Press, 2009).

15. Adam Hochschild, *The Unquiet Ghost: Russians Remember Stalin* (New York: Viking, 1994), 281.

16. Jeremy Azrael, "Varieties of De-Stalinization," in Chalmers Johnson, ed., *Change in Communist Systems* (Palo Alto, CA: Stanford University Press, 1970): 135–51.

17. Pyotr Cheremushkin, "Destalinizatsiya Rossii: Tret'ya Volna," *Golos Ameriki*, October 20, 2010. Web. https://www.golosameriki.com/a/russia-stain-2010-10-20-105341173/189506.html.

18. "President Vladimir Putin, Press Conference after Visiting the Butovo Memorial Site," Kremlin.ru October 30, 2007. Web. http://archive.kremlin.ru/eng/speeches/2007/10/30/1918_type82912type82915_149844.s html. [NB: In "The Stalin Puzzle" article authors note that emotional words such as "insanity," "why," were deleted from the official transcript shortly after its initial publication. See: "The Stalin Puzzle: Deciphering Post-Soviet Public Opinion" (Washington, DC: Carnegie Endowment for International Peace, 2013).]

19. "Speech by President Dmitri Medvedev: Pamyat' o natsional'nykh tragediyakh tak zhe svyashchenna, kak pamyat' o pobedakh," Kremlin.ru, October 30, 2009. Web. http://kremlin.ru/video/256.

20. "Stalin's Approval Rating Among Russians Hits Record High," RBC News, April 16, 2019. Web. https://www.rbc.ru/politics/16/04/2019/5cb0bb979a794780a4592d0c.

21. Ibid.

22. Matthew Sharpe, "Alexander Dugin, Eurasianism, and the American Election," *Conversation*, November 13, 2017. Web. https://theconversation.com/alexander-dugin-eurasianism-and-the-american-election-87367.

23. Dugin, "Iosif Stalin: Velikoye 'Da' Bytiya," *Ulpressa*, March 5, 2013. Web. https://ulpressa.ru/2013/03/05/aleksandr-dugin-iosif-stalin-velikoe%DAbyitiya/.

24. Dugin, interview with author, December 15, 2020.

25. Ibid.

26. Ibid.

27. Ibid.

28. Richard Ned Lebow, "The Future of Memory," *The Annals of the American Academy of Political and Social Science*, vol. 617 (May 2008): 39.

29. "George Washington Statue Toppled by Protesters in Portland, Oregon," CBS News, June 19, 2020. Web. https://www.cbsnews.com/news/protesters-portland-oregon-topple-george-washington-statue/.

30. Dan Sabbagh and Vikram Dodd, "BLM Organisers Call Off London Event to Avoid Clashes with Far Right," *Guardian*, June 11, 2020. Web. https://www.theguardian.com/uk-news/2020/jun/11/blm-organisers-call-off-london-event-to-prevent-clashes-with-far-right.

31. "Statue of Queen Victoria Defaced in Hyde Park, Leeds," BBC, June 9, 2020. Web. https://www.bbc.com/news/uk-england-leeds-52985627.

32. Serhii Shebelist, "Leninfall: The Lack of Adequate Commemoration Policy in Ukraine Provokes the New Tide of the War of Monuments," *Day.Kyiv.ua*, September 30, 2013. Web. https://day.kyiv.ua/en/article/society/leninfall.

33. "Vid Leninizmu do leninopadu," Radio Svoboda, December 12, 2014. Web. https://www.radiosvoboda.org/a/26770232.html.

34. For more on the four varieties of truth, see International Coalition of Sites of Conscience, https://www.sitesofconscience.org/en/home/.

35. David A. Graham, "Where Will the Removal of Confederate Monuments Stop?," *Atlantic*, June 28, 2017. Web. https://www.theatlantic.com/politics/archive/2017/06/where-will-the-removal-of-confederate-monuments-stop/532125/.

36. Vamık D. Volkan, "Chosen Trauma: The Political Ideology of Entitlement and Violence," paper presented at Berlin Meeting, June 10, 2004; Volkan, "Le trauma massif: l'idéologie politique du droit et de la violence," *Revue française de psychoanalyse* 71, no. 4 (2007): 1041–59.

37. Kevin M. F. Platt, *Terror and Greatness: Ivan and Peter as Russian Myths* (Ithaca, NY: Cornell University Press, 2011).

38. Kevin M. F. Platt, interview with author, October 23, 2020.

Chapter V

Cult of Personality

The death of an authoritarian leader resulting in political chaos and societal turmoil, the complex plotting and manipulation ridden with twists and turns as the apparatus, in its frantic state, tries to choose a successor to the great dictator is not only a scenario for an engaging satirical motion picture but, as the release of *The Death of Stalin* would demonstrate, also one of the deepest, darkest nightmares of the current leadership at the helm of the Kremlin. "In Russia, *The Death of Stalin* is no laughing matter,"[1] a *New York Times* headline proclaimed with the US release of the satirical comedy in early 2018.

An adaptation of Fabien Nury and Thierry Robin's graphic novel by the same title, Armando Iannucci's film chronicles the immediate aftermath of the tyrannical dictator's death from a stroke in March of 1953, and shows his parasitic cronies—the Soviet postwar elite—frantically struggling to claim the newly vacated seat. What follows thereafter are a series of terrifyingly absurd and mordantly funny pursuits of power, as the members of the Politburo scurry around in desperate and often darkly comic attempts to shore up their positions at the helm of the Soviet throne. The provocative portrayal is primarily concerned with the ruling clique depicted as brutal, power-hungry buffoons, rather than Stalin himself, who is onscreen only for several minutes. The narrative avoids delving into the iconography of Joseph Stalin, instead focusing on the chaos of the regime after his demise—the pathology of power, the critique and at times even unsubtle mockery of authoritarianism, and the constant fear among both the general Soviet public and the ruling elite.

While the dark comedy from the creative force behind the HBO satire, *Veep*, Armando Iannucci, received largely positive feedback from British and American moviegoers and critics alike, in Russia, *The Death of Stalin* was not welcomed with open arms—quite the contrary. In January of 2018, the Ministry of Culture of the Russian Federation received a letter cosigned by twenty-two state officials and Russian film directors who, in a unified statement, denounced *The Death of Stalin* and its content for "blackening the memory" of Soviet Russians who fought and sacrificed their lives in the Great Patriotic War. In a follow-up statement, the Russian Ministry of Culture criticized the film for inciting hatred and enmity in the viewers and revoked the distribution license just two days before its national premiere. Iannucci's satirical comedy was ultimately banned in Russia on the grounds of "extremism,"[2] and condemned for exaggerating and distorting the Soviet past, all the while failing to adequately recognize Joseph Stalin's and the Soviet Union's contribution to the global victory of the free world over fascism.[3]

Coincidentally, the controversy around the satirical black comedy erupted during a momentous year for Russia's past, present, and future. In 2018, Vladimir Putin was preparing for his fourth presidential election, which would extend his eighteen-year rule by an additional six years, thus making him the longest-serving leader since Joseph Stalin. That same year, the successor of the Soviet Union marked the seventy-fifth anniversary since its revered victory in the Battle of Stalingrad in 1943, a turning point in the Great Patriotic War.

The Russian Minister of Culture, Vladimir Medinsky openly denied that banning the film from Russian distribution was an act of censorship or, moreover, a reflection of the state's fear of negative assessment of Russia's history. Instead, he emphasized that the decision was rooted in the question of morality, particularly during a moment in time when the nation is celebrating the victory of its people who fought and died for a city that bore the name of Stalin. "Many people of the older generation—and not only—will regard [this film's release] as an insulting mockery of the Soviet past, of the country that defeated fascism and of ordinary people, and what's even worse, even of the victims of Stalinism,"[4] Medinsky elaborated in his official statement.

However, a more rounded explanation behind the Russian authorities' verdict to ban the British comedy may lie deeper than the Kremlin's officially publicized narrative. Even more so than an attempt to discourage disrespect toward the Soviet Union's role in defeating Nazi Germany and the overall critical appraisal of Russia's history, the decision bears traces of a total rejection of the unknown, the utter chaos and fear of an entire destabilization and lawlessness that Russia could encounter if and when Vladimir Putin—the only alleged force that continues to hold the entire country together—is replaced or otherwise removed from the vertical of power. This fear of the unpredictable is not only present in the Russian political culture and continuously spreading among the members of society writ large but, increasingly so, is likewise prevalent in the West that has also contributed to shaping the very figure of Vladimir Putin as Russia's irreplaceable leader, either knowingly or unknowingly dismissing the very notion of a viable alternative.[5] Even as dissent continues to grow in Russia and the decline of Putin's popularity persists and even increases, particularly among the young,[6] the paradox lies in the lack of a viable alternative to Putin, which permeates social discourse, including the more critical slivers of society that do not support the ruling regime.[7]

As evidenced by Stalin's unexpected demise in the film, the unpredictability of a country thrown into chaos overnight is a potential reality that Russia, at least to its best knowledge, is unprepared for—not in the least due to a narrative promoted by the Russian state over the past two decades of Putin's leadership. As Masha Gessen, a Russian-born American journalist notes, the prevailing fear not only in Russia but also in the United States is that "when Putin is gone, someone worse—more aggressive, more repressive, and more anti-American—will come to power."[8] *The Death of Stalin* illuminates and further aggravates these very anxieties which, in turn, prompt the Russian state's growing uneasiness with the sensitivity of the content that could potentially stir chaos in the country, particularly as the ruling regime wrestles with growing dissent, decreasing oil prices, and an otherwise weakened economy.

Historically, if we momentarily take Boris Yeltsin's resignation on New Year's Eve in 1999 out of the equation, change of power has always been accompanied by a wave of destabilization and eventual chaos in the Russian political culture of the twentieth century. Thus, the most vulnerable targets and simultaneous villains of the film, contrary to Medinsky and the state officials, are not the Russian people or the veterans of the Great Patriotic War. Neither is it Stalin himself, but rather—it is instead the *nomenklatura* of a political clique that is power-hungry, insatiable, and often brutal. The very subject of "power" is handled with utmost care in the Russian media. Over the past decades, it has become a delicate matter, a taboo of sorts that is safest left unchallenged. Continuity and change in the Russian political culture are often equated with stability and stagnation on the one hand, and chaos and destruction on the other. Political transitions of any description in the living memory of the majority of the Russian population are associated with unpredictability and broken promises, ultimately producing a strong current of cynicism that still remains vividly sore decades after the tumult and disappointment of the 1990s.

In contrast with the Russian reaction, in his native Georgia, *The Death of Stalin* was met if not with fanfare, at the very least with significant enthusiasm—less as a black comedy and much more so as a common tragedy and relevant commentary on this critical period in the nation's history. "We just don't know what to do with Stalin,"[9] says Natalia Antelava, a Georgian journalist whose successful media start-up, Coda Story, has been focused on investigating Russian disinformation campaigns. "One thing the West probably does not understand is how relevant this film is for this part of the world."[10]

"It was truthful, it was accurate,"[11] Giorgi Kandelaki, a member of the Georgian Parliament from the opposition's side who, following the 2008 Georgian-Russian war, personally participated in the ill-fated attempt to revamp the Stalin Museum in Gori, said of the film. "The use of black humor really shows what it was like. How mad it was."[12] Instead of being viewed as an attempt to mock the late dictator, from the Georgian audience's perspective, Iannucci's black comedy became a long overdue instrument for reckoning with Georgia's complex identity that remains deeply entrenched in the Stalin epoch.

A similar attempt was already made in cinematography during Gorbachev's glasnost' years when the late Georgian film director, Tengiz Abuladze produced an emotional denunciation of the crimes of the Stalin years in what was hailed as both a cultural and political milestone. The film shattered many taboos, including one poignant, albeit deliberately subtle social criticism and denunciation of Georgia's native son who is not explicitly named but is instead constantly referenced in a subtle manner throughout the narrative—Joseph Stalin. While the main premise of the surrealistic film explores terror in the face of evil—Georgia's Stalin problem and the unresolved puzzle—the portrayal of the main character, Varlam Aravidze (translated from Georgian as "Varlam No Man") also encompasses different elements of Beria, Hitler, Mussolini, and, to a subtler degree, particularly in terms of physical likeness, even Charlie Chaplin's "great dictator." The explicit references in the film to Georgia's infamous son, Ioseb Jughashvili, are mostly limited, as are the specific problems of Stalinism in Georgia—an issue deliberately generalized in the narrative to avoid the growing tendencies during the glasnost' years to equate all crimes of the period with Stalin himself. In this balancing act, Abuladze gradually excites and seduces his Georgian audience by revealing similarities with the Soviet dictator, all the while carefully "pacifying" them with sufficient differences and offering the viewer enough time to ponder "to what extent was Stalin a Georgian" and "to what extent was Stalin good to and for Georgia and its history."[13]

One of the strongest links between Abuladze's Varlam and the Soviet Georgian tyrant is the chameleon-like ability of Ioseb Jughashvili turned Joseph Stalin to constantly don masks and navigate with great ease and flexibility between his many identities: from a great patriot to a sadistic, tyrannical pervert, from a megalomaniac to an enlightened, deeply caring father of the nation. Deliberately eschewing the facts and concealing historical knowledge in surrealism, instead of recreating the past events, Abuladze agonizes the viewer by recreating the deeply seated albeit unreconciled sentiment of fear in the face of terror.

Abuladze's phantasmagoric *Repentance* was suppressed by Soviet censors for two years after its completion in 1984,[14] released for closed screenings in Tbilisi and Moscow in 1986, and finally premiered Union-wide in January 1987.[15] The anti-Stalin film was less critical of the Soviet regime per se and more so introspective, self-critical, and sobering, above all, for Georgian audience members—those who were simultaneously the victims and active participants, particularly on the elite level, in the bloody regime under Stalin's leadership. The cult of dictatorial personality is still traced throughout the film, and its effects remain both chilling and destructive for the nation and its identity. Decades after its inception, the film demonstrates that not only at the dusk of the waning Soviet era but also in its aftermath and to this very day, full reckoning with the past remains unachieved. Alas, the time for repentance has not yet come even despite the eradication of censorship rules and restrictions.

The "Cult of Personality" vis-à-vis that era as a whole was not only present in Soviet Russia but also throughout the rest of the fellow republics under the Soviet umbrella, the eastern bloc more generally, and communist as well as post-communist dictatorships more specifically not only pertaining to Stalin but also in relation to other leaders in the region,[16] including "minor" leaders such as Kliment Voroshilov, the People's Commissar for Defence and a prominent Marshal of the Soviet Union in the 1930s. Georgia, of course, was no exception—if not one of the most striking examples as the nation that birthed the dictator.

What we witness in Russia today is a rebirth of another Stalin-era legacy— the "Cult of Personality," perhaps one of the few phenomena present and evergreen across all three of the Stalins nestled inside this matryoshka. A strong, even ruthless national leader who emerged out of the ashes of destruction and disillusionment amid shattered hopes for change and new beginnings is not an unknown concept to this nation. In general, comparisons between cults of personality past and present are more accurate vis-à-vis "cults" rather than "personalities." The connotations of the term were formerly perceived as mostly negative, but now, under the ongoing two-decade-long leadership of Vladimir Putin, the concept is frequently interpreted in a largely positive light.

British academic, E. A. Rees ties leader cults to the founding myths of new states,[17] whereby the new power that be is symbolically depicted and even celebrated in "flags, hymns, and anthems, medals, awards, prizes, stamps and coins, in the renaming of towns, streets and institutions."[18] Art historian

Anita Pisch further elaborates on this notion, stating that within a state such as the Soviet Union (and, for the sake of our analysis, post-Soviet Russia in particular) in the process of reinventing and repositioning itself, the leader cult evolves into "the means by which new rituals and traditions are instituted, employing symbols to bring consensus and a sense of shared identity in societies beset by latent conflict or indifference to the dominant ideology."[19] Following this narrative in conjunction with an array of narratives that the Soviet Dictator was single-handedly instrumental in crafting himself, his post-mortem persona has evolved into a "symbolic vessel"[20] of a leader who mobilizes, unifies, modernizes, and yet is also cognizant of traditions and thus remains at once conservative and simultaneously focused on progress.

In 1971, Tbilisi-born Soviet dissident Roy Medvedev wrote that particularly at the peak of the tumult, unpredictability, and tragedy of the Great Patriotic War, "Stalin's image became a sort of symbol existing in the popular mentality independently from its actual bearer."[21] Thus, in the war-torn Soviet Union, the very name of Stalin, and what Medvedev believed was also a great degree of faith entrusted in his leadership, ultimately helped pull the Soviet people together "giving them hope of victory"[22] which was eventually achieved and presented to the nation not only as Stalin's personal victory but to an equal degree also the victory of togetherness and of the union as such. In keeping with the logic behind the cult of personality and leadership, not dissimilar to the Georgian case, in Russia, the atrocities and defeats of the military and political vertical of power are often displaced from Stalin and attributed to "other commanders or to treason."[23] Meanwhile, Medvedev writes that, in contrast, the victories are, in turn, celebrated as a direct responsibility of Comrade Stalin. Although the "inexorable"[24] facts of the senseless, extravagant errors of the commander and his decision-making are not blindly dismissed, the wartime events of World War II remain linked to the mythical image of Stalin as the Great Father of the nations.

Alexander Dugin sees the "Cult of Personality" not as a historical construct or a concept rooted in the past but, instead, as a modern-day depiction of Russia and to a degree also of Georgia. Moreover, in both cases, he considers this phenomenon to be fundamentally constructed in a bottom-up—not a top-down—fashion, born at a grassroots level and working itself up through the various echelons of power.[25] In addition, Dugin views Stalin's Georgianness as a unique and important component of this "Cult of Personality": "We, the Russian people, contrary to what others may say, are not chauvinists by nature," he insists on dispelling one of the liberal media's criticisms of his own work and philosophy. "Instead, we worship other nations and look up to them, and here, Georgia is no exception but rather a clear and vivid example of this." Thus, the Eurasianist philosopher believes the polemic narratives revolving around Stalin to be rooted in mythology and metaphysics more so than history per se, which, among other attributes, also offers a glimpse into the complicated history of Russo-Georgian relations. Highly complex and tangled though the relationship may be, Dugin claims that neither views the "other" with emotional indifference or carelessness. "This love and adoration of Stalin is at times also reflective of Russia's deep love and adoration for the Georgian people and the Georgian culture as a whole," argues Dugin, who has been frequently condemned by Stalin's compatriots for attempting to pit Georgian patriotism against European civilization and, in doing so, placing Georgia within the "Russian world" or *Russkiy mir*.[26]

The Russian President, on his part, has been vocal to dismiss any attempts of circulating narratives around his growing cult of personality in Russia's political environment.[27] His spokesperson, Dmitry Peskov, recently noted that "the cult of personality of Vladimir Putin is something that Vladimir Putin categorically disagrees with." Peskov reiterated that Vladimir Vladimirovich "doesn't like it and he doesn't agree with it."[28] There is likely a degree of truthfulness to this statement as, historically, the traditional concept of a leader's personality cult carries pejorative undertones, and the term itself immediately evokes tainted imagery of dictators, such as Stalin, Hitler, Mao, to name but a few. After all, the phrase "Cult of Personality" was used by Nikita Khrushchev in 1956 to discredit and condemn the hero-like worship of Joseph Stalin. However, the construction and continued formation of the cult of Putin as the "national leader" has permeated the Russian pro-government media discourse. The cult of Stalin in his media portrayal[29] and within the public discourse was a "deliberately constructed and managed mechanism" built upon the "closure of the public sphere"[30] and driven by eliciting both enthusiasm and fear primarily from the Soviet population. The aim of the construct becomes the "integration of the political system around the leader's persona,"[31] as opposed to the leader serving the system and the nation. This mechanism is adapted in modern Russia vis-à-vis Vladimir Putin with a dual goal: to elicit enthusiasm and adulation in the relationship between the leader and his followers on the one hand, and on the other, to project fear both domestically and, even more so, beyond the borders of Mother Russia.

Like Stalin, who publicly disavowed his cult but ultimately embraced and even found it useful in ruling the Soviet Union and projecting his strength and absolute power abroad, Putin has also inspired expressions of adulation as the great and all-knowing leader of the Russian people "offering psychological and emotional reassurance, a focus of stability and unity, in a world of uncertainties,"[32] all the while ruling in a ruthless and at times merciless manner in the name of protecting the sovereignty of the nation against foreign threats and aggression from without. Even though social control in the Putin era is far less pronounced and the construction and promotion of the leader's personality cult is no longer conducted through ruling party-mandated coercion, the officialdom's desire to replicate familiar sentiments in the form of nostalgia for the Soviet past among society is seen through the depiction of Putin as the generous and all-powerful "father of the Russian nation."

Therefore, the more appropriate terms here are either "Putinism" or "Putinmania,"[33] rather than "Cult of Personality," even if the cult of leadership continues to define and drive the Putin leadership. This phenomenon and its relevance in Russia then and now is explained, at least partially, by historian Stephen Kotkin's suggestion that a cyclical pattern, which has persisted in Russia's historical development, whereby spurs of modernization are inevitably followed by waves of authoritarianism and repressions, in turn, resulting time and again in destruction or collapse, is largely due to an inherent gap between Russia's aspirations and its capacity.[34] This cycle is then unavoidably succeeded by another wave of authoritarianism that brings to the fore the need for an autocrat—be it a Tsar, a General Secretary, or a President of a strong and, if need be, a coercive state apparatus. Russia is both dominated by and accustomed to this governing approach and, therefore, explaining this tendency observed in Vladimir Putin's ruling style as a recent evolution means oversimplifying the complex phenomenon.

Faith in the Tsar as the single great protector of the nation was shaken by 1905 events, but the need for an autocratic, iron-fisted, and, if need be, ruthless ruler has continued to persist and has even outlived the Russian tsar. However, we must be cautious with a frequently overused and oversimplified statement that has evolved into a widespread cliché, which posits that Russia has a historical predisposition to and even a degree of hunger for autocracy. "In today's climate of confrontation, people want to see a strong leader, even if not always humane, which is why attitudes toward Stalin are improving, as evidenced by the results of various polls,"[35] Alexei Grazhdankin, deputy director of the Levada Center, told the Russian newspaper, *Kommersant* back in 2015.

Aside from "Putinism" and "Putinmania," it may also be appropriate to refer to the personality cult phenomenon under Vladimir Putin's presidency as the "Leader Cult," which, according to historian E. A. Rees is "an established system of veneration of a political leader, to which all members of society are expected to subscribe, a system that is omnipresent and ubiquitous and one that is expected to persist indefinitely. It is thus a deliberately constructed and managed mechanism, which aims at the integration of the political system around the leader's persona."[36] As the term "cult" is embalmed with religious connotations, it is not surprising that personality cults surrounding political leaders are, in the most extreme of examples, equated with religious worship.

Historian of modern and contemporary history at the University of Bern, Marina Cattaruzza observes that "political religion"[37] is a phenomenon that is most frequently associated with the 1930s and totalitarian rulers who dictated the world order during that era, including Stalin, Hitler, and Mussolini. Personality cults of leaders in authoritarian regimes stabilized the political and societal order, and provided a sense of predictability and a structured ritual in the relationship between the ruler and his people, further legitimizing the leadership. Today, we are witnessing a similar trajectory in Putin's Russia where, instead of personal and political rituals replacing the religious rituals as they once did under Stalin, in modern-day Russia, these rituals are frequently conducted in tandem with the Russian Orthodox Church. And lest we forget, Alexander Dugin reminds us that the paradox behind the Russian Orthodox Church's embrace of Stalin and his personality cult today has permeated the ROC at every level of management and leadership—even despite the atrocities conducted against the orthodoxy and religion by Stalin during his rule.[38]

In exploring "Cults of Personality" in the Soviet history during the span of the twentieth century, it is important to momentarily turn to the quasi-religious cult of Lenin as a god-like, messianic figure with a historic mission of guiding the Soviet people toward Socialist Utopia who, for the greater part of the twentieth century, was deemed immortal. At its core, Mikhail Gorbachev's glasnost' and perestroika were not directly concerned with debunking the myth of Leninism as such. In fact, according to Mikhail Sergeevich, Lenin himself had frequently used the term glasnost', and, in Gorbachev's words, the very concept of perestroika was rooted in Vladimir Ilyich's "immortal ideas."[39] Moreover, in 1985, Mikhail Gorbachev reassured the Soviet people on the brink of change that "the great perestroika revolution is the direct successor of the works of October [of 1917] and the deeds of Lenin," furthering arguing that "perestroika brings us closer to Lenin, and brings Lenin closer to us."[40] However, by the very act of putting these drastic policies into motion, Gorbachev not only issued a death sentence to an already withering Soviet regime but, furthermore, also granted a death sentence to the cult of Leninism that was, to a large extent, constructed upon myths which could only be sustained under a tightly controlled state apparatus that was fast losing its former power, grandeur, and overall appeal.

As Lenin and the Soviet state were intimately linked, the disintegration of the national cult of Lenin was thus directly paralleled with the drastic decline of the Soviet state authority and popular support for the governing apparatus. This was not solely apparent in the political rhetoric of the state authorities of that era, but grew increasingly so by the demise of the USSR. Furthermore, the decline also became visible in the gradual disappearance of physical vestiges, such as monuments and portraits of Vladimir Ilyich that slowly but surely started to lose their former allure and weight. During the transitional decade of the 1990s, Lenin rejoined the "ranks of the mere mortals,"[41] leaving a lesser mark on the political culture of Russia and other former Soviet states. Meanwhile, his successor, Joseph Stalin, not only continues to grow more popular but also persists in influencing and even shaping the political rhetoric, further driving societal viewpoints with his polyphonic legacy that, with time, becomes even more—not less—complex and convoluted.

While Stalin's "Cult of Personality" in the twentieth century rested primarily on the pillars of fear and social control, under Putin and into the new millennium, the phenomenon became less concerned with explicit coercion. This is not to say, however, that the pillars of fear and social control are entirely absent from the Russian political culture as its distinct features. Through continuously invoking at times artificially constructed fear and claiming that only the governing body has the means and the right to protect its people from threat emanating from both within and without, the regime continues to hold on to power by constantly tightening its grip on unmanaged freedom in the name of avoiding chaos and, thus, performing the greater good.

Furthermore, unlike the classic authoritarian model, in the construction of the geopolitical iconography of contemporary Russia, Vladimir Putin's image is presented as that of a "strong leader" of an orderly state and a reemerging global power that protects its sovereignty, statehood, and identity, at once responding to the interests of the pragmatic political elites and the romantic aspirations of greatness of the mass population. Through what scholars Dimitry Filimonov and André Filler describe as "power branding" that presumes "labeling the exercise of power"[42] beyond the mere individual factors or an official juridical framework of the supreme function, the image of Vladimir Putin at the constant helm of the vertical of power of modern Russia aims to minimize the threat of an abrupt change of leadership.

In his quest for a strong state, it is no secret that Vladimir Putin has curbed all remnants of Russia's brief flirtation with open democracy and swiftly put an end to any diffusion of power within the government that preceded his presidency. The restoration of the Soviet-era "vertical of power" that establishes a chain of hierarchical authority has evolved over the years of Putin's leadership to a version of a "circle of shared responsibility."[43] However, the one constant condition remains unchanged and largely unchallenged—the leader at the helm of the vertical. The decision-making processes in Russia continue to show Putin in a position of complete control, but through this absolute consolidation of power and gradual reversal to authoritarianism,

Russia has also found itself without a viable civil society as such. Moreover, with a goal of continuously legitimizing the current political regime, the Kremlin has demonstrated a willingness and propensity to repress (not on the scale of the explicit and often vulgar Stalinist repressions, but on a limited and selective basis) as a means of responding to and mitigating both internal and external threats to redistribution of power and its legitimation.

In addition to returning in the early 2000s to the policies of illiberalism and traces of anti-democratic styles of political ruling, the dawn of the new century in Russia also demonstrated political and decision-making tendencies rooted less in conservatism and much more so geared toward archaism. As the director of the Levada Center Lev Gudkov says, the regime of "Putinism" also promotes the return to de-modernization and anti-modernization of society.[44] This, above all, according to Gudkov, is Russia's response to the failure of democracy and democratization of the system and its society at the tail end of the last century.[45]

The days of gulag-type repressions have given way to the more subtle forms of political repressions that are still rooted in the many original forms present in the Soviet-style regime of politics of fear. Repressions were utilized by the Stalin regime as a dissent-mitigating instrument. However, in the early 2000s, as Putin's popularity was further fueled by Russia's economic growth, the citizens' loyalty and approval of the ruling regime minimized the need to revert to the "old practices" on a large scale. The 2010 Arab Spring revolutions followed by anti-Putin demonstrations in Russia in the winter of 2011–2012 vividly showcased the effectiveness and impact of social media and information-sharing websites, such as Facebook and Twitter, on mobilizing protesters, and thus began to pose a direct threat to the ruling regime. This, in turn, resulted in a political crackdown on civil society and all movements of or even the slightest attempts at dissent. As the government was no longer able to "buy" public support and loyalty due to the economic consequences stemming from Russia's withering economy, the state was forced to look for avenues to mitigate discontent and disloyalty among both elites and citizens at large. Public discreditation of opposition leaders, dissidents, and other anti-Putin activists became the new norm of managing pressure and discontent from the public.

Russian political scientist, Vladimir Gel'man notes that it was precisely on May 6, 2012, that Russia's "politics of fear"[46] became the new policy for the Kremlin and thus signaled a strengthening of its repressive policies. The crackdown on political and civil activity in opposition to the ruling party was no longer solely targeting journalists and politicians against the Putin regime. The circle had expanded to include anyone criticizing the leadership, including those showcasing tendencies of dissent on the internet. Since the

2011–2012 demonstrations, through closely monitoring internet user habits, the federal services have been both implicitly and explicitly influencing user behavior, in turn spreading a heightened level of self-awareness among citizens in terms of *what* they post and *where* they post it. Moreover, self-censorship is constantly being encouraged by selective and widely covered arrests and fines of individuals—both political figures and regular civilians—who publicly voice their criticism of the ruling regime, and particularly of President Putin.

One of the most recent cases of the above policy took place in August 2019, when a resident of the Krasnoyarsk region, Yevgeny Noskov, was fined 30,000 rubles (approximately $450) for disrespecting the ruling regime in his VKontakte[47] post, in which he complained about his low salary and directly insulted president Vladimir Putin. In a similar vein, a resident of the Novgorod region, Yury Kartizhev, was also fined 30,000 rubles after insulting Vladimir Putin on his social media homepage.[48] The Russian President signed the law on "Disrespect of Authorities" on March 18, 2019.[49] Rigid and systematic individual pressure on opposition forces has gone beyond mere criticism of dissent even if, for the time being, the number of political arrests and subsequent trials remain relatively low compared to other authoritarian regimes.[50]

A failure to fall in line with the regime's tough restrictions, while not directly linked with one's inevitable downfall, is still frequently associated with falling out of grace with the state authorities—a phenomenon, albeit in a much lighter form, borrowed from the Stalinist era, even if we continue to posit that Putin's Russia is not Stalin's Soviet Union. Yet, we already predict that similar to how the system under Stalin's rule outlived the Soviet Dictator, *sistema* or a system of governance of Putin's Russia as an undeniable attribute of Russian culture beyond mere politics and political ideology could persist even after the inevitable end of Vladimir Vladimirovich's leadership, not in the least for biological reasons.[51]

This state-controlled *sistema* pursued by the Putin administration continues to share familiar features with the Stalin period as its direct legacy: fear and uncertainty of Russia after its longtime ruler and the father of the nation is no longer at the vertical of the Kremlin's powerhouse. However, unlike its Soviet prototype rooted in theoretical tenets of socialism, such as political and ideological rigidity, lack of private property, a centralized system of planning, etc., the concept of *sistema* has transformed and adapted to reflect global and domestic changes.

In the Soviet days, the term *sistema* primarily described the triangular relationship between the state, the Communist Party apparatus more broadly, and the Soviet people. The informal governing *sistema* that characterizes Putin's Russia today is, above all else, focused on economic growth through monetization of the economy and concentration of power through privatization and increase of private wealth.[52] Although a largely fluid and flexible concept, *sistema* in both its Soviet and modern-day Russian variants enjoys one constant—a ruling regime that protects its grip on the levers of power against the threat of losing control and descending into chaos.[53] As political scientists Gleb Pavlovsky and Alena Ledeneva argue, *sistema* as an important attribute of the Russian political culture beyond politics and ideology had existed in Russia prior to the ascent to power of Vladimir Putin, dating back to the Soviet period, and thus will more than likely outlive the Putin regime.[54] It is therefore highly probable that as a result of the total privatization of Russian politics and centralization of control at the helm of the vertical of power, should Vladimir Putin step down from the presidential throne, irrespective of who may replace him, the presiding team of modern Russia will only be able to rule through *sistema*.[55]

NOTES

1. Matthew Luxmoore, "In Russia, 'The Death of Stalin' Is No Laughing Matter," *New York Times*, January 24, 2018. Web. https://www.nytimes.com/2018/01/24/movies/death-of-stalin-banned-russia.html.

2. Denis Pinchuk and Andrew Osborn, "Russia Cancels Release of 'Insulting' Film about Stalin's Death," Reuters, January 23, 2018. Web. https://www.reuters.com/article/us-russia-film-stalin/russia-cancels-release-of-insulting-film-about-stalins-death-idUSKBN1FC1X6.

3. "Kosh'unstvo i glumleniye: fil'm 'Smert' Stalina' ne pustili v prokat," RIA Novosti, January 23, 2018. Web. https://ria.ru/20180123/1513179176.html.

4. Pinchuk and Osborn, "Russia Cancels Release of 'Insulting' Film about Stalin's Death."

5. On arguments in Russian academic sources about Russia's unpreparedness to replace Vladimir Putin and the lack of a viable alternative leader, see: Svetlana Babaeva i Georgiy Bovt, "Prezidentom Rossiyskoy Federatsii snova izbran V. V. Putin," *Izvestiya*, March 15, 2004; Antonina V. Seleznyova, "Obraz prezidenta Rossii V.V. Putina v soznanii rossiyskikh grazhdan," *Russkaya Politologiya* (2018): 4–11; Vladimir Ilyin i Mikhail Morev, "Chto ostavit V. Putin svoyemu priyemniku v 2024 godu?" *Ekonomicheskiye i sotsialniye peremeny: fakty, tendentsii, prognoz* 11, no. 1 (2018): 9–30; Nadezhda Oktyabr'skaya, "Putin sozdal problemy, a komu ikh reshat'?", *Zdorovye—osnova chelovecheskogo potentsiala: problem i puti ikh resheniya* (2020): 1227–30; Pyotr Panov, " Poleticheskiy poryadok i problema proizvodstva vlasti: institut preemnika," *Politicheskaya ekspertiza: Politeks* 6, no. 3 (2010): 19–33.

6. When asked if they would like Vladimir Putin to step down from his post in 2024, 41% of young Russians between the ages of 16 and 34 responded "definitely yes" while 20% answered "probably not." See: Gwendolyn Sasse and Félix

Krawatzek, "Young Russians Want Putin to Step Back from Power," Carnegie Europe, June 24, 2020. Web. https://carnegieeurope.eu/2020/06/24/young-russians-want-putin-to-step-back-from-power-pub-82357.

7. In 2014, Levada Center published results of a poll surveying over 1,600 Russian respondents about possible political alternatives to Vladimir Putin: 31% of the respondents said that they do not believe they see an alternative to Putin at the presidential helm, even though 47% of them admitted that they would like to see another leader replacing Putin after 2024. See: "Vozmozhniy preemnik V. Putin na postu prezidenta Rossii," Levada Center, January 20, 2014. Web. Another Levada Center poll conducted ahead of the 2018 Presidential Elections in Russia showed that more than half or 51% of Russian respondents would like to see Putin at the top of the vertical of power, while 27% would prefer if the incumbent left his post earlier than planned. Nonetheless, 57% unanimously stated that "decisive, full-scale changes" were needed in the country with or without Putin as the leader. See: "Izmeneniya i peremeny," Levada Center, June 19, 2018. Web. https://www.levada.ru/2018/06/19/izmeneniya-i-peremeny/. Ahead of a constitutional reform vote held shortly after the outbreak of COVID-19 in 2020, only 25% of the respondents surveyed by Levada Center named Vladimir Putin as the most trusted politician, demonstrating a dip in his approval ratings, which comparatively is still higher than the popularity of other politicians in the country. See: "Doveriye politikam," Levada Center, May 29, 2020. Web. https://www.levada.ru/2020/05/29/doverie-k-politikam/. For analyses of public attitudes toward the possibility of Putin's departure from the political arena, see: "Chto, uzhe ukhodite? Kak rossiyane otnosyatsya k otstavke Putina v 2024 godu," Levada Center, March 5, 2020. Web. https://www.levada.ru/2020/03/05/chto-uzhe-uhodite-kak-rossiyane-otnosyatsya-k-otstavke-putina-v-2024-godu/, and Denis Volkov, "Podberut cheloveka: chto dumayut rossiiskiye izbirateli o probleme-2024," RBC, May 14, 2019. Web. https://www.rbc.ru/opinions/politics/14/05/2019/5cda6f089a794770fbfb5ec9.

8. Masha Gessen, "'The Death of Stalin' Captures the Terrifying Absurdity of a Tyrant," *New Yorker*, March 6, 2018. Web. https://www.newyorker.com/news/our-columnists/the-death-of-stalin-captures-the-terrifying-absurdity-of-a-tyrant.

9. William Dunbar, "What Georgians Make of 'The Death of Stalin,'" *Economist*, February 16, 2018. Web. https://www.1843magazine.com/culture/the-daily/what-georgians-make-of-the-death-of-stalin.

10. Ibid.

11. Ibid.

12. Ibid.

13. Julie Christensen, "Tengiz Abuladze's Repentance and the Georgian Nationalist Cause," *Slavic Review* 50, no. 1 (Spring 1991): 168.

14. One of the events that delayed the approval for the film's release was the growing tension between Tbilisi and Moscow when halfway through the filming of *Repentance*, on November 18, 1983, a group of seven young people from prominent Georgian families, including one of the lead actors from the film, Gega Kobakhidze, and his wife, Tinatin Petviashvili, highjacked an Aeroflot flight 6833 en route from Tbilisi, Georgian SSR to Leningrad, Russian SFSR. The group's aborted attempt

to flee the Soviet Union and escape the communist regime highlighted the ideological alienation of the youth in the USSR, reviving nationalist and anti-colonialist sentiments among young people. The incident claimed the lives of three innocent members of the Aeroflot crew and two passengers, as well as three of the hijackers. Kobakhidze and his friends, accused of using "Nazi tactics," were arrested by the Alpha Group, the counterterrorism task force of the KGB, and sentenced to the death penalty. This decision resulted in a petition signed by over 3,000 members of the Georgian intelligentsia elites calling for their commutation. With the hijackers' fate still unknown, the filming of *Repentance* resumed and Kobakhidze was replaced with a young theater actor, Merab Ninidze. At the time, over the next three years, the film remained shelved until it was ultimately approved for a public premiere in 1987. For more on the hijacking of the Aeroflot flight and the fate of the young hijackers, see: Nino Gozalishvili, "The Late Cold War and Cracks in the Iron Curtain for Georgian Youth in the 1980s: The Subcultural Nature of the 'Jeans Generation,'" *Corvinus Journal of International Affairs* 3, no. 2 (October 2018): 42–54; Sergey Turchenkp, "Krovaviy reys #6883," *Trud*, February 8, 2000. Web. https://archive.is/20130416214702/www.fsb.ru/fsb/history/author/single.htm!id%3D10318151@fsbPublication.html#selection-281.14-281.16; "At Least Seven Die in Shootout After Hijacking of a Soviet Plane," *New York Times*, November 23, 1983. Web. https://www.nytimes.com/1983/11/23/world/at-least-seven-die-in-shootout-after-hijacking-of-a-soviet-plane.html.

15. Later that year, the film received the Special Jury Prize at the 1987 Cannes Film Festival.

16. For more background and documentation of leadership cults in the Eurasian region and beyond in pre-communist, communist, and post-communist periods, see: E. A. Rees, "Introduction: Leader Cults: Varieties, Preconditions and Functions," in Balázs Apor, Jan C. Behrends, Polly Jones and E. A. Rees, *The Leader Cult in Communist Dictatorships: Stalin and the Eastern Bloc* (Hampshire, UK: Palgrave Macmillan, 2004); Xavier Márquez, "The Mechanisms of Cult Production: An Overview," in Kirill Postoutenko and Darin Stephanov, eds., *Ruler Personality Cults from Empires to Nation-States and Beyond: Symbolic Patterns and Interactional Dynamics*, 21–45 (New York: Routledge, 2021); Andrea Orzoff, "The Husbandman: Tomáš Masaryk's Leader Cult in Interwar Czechoslovakia," *Austrian History Yearbook* 39, no. 1 (April 2008): 121–37; Balázs Apor, "National Traditions and the Leader Cult in Communist Hungary in the Early Cold War Years," *Twentieth Century Communism* 1, no. 1 (June 2009): 50–71; Abel Polese and Slavomir Horák, "A Tale of Two Presidents: Personality Cult and Symbolic Nation-Building in Turkmenistan," *Journal of Nationalism and Ethnicity* 43, no. 3 (May 2015): 457–78.

17. It is noteworthy, however, that contrary to E. A. Rees' theory about the founding myths of new states focused on their founders, neither Joseph Stalin nor Vladimir Putin were the founders of their "new" states. Both Stalin and Putin took over the throne following the passing of Lenin and Yeltsin respectively and, in the aftermath, are believed to have imposed order, stability, and curbed the revolutionary ferment and chaos of the transition period.

18. E.A. Rees, "Introduction: Leader Cults: Varieties, Preconditions and Functions," 7–8.

19. Pisch, *The Personality Cult of Stalin in Soviet Posters, 1929–1953*, 193–94.

20. Ibid., 259.

21. Roy Medvedev, *Let History Judge: The Origins and Consequences of Stalinism* (New York: Knopf, 1971), 749.

22. Ibid.

23. Ibid.

24. Ibid.

25. Dugin, interview with author.

26. Valeri Chechelashvili, "Dugin Has Come Out as a Supporter of Georgia: How Did This Happen?", Georgian Foundation for Strategic and International Studies, June 20, 2019. Web. https://www.gfsis.org/blog/view/956; Alexander Dugin, "Manifest o prisoyedeneniiy Gruzii k Rossii," Dugin.ru via Tsargrad.tv., n.d. Web. http://dugin.ru/video/manifest-o-prisoedinenii-gruzii-k-rossii.

27. Julie Cassiday and Emily Johnson identified the earliest use of the phrase "cult of personality" in conjunction with Vladimir Putin in William Safire's essay on Putinism, in which the American author and Richard Nixon's former speechwriter observes that "an instant cult of personality has been created for Putin—tough-minded and lean-bodied, in contrast to the staggering Yeltsin." See: William Safire, "Essay; Putinism Looms," *New York Times*, January 31, 2000. Web. https://www.nytimes.com/2000/01/31/opinion/essay-putinism-looms.html.

28. Stepan Kravchenko and Andrey Biryukov, "Putin Doesn't Like Cult of Personality of Putin, Kremlin Says," *Bloomberg*, March 13, 2020. Web. https://www.bloomberg.com/news/articles/2020-03-13/putin-doesn-t-like-cult-of-personality-of-putin-kremlin-says.

29. For more detailed analysis comparing the personality cults of Stalin and Putin, Evgeniy Kablukov in "Joseph Stalin and Vladimir Putin: Practices of the Image Construction of a Political Leader in the Discourse of Soviet and Russian Media" observes that the gatekeeping practices vis-à-vis the mass media and the depiction of these two leaders' images in various discourses are fundamentally different. Kablukov argues that one of the contradictions in their portrayals is revealed in the contrasting differences between the formation and promotion of the "celebrity image" of Putin through spectacular breaking news coverage with Vladimir Vladimirovich as the "star," whereas the Soviet media refused to focus on sensationalism, instead covering official and routine events with Stalin's participation, highlighting these "ordinary actions" and portraying him as a "deified father." See: Evgeniy Kablukov, "Iosif Stalin i Vladimir Putin: praktiki konstruktirovaniya obraza politicheskogo lidera v diskurse sovetskikh i rossiyskikh media," *Przegląd Wschodnioeuropejski* 11, no. 2 (2020): 73–84.

30. Rees, "Introduction: Leader Cults: Varieties, Preconditions and Functions," 4.

31. Ibid.

32. Ibid.

33. Julie A. Cassiday and Emily D. Johnson, "Putin, Putiniana and the Question of a Post-Soviet Cult of Personality," *Slavonic and East European Review* 88, no. 4 (October 2010): 681–707.

34. Stephen Kotkin, "Russia's Perpetual Geopolitics: Putin Returns to the Historical Pattern," *Foreign Affairs* 95, no. 3 (May–June 2016): 2–9. Web. https://www.foreignaffairs.com/articles/ukraine/2016-04-18/russias-perpetual-geopolitics.

35. "V SPCH opasayutsya, chto Iosif Stalin raskolet obshestvo," *Kommersant*, March 30, 2015. Web. https://www.kommersant.ru/doc/2698033.

36. Rees, "Introduction: Leader Cults: Varieties, Preconditions and Functions," 4.

37. Marina Cattaruzza, "Introduction to the Special Issue of *Totalitarian Movements and Political Religions*: Political Religions as a Characteristic of the 20th Century," *Politics, Religion & Ideology* 6, no. 1 (2005): 2.

38. Dugin, interview with author.

39. "M. S. Gorbachev," *Moskovskii Komsomolets*, March 12, 1985, 1; Trevor J. Smith, "Lenin for Sale: The Rise and Fall of the Personality Cult of V. I. Lenin in Soviet Russia, 1935–1995," Master's thesis, University of Ottawa, 1995, 34–96; Galina Mukhina, ed., V. 1. *Lenin o Glasnosti* (n.p.: Moscow, Russia, 1989); *Moskovskii Komsomolets*, April 22, 1989, 1.

40. *Moskovskii Komsomolets*, November 1, 1989, 1; April 23, 1988, 3.

41. Trevor J. Smith, "The Collapse of the Lenin Personality Cult in Soviet Russia, 1985–1995," *Historian* 60, no. 2 (Winter 1998): 343.

42. André Filler and Dimitry Filimonov, "Vladimir Putin: A Geopolitical Representation? From the Image to Usage," *Hérodote* 166, no. 3 (2017): 51–67.

43. Andrew Monaghan, "The Russian *Vertikal*: the Tandem, Power, and the Elections," Russia and Eurasia Programme Paper REP 2011/01, Chatham House, June 2011. Web. https://www.chathamhouse.org/sites/default/files/19412_0511ppmonaghan.pdf

44. S. Medvedev, "Jughaphilia."

45. Ibid.

46. Vladimir Gel'man, "Politics of Fear," *Russian Politics and Law* 53, nos. 5–6 (September–December 2015): 6–26.

47. A popular Russian social media platform.

48. "Zhitelya Krasnoyarskogo kraya otshtrafovali na 30 tysyach rubley za slova o Putine," *Svoboda*, August 13, 2019. Web. https://www.svoboda.org/a/30107224.html.

49. "Russia's Putin Signs Law Banning Fake News, Insulting the State Online," Reuters, March 18, 2019. Web. https://www.reuters.com/article/us-russia-politics-fakenews-idUSKCN1QZ1TZ; "Sibiryaku, napisavshemu pro nizkuyu zarplatu i nazvavshemu Putina na bukvu 'P,' naznachili shtraf za oskorbleniye vdvoye vyshe zarobotka," News.ru, August 13, 2019. Web. https://www.newsru.com/russia/13aug2019/noskov.html.

50. Gel'man, "Politics of Fear," 19.

51. Gleb Pavlovsky, "Russian Politics Under Putin: The System Will Outlast the Master," *Foreign Affairs* 95, no. 3 (May–June 2016): 14.

52. For more on the concept of *sistema* in Putin's Russia, including contrasts and parallels between the systems of governance in the Soviet era and modern Russia, see:

Alena V. Ledeneva, *Can Russia Modernise? Sistema, Power Networks and Informal Governance* (London: University College London, 2013).

53. Pavlovsky, "Russian Politics Under Putin: The System Will Outlast the Master," 15.

54. Ibid.; Alena C. Ledeneva, "Cronies, Economic Crime and Capitalism in Putin's Russia," *International Affairs* 88, no. 1 (January 2012): 149–57.

55. Pavlovsky, "Russian Politics Under Putin: The System Will Outlast the Master," 17.

Chapter VI

Trauma and Nationalism

As argued thus far, the controversial legacies of Joseph Stalin and the Soviet era under his leadership are very different in their Russian and Georgian variants. One is largely depersonalized and mythologized through the legacies of the historical achievements of the Soviet Union under Stalin's rule, whereas the other tends to be exclusively focused on the man behind Stalin—Georgian Koba, whose complex figure as a local folk hero continues to be colored by historical myths and "facts" that are often portrayed beyond recognition.

An important element of the Third Stalin as a mirror image of the self in the portrayal of Stalin's mythological figure is Vamık D. Volkan's proposed "chosen trauma" described as a reflection of an "infection" of a large group's mourning of a catastrophic loss or humiliation from the adversary.[1] According to Volkan, the reactivation of this "infection" serves as a unifying thread between the members of a given collective that historically share this chosen trauma. But what if the mourning process following a loss or humiliation at the hand of the enemy was never properly initiated—much like de-Stalinization, which, as this work argues, was never fully carried out in the successor state of the USSR, Russia? What if mourning as a process was not permitted, or at the very least frowned upon by post-occupied Georgia, and thus society transitioned from collapse and destruction straight into a post-traumatic disorder? One could argue that a lack of an appropriate mourning process following a chosen trauma does not link but rather divides and splits members of a unified group sharing the trauma with this disease and its numerous side effects.

Another vulnerability of a given society that acquires this infection, either as a DNA-like inheritance from predecessors or as an accidental victim of a widespread contagion, is that its reactivation is used and frequently even abused by political actors as a way of achieving their own goals and interests by promoting social movements, which, Volkan notes, are more often than not "deadly" and "malignant."² We saw one such example of many in post-Soviet Georgia when incoming nationalist leader Zviad Gamsakhurdia successfully initiated the reaction of chosen trauma targeting the Georgian nation from the hands of the enemy, Soviet Russia, in order to both fuel and exploit ultranationalist ideologies rooted in simultaneous entitlement and victimhood.

The tragic April 9, 1989 events in Tbilisi, Georgia—when Soviet military forces brutally broke up a demonstration in the Georgian capital organized by Gamsakhurdia's National Liberation Movement³—marked a turning point in the republic's history. This national tragedy has since evolved into the "chosen trauma" of Georgian national identity as a "shared mental representation of the historical traumatic event," turning it into "a significant marker for the large group identity."⁴ The "chosen trauma" syndrome was further amplified during the referendum on the restoration of Georgian independence two years later as the "latest manifestation" of the bloody terror and repressions of the Soviet Union.⁵

Gamsakhurdia's public statements from the late Soviet and early post-Soviet era demonstrate a domination of the nationalist rhetoric, although he preferred to characterize himself as a "patriot."⁶ He described Georgia's declaration of independence on April 9, 1991, as "restoration" of what had already been in place all along: "Georgia declared its independence in 1918 and it is still legitimate. Therefore, we do not need to announce our independence again."⁷ In his televised New Year's message on January 1, 1991, Zviad Gamsakhurdia addressed his Russian counterpart, Boris Yeltsin, and urged his leadership to openly admit that Georgia had been occupied by Russian forces in the form of a bilateral treaty. "After the fall of the Soviet Union, the only legitimate framework for relations between the Russian Federation and Georgia moving forward can be the treaty signed between Soviet Russia and the Democratic Republic of Georgia in Moscow on May 7, 1920," ⁸ Gamsakhurdia extended as an ultimatum to the Kremlin. However, official Moscow declined to sign the treaty, and thus, the Gamsakhurdia leadership publicly declared the Soviet Union and its successor state, Russia, an occupying force.

Aside from rebuilding Georgia's post-Soviet identity on the basis of rejecting the Russian occupying forces and in the emergence of entitlement and victimhood, Gamsakhurdia also capitalized on Georgia's Christianity as a vital component of the nation's identity. He went so far as to equate the Georgian Orthodox religion with the nation's historical ethnicity, further alienating many Georgian citizens by rejecting the possibility of reaching a national consolidation in the country's diverse ethno-religious population. In his statements, he not only linked Georgian ethnicity with Christianity but also issued an ultimatum for one's belonging and rightful membership within the nation of Georgia:

> Georgian nation, you have two paths in front of you. Your national-independence movement is at a crossroads. There is a path of Ilia Martali, path of holiness, morality, democracy, truth, and innocence, and there is a path of robbery, insidiousness, and terrorism! Georgian nation and Georgians choose the path of Christ and kindness, [we] choose the path of Ilia Martali because it will lead [us] to purgatory! And whoever picks the path of destruction, the path of Barabbas, will be cursed for eternity.[9]

When criticized for suggesting the impossibility of ethno-religious diversity in the population, Gamsakhurdia described disinformation and rumors spread by "Georgia's enemies" both within and outside of the country as a crude attempt to "create negative public opinion"[10] and thus derail Georgia's independence. Through the process of post-Soviet Georgian identity reformation, Gamsakhurdia brought to the fore the "chosen trauma" experienced by the Georgian society and their ancestors who fought for many decades against the occupying Soviet forces, and in doing so, he reignited the fear that the newly independent status and way of life were once again under threat. The ultranationalistic policies pushed by the Gamsakhurdia regime emphasized the patriotic sacrifices made by the ancestors, in turn highlighting that the survival against the occupier by using the weapon of ultranationalism and the power of a strong identity was part of the divine force. Within the context of the Georgian-Abkhaz conflict reignited under Gamsakhurdia's leadership, the Russian side, the main culprit, was presented as the occupying force with inherently imperialist ambitions while Georgia was positioned as the answer to Abkhazia's self-preservation against the classic Russian enemy. As for South Ossetia, Georgia's other breakaway region, the creation of the autonomous republic that began to actively demand separation from Georgia after the collapse of the Soviet Union, Gamsakhurdia insisted, was "the result of the Red Army's invasion,"[11] although the first President of the newly independent Georgian republic did not specify precisely how South Ossetia's separatism and the Red Army's invasion were linked.

Professor of Slavic in the Department of Modern Languages and Linguistics at Florida State University, Lisa Ryoko Wakamiya, who examines post-Soviet Russian appropriations of traumatic memory, delves into the political significance of trauma as a theory and notes that, paired with nostalgia, trauma is used as a political instrument by post-Soviet actors, be it state-operated and -funded media operatives or actual political figureheads at the helm of the vertical of power, to advance their particular political interests.[12]

Therefore, Volkan's chosen trauma model becomes institutionalized and contested which, in turn, allows state authorities to both forge and promote nationalistic agendas and policies.

In the early years of post-Soviet Russia, mythological past and cultural memory depicted in a series of television advertisements served as a tool for surviving the present trauma. In the midst of the chaotic transition from the remnants of communism of the late 1980s into the wilderness of the capitalism of the early 1990s, the nation's overall identity crisis was also reflected in the crisis toward attitudes pertaining to consumption, whereby capitalist consumption or *veshchizm*[13] replaced the socialist ideal of rational consumption and what was presented to the collective society as a socialist value system.

In 1992, a series of award-winning commercials for Russia's Imperial Bank directed by Timur Bekmambetov were launched less for commercial purposes and more so, according to the state bank's president, Sergei Rodionov, as a means of providing emotional "therapy" for the nation in the midst of an identity crisis. Instead of focusing on the great power narratives pertaining to the Great Patriotic War, a leitmotif that became a signature of Putin's 2000s, the Bank Imperial campaign featured highlights of the history of the Russian Empire placed at the heart of the broader canvas of world history, from Prince Dmitry Donskoi, Russia's fourteenth-century liberator from the Mongols, to Catherine the Great and General Suvorov.[14]

Scholar Elizaveta Mankovskaya observes that the advertisement dealt with the trauma of losing prerevolutionary Russia and, by focusing on the legacy of Imperial Russia rather than its successor, the Soviet Union, the nation was able to dive into the lost utopia, a safe haven that bore no traces of the trauma of civil war, Stalin's purges, and the economic devastation of the late Soviet and post-Soviet periods.[15] Mankovskaya notes that the slogan of the campaign itself "Vsemirnaia istoriia—Bank Imperial"[16] simultaneously shows nostalgia for the old, pre-1917 Russia and conveys hopefulness for the new post-Soviet Russia. Prerevolutionary heroes portrayed in this cultural project tell the 1990s' audience about the pre-Soviet world and, in doing so, the episodes provide viewers with a tool for dealing with the trauma through "narrative fetishism." The concept of narrative fetishism introduced by Eric Santner deals with "the construction and deployment of a narrative consciously or unconsciously designed to expunge the traces of the trauma or loss that called that narrative into being in the first place."[17] By reminding society about the difficulties overcome by the nation through a vivid depiction of heroic, victorious historical events, lessons learned are equated with the chaos of the 1990s following the geopolitical disaster of the collapse of the Soviet Empire, and serve as a reminder of the great resilience of the Russian people. Through creating a link between prerevolutionary and post-Soviet Russia, the viewers are reminded that in a time of cultural, economic, and political chaos, a sense of relative stability is sought not through money and *veshchizm* but rather through timeless values that "smooth the rupture between the epochs"[18] and transcend chaos of transition period.

The collective result is a psychological trauma shared, to varying degrees of intensity, by all of the nations under the unifying umbrella of the Soviet Socialist Republics. The trauma has been unique for each of these countries, as was their actual national and cultural identity underneath the forced collective identity presented on the global stage as a collective whole, equally shared by all. On a ladder of the hierarchy of Soviet suffering, Georgia's trauma pertaining to this period was inevitably different—no greater or lesser than that of neighboring Russia, Azerbaijan, or Armenia—but simply different. The hierarchy of suffering[19] of the tumultuous era, be it through the Great Purges or the losses during the Great Patriotic War, every nation under the broad Soviet umbrella experienced and each continues to experience its own suffering and thus its own, unique post-traumatic syndrome in a unique way, simultaneously wrestling with and embracing these legacies as irreplaceable and irreversible parts of its identity. The uniqueness of each victimized society's trauma does not necessarily fade with time and further dissipate from one successor generation to another. It is rather the memory that begins to acquire different shades, contrasts, and fabrics that, from one generation to another, inevitably includes new attributes, in the process shedding previous notions and connotations but by no means losing its core attribute. This attribute is the sense of self and the location of oneself within the narrative cycle, with the environment, setting, window-dressing, and the embroidery on the wallpaper changing with time and circumstance. But the sense of one's place in this history as a fluid construct is largely unphased by temporal, spatial, and political factors.

In Putin's Russia, the nation's greatness and stability are frequently, if not always, linked to the Great Patriotic War as an overarching idea that unites the nation, in turn legitimizing the current political regime rooted in authoritarian elements rather than democratic values. Through this narrative, Stalin becomes a unifying instrument, depicted as a quasi-mythological figure who led the Soviet people in unison toward a great victory against Nazism, and the leader who brought glory to the Soviet Union by tightening the grip on the nation as a whole. The Great Terror—an unprecedented, large-scale massacre organized by CPSU leadership with Comrade Stalin at its helm in 1937–1938—is presented today as an unfortunate, albeit unavoidable, side effect, for national authority that mobilizes and unifies the peoples cannot be expressed without violence in the name of glory. Millions of peasants, priests, nobles and aristocracy, individuals who were suspected of ties with counter-revolutionaries, and countless members of opposition political parties, among others, were arrested and deployed to prison camps, many were repressed and more still disappeared with no further notice. Therefore, based on this narrative, the appropriate use of measured force and the inevitable losses in a struggle toward this ultimate glory were precisely that—inevitable.[20]

Today, the official Russian narrative posits, time and again, that the historical greatness of the USSR was anchored in and constantly motivated by the devotion to the Fatherland and relentless service to the nation in the name of patriotism, declared by Vladimir Putin as the only "national idea"[21] that drives modern-day Russia under his leadership. And to this end, the private concerns and desires are sacrificed in this model toward something grander than life—the great national project. During Putin's third presidential term (2012–2018), politics of memory and the historical propaganda of the Great Patriotic War "coincided" with the economic slowdown and the financial crisis, Ukraine's Euromaidan Revolution in 2013 followed by the outbreak of war in Eastern Ukraine and Russia's annexation of Crimea, and last, but certainly not least, the declining living standards and increased public protests across Russia.[22] The "sacred, messianic" portrayal of the Great Patriotic War as a neo-imperial historical narrative of Russia's greatness as the savior of the world from the absolute evil of Nazism was brought to the fore during Putin's fourth (and current) presidential term. The Kremlin's official reinterpretation of the protocols pertaining to the historic Molotov-Ribbentrop Non-Aggression Pact were presented under Putin as positive. Although during the late Soviet years, authorities entirely denied the existence of protocols that aimed to divide Central and Eastern Europe into zones of influence for Nazi Germany and the Soviet Union, by 2015, during a joint conference with German chancellor Angela Merkel, Vladimir Putin firmly assessed the pact as "vitally important for the USSR's national security."[23] Four years later, in June 2019, the original Soviet copy of the non-aggression pact was displayed at an exhibition at the State Archive of the Russian Federation, and presented as a symbol of Soviet diplomacy and a source of great pride for the Russian people, with Stalin at the helm of the victorious decision-making throne.[24]

For Georgians, however, the dominant version of the Stalin narrative revolves around the legend of the "great man"—a Georgian man, first and foremost. What complicates his controversial legacy even more is the fact that Georgians are still wrestling with their own post-Soviet identity. The remnants of their Soviet history remain both categorically rejected and permanently present in Georgia's modern political culture. Georgia is simultaneously dealing with the Stalin legacy as both the victim of his regime as well as its complacent and active participant.

We witness a similar pattern in the complex legacy of Georgia's other leader, Eduard Shevardnadze, who is both admired and severely criticized in Georgia today.[25] Prior to becoming the second President of the post-Soviet Republic of Georgia, Shevardnadze served as the Minister of Foreign Affairs of the USSR under Mikhail Gorbachev. Upon assuming presidency following Zviad Gamsakhurdia's turbulent leadership, he was revered as the great messiah who would rescue Georgia from his ultranationalist predecessor's tumultuous and despotic rule. Today, few recall that several years after assuming presidency, in commemoration of the fiftieth anniversary of the free world's victory against Nazi Germany, Eduard Shevardnadze visited the Stalin Museum in Gori and announced the opening of a research institute "dedicated to the phenomenon of Stalin"—an "ambitious promise,"[26] according to historian Lasha Bakradze, that never came to pass.

Shevardnadze continues to be less than popular among the majority of Georgians today. He is often held responsible for the unresolved frozen conflicts in the country's breakaway regions of Abkhazia and South Ossetia, and is harshly criticized for the economic hardships and corruption that served as constant leitmotifs in Georgia of the 1990s under his presidency. Not dissimilar to Stalin who is both revered and hated as both a messiah and a source of all evil, the dual appraisal of the Shevardnadze years still divides Georgian society to this day. While his eleven-year rule is characterized by corruption, economic decline, and criminalization among the majority of population, those in the minority view him as a pro-Western leader who helped shape Georgia's pro-Western course in the aftermath of the Soviet occupation and Gamsakhurdia's ultranationalist policies.

Both in Russian and Georgian variants of the Stalin question, the theme of "patriotism" appears as a common thread, albeit painted with strokes of contrasting, if not divergent, undertones—in one case, embracing the Soviet legacies and the greatness of the former empire and, in the other, categorically and unequivocally rejecting it.

In Russia's chaotic nineties' chapter, the reassessment of the turbulent events of Soviet history and its failed ideologies was a brief process. In this process, the dismantling of communist legacies and a reintroduction of de-Stalinization more specifically were halted by the socioeconomic hardships of the decade. In 1992, the Yeltsin administration made a brief attempt to condemn the Communist Party for atrocities committed in the Soviet epoch through a trial that ultimately failed to produce a verdict on the brutal crimes of the regime. In lieu of looking back and reconciling the past with the present, the leadership during Boris Yeltsin's first term decided that the only path for Russia in the current environment was forward. Hence, the country saw an emergence of debates pertaining to a new "Russian Question"—a lingering crisis of post-Soviet Russian national and cultural identity that followed glasnost' and perestroika, which culminated with the collapse of the Soviet Union in 1991.

Perhaps the starkest differences between Yeltsin's and Putin's tools for healing the nation after the radical rupture of 1991 in one case and Russia's global humiliation of the 1990s more generally in the other are rooted, above all else, in Yeltsin's gaze toward the future and denial of the past and Putin's utmost reliance on Russia's prowess and magnitude as historical tropes and the unavoidable return to the country's greatness as its only way forward into the future.

Prior to analyzing the revision and renaissance of history under Putin, it is worth mentioning that Yeltsin's radicalism of breaking away from the chains of the Soviet past was meant to produce a complete loss of the collective past through rejection instead of acceptance—an impossible task, as it turned out. In hindsight, the emergence of the project aimed at recreating the new Russia's national idea was not necessarily an ideological catalyst for the political regime but instead a quick fix—a Band-Aid—that was supposed to mend the wounds produced by the rupture of the Soviet Union, at least for the time being, until a more permanent treatment was discovered or created by the new *nomenklatura*. Yeltsin's attempt to create a committee that would build—not rebuild but rather construct from scratch—upon a land that suffered from structural failures and collapses, a fallen empire that started to disintegrate with cavities that eventually breached the ground surface, creating sudden and dramatic sinkholes and, soon enough, a complete and irreversible collapse—a new foundation by manufacturing a national idea in a matter of twelve months was quickly dismissed as unrealistic.

Soon thereafter, in 1996, Yeltsin appealed to the nation through the pages of *Rossiyskaya Gazeta* newspaper, announcing a competition for the new Russian "national idea," an all-uniting narrative based on the common values aimed at bringing the nation together in the midst of instability and chaos. "Boris Yeltsin thinks Russia needs a new national vision, so he is asking his compatriots to come up with one," the Associated Press reported in August of 1996. "Something, perhaps, to rival the American Dream. Something so inspiring it would erase all memories of 'Glory to the Communist Party of the Soviet Union.'"[27]

However, forging a national idea through nation-building upon the newly reformed sacral idea of "the Russian way" was tarnished before any real attempts were made to this end. As author and historian Kathleen E. Smith argues in her work, *Mythmaking in the New Russia*, "images of the past are not infinitely malleable, [and] the Russian experience shows that politicians can neither escape the past nor mold it completely to their will."[28]

Yet, while Smith's words may be true for Yeltsin's Russia, what we have witnessed over the past two decades—and counting—of Vladimir Putin's rule has shown that the same may not apply to the current tsar of the Kremlin Palace. Russia's underlying quest for an all-unifying national idea constructed upon the ruins of a failed Soviet Empire persisted and led Yeltsin's eventual successor, Vladimir Putin to embrace the historical greatness of the nation and identify "patriotism" as the moral and cultural basis for the "consolidation of society and the strengthening of the state."[29]

At the annual plenary meeting of the Valdai International Discussion Club in 2013, Putin reminded his international audience of how, following the collapse of the Soviet Union, there was an illusion that a new national ideology would "simply appear by itself."[30] However, Putin also reminded his audience, the Russian state apparatus under Boris Yeltsin—including government authorities, intellectual, and political classes—"virtually rejected engaging in this work, all the more so since previous, semiofficial ideology was hard to swallow."[31] Vladimir Vladimirovich added that inevitably, among other downsides, the lack of a collective national idea "profited the quasi-colonial element of the elite—those determined to steal and remove capital, and who did not link their future to that of the country."[32]

For the Putin regime, patriotism is firmly built upon three main pillars: religious faith and the Russian Orthodox Church; history and in particular the achievements during the Great Patriotic War; and national identity, which is ultimately a combination of the previous two elements with additional components sprinkled throughout, eventually producing a fleeting concept in Russia's context throughout the twentieth century that had to be reclaimed in order to allow modern Russia to flourish to its fullest potential.

By the same token, Vladimir Putin emphasized that a national idea cannot and should not be "imposed"[33] or fabricated from the top. Some, particularly those in direct opposition to the President's political order, would go so far as to argue that it is not patriotism but rather nationalism that has become the unifying idea under his Russia. Therefore, it is important to separate these two concepts that are often, albeit erroneously, used as synonyms.

According to the German political scientist, Volker Kronenberg, while nationalism and patriotism both require identification with the nation, these concepts ultimately diverge as they support different pillars of three important components: nation, state, and regime. Moreover, the two concepts define different social objectives and produce different, at times irreconcilable, models of behavior. While, according to Kronenberg, both nationalism and patriotism are, in the end, "forms of positive assessment of one's own group," nationalism is largely rooted in "internal homogeneity, blind allegiance, and an idealized appraisal of one's own nation (being superior)," whereas patriotism is more concerned with "internal social heterogeneity and critical distance from the state and the regime."[34] To this end, it is not at all surprising that in the Soviet as well as Russian contexts, the term "nationalism" is predominantly tainted by negative connotations far more so than "patriotism"—hence the constant emphasis on the latter concept in lieu of the former as an inherent ingredient of the Russian identity.

Meanwhile, in the tangled web of Georgian post-Soviet national identity, the Stalin question sheds light on patriotism from a different angle—one that highlights Georgia's unique place in the region's history and geopolitics. The lingering cult of Joseph Stalin in his native country is intertwined, first and foremost, with national pride. The paradox of Georgian post-Soviet identity lies in the rejection of Soviet vestiges and simultaneous embrace of Stalin as a Georgian, not a Soviet man. While in Russia, he is viewed as a byproduct of the communist system, in Georgia, he is seen as an offspring of a ground he trod as a child but ultimately, like Judas, sold to the socialist project.

Even in those contexts where Joseph Stalin is no longer portrayed as a national symbol in Georgia but instead presented as an enemy of his own people, paradoxically, the great tyrant remains fanatically revered as an embodiment of local patriotism in his hometown. This dualism of emotions pertaining to his legacy occasionally comes in direct conflict with patriotism and national identity—"Georgianness" in lieu or perhaps in spite of "Sovietness" in assessing Georgia's seventy-year occupation under the firm Soviet rule. But instead of allowing Georgia to come to terms with its tumultuous past and embrace—or, perhaps to begin with, learn to accept—its post-Soviet national identity, the complicated topic of Stalin persists as a foundation of the uncomfortable and unresolved conflict of post-Soviet national identity.

The abruptness of a breakup of ideologies, beliefs, and a total collapse not only of a system but also of a psyche is simultaneously liberating and deeply, albeit darkly, motivating; yet this radical rupture and destruction of the past is inevitably traumatic for the traumatized. While perusing through the mysterious rubble and painful ruins of an unresolved past, we are now breathing the dust of dreams of socialism and once promised utopia that we ourselves never chose but rather, it was imposed upon us as a prison mentality through coercion and force. Amid this haze, we find the one barely tangible omnipresent ghost that we mold to our own likeness—be it through greatness or evil, respect or fear—and use this historical and cultural trope to justify, reject, condone, and condemn, and, most importantly, attempt to explain the fading past . . . a past that is predominantly colored by nostalgia.

NOTES

1. Vamık D. Volkan, "Large Group Identity and Chosen Trauma" *Psyche* 54, no. 9 (2000): 931–53.
2. Ibid.
3. See chapter 2 for more on the April 9, 1989, events in Tbilisi, Georgia.
4. Volkan, "Chosen Trauma: The Political Ideology of Entitlement and Violence."
5. Helen Partsvaniya, "Georgia: 20 Years of Independence," *Institute of World Policy*, February 28, 2001. Web. http://georgia.iwp.org.ua/eng/public/133.html.
6. "Zviad Gamsakhurdia's Interview," *Sakartvelos Respublika* 36:56, February 22, 1991, 1.
7. "Sakartvelos umaghlesi sabchos tavmjdomaris Zviad Gamsakhurdias saakhaltslo mimartva televiziit" ("The Head of Supreme Council of the Republic of Georgia Zviad Gamsakhurdia's New Year Address on TV"), *Sakartvelos Respublika* 1, no.12 (January 1, 1991.)
8. Ibid.
9. "Zviad Gamsakhurdia's Speech of May 26, 1990," (full text), July 2, 2010.
10. "Zviad Gamsakhurdia's Interview," *Sakartvelos Respublika* 39:59, February 27, 1991, 1–2.
11. Mikheil Saluashvili, ed. *Otkhmotsdatertmeti: sakartvelos prezidenti Zviad Gamsakhurdia (Ninety-One: President of Georgia, Zviad Gamsakhurdia)* (Tbilisi, Georgia: Khma Erisa, 1995), 121–22.
12. Lisa Ryoko Wakamiya, "Post-Soviet Contexts and Trauma Studies," *Slavonica* 17, no. 2 (November 2011): 134–44.
13. In Russian: *thing-ism* or a "predilection for material values to the detriment of spiritual values." See: Sergei I. Ozhegov and Nataliia Iu. Shvedova, eds., *Tolkovyi slovar' russkogo iazyka: 72,500 slov i 7,500 frazeologicheskikh vyrazhenii*, (Moscow, Russia: Az, 1995).
14. Out of the fourteen available episodes, eight are focused on portraying historical narratives that take place outside of the Russian Empire, while six are dedicated specifically to Russian history.
15. Elizaveta Mankovskaya, "Mythologizing the Past to Survive the Present: Trauma and Cultural Memory in Timur Bekmambetov's Imperial Bank Commercials (1992–1997)," *Ulbandus Review* 17, no. 1 (2016): 86–107.
16. In Russian: "World history—Imperial Bank."
17. Eric Santner, "History Beyond the Pleasure Principle," in Saul Friedlander, ed., *Probing the Limits of Representation: Nazism and the "Final Solution"* (Cambridge, MA: Harvard University Press, 1992), 149.
18. Mankovskaya, "Mythologizing the Past to Survive the Present," 107.
19. This is a largely medical term that has been appropriated in other disciplines and is the subject of continued debate. On the use of the term of "hierarchy of suffering" in the context of Holocaust survivors and its manifestation and impact on surviving individuals, see: Hester Maria Shantall, "A Heuristic Study of the Meaning of Suffering Among Holocaust Survivors," University of South Africa (June 1996.)

20. Although 1937 saw a sudden surge in purges which continued through 1938, meticulous planning of these terror campaigns had reportedly begun by the early 1930s.

21. "Putin Declares Patriotism Russia's Only National Idea," *Moscow Times*, February 4, 2016. Web. https://www.themoscowtimes.com/2016/02/04/putin-declares-patriotism-russias-only-national-idea-a51705.

22. For an exploration of the Great Patriotic War and the sacralization of Soviet victory over Nazism as the Kremlin's soft-power tool, see: Maria Domańska, "The Myth of the Great Patriotic War as a Tool of the Kremlin's Great Power Policy," *Center for Eastern Studies* 316, no. 1 (December 2019): 1–10.

23. "Putin soglasilsya s Medinskim po paktu Molotova-Ribbentropa," Interfax, May 10, 2015. Web. https://www.interfax.ru/russia/440996.

24. The historical propaganda campaign on the memory politics of the Great Patriotic War was relaunched in time for the seventy-fifth anniversary of the end of the Second World War, although the celebration agenda was largely disrupted by the outbreak of the COVID-19 pandemic and the first mass lockdown imposed in Moscow and other parts of the country in late March 2020.

25. For more on the rise and fall of Shevardnadze's popularity in Georgia after the collapse of the Soviet regime and his ascent to power in post-Soviet, independent Georgia, see: Nina Dadalauri and Lars Johannsen, "Shevardnadze's Political Strategies: The Rise and Fall of the Incumbent," in Karin Hilmer Pedersen and Lars Johannsen, eds., *Pathways: A Study of Six Post-Communist Countries* (Aarhus, Denmark: Aarhus University Press, 2009): 52–68.

26. Bakradze, "Past and Future of the Stalin Museum in Gori," 10.

27. Julia Rubin, "Meditations on Russia: Yeltsin Calls for a New National Idea," Associated Press, August 2, 1996. Web. http://www.apnewsarchive.com/1996/Meditations-on-Russia-Yeltsin-Calls-for-New-National-Idea-/id-122cd732a8cf8b35989afeec4db69dcd.

28. Kathleen E. Smith, *Mythmaking in the New Russia: Politics and Memory in the Yeltsin Era* (Ithaca, NY: Cornell University Press, 2002): 184.

29. Gosudarstvennaya programma "Patrioticheskoye vospitanie grazhdan RF na 2006–2010 gody," 2010, Russian Federation. Web. http://www.ed.gov.ru/junior/new_version/gragd_patr_vospit_molod/gosprog/.

30. Vladimir Putin, "It is impossible to move forward without spiritual, cultural and national self-determination," Russia Today, September 20, 2013. Web. https://www.rt.com/russia/official-word/putin-valdai-national-idea-142/.

31. Ibid.

32. Ibid.

33. Ibid.

34. Volker Kronenberg, *Patriotismus in Deutschland: Perspektiven für eine weltoffene Nation* (Wiesbaden: VS Verlag für Sozialwissenschaften, 2006), 45–46.

Chapter VII

Nostalgia

Even the most somber, burdening memories of the darkest hours of historical significance have failed to deprive the locals in Gori of a deeply rooted sense of pride. These timeless relics continue to serve as a reminder that Koba, or Soso, as his mother affectionately called the future autocrat, was one of the flock. Carefully justifying the historical misfortunes of the era, the widely accepted consensus throughout Stalin's Museum—and his hometown more generally—is that Soso was ultimately the man who made his small country famous around the world.

This, in turn, brings to light a sentiment reminiscent of nostalgia for Georgia's significance experienced vicariously through its prodigal, if infamous, son. Both the triumphant successes and atrocities of Stalinism, the irreversibly catastrophic failures of de-Stalinization, countless effects and ramifications of historical and collective memory, the complex relationship between the political state and its society are just a few of the visible aspects of the Soviet past that have infiltrated the modern-day political and societal realities of Georgia and other former Soviet countries. Whether the governing body of this independent country is a pro-Western ruler or a more Russian-friendly state, the lasting memory and an indelible legacy of the nation's seventy-year history continues to play a major role in the active formation of its political culture and the revision of national identity as a byproduct of a not-so-distant Soviet past.

These sentiments reminiscent of a postmodern nostalgia can also be traced in the current Russian narrative, if only with different undertones. According to Levada Center sociologist Karina Pipiya, Russia is experiencing a growing nostalgia for the Soviet period and Stalin as the nation's leader[1] "who defeated fascism and thus gets the honors for [the Soviet Union's] victory in the Great Patriotic War."[2] This victory, Pipiya emphasizes, is both a source and a symbol of national pride for all Russians, "even for those born in the post-Soviet period."[3] The Levada Center poll on public attitudes and nostalgia for the Soviet Union referenced by Pipiya was conducted in March 2019 and surveyed over 1,600 Russians aged 18 and above in 137 towns and cities across the Russian Federation. The findings demonstrated that over the past decade, positive evaluation of the Soviet past has increased by nearly 25%.[4] Furthermore, 65% of the respondents admitted they "regret"[5] the collapse of the Soviet Union and believe that the Union's demise was not unavoidable. In the midst of the growing nostalgia, however, only 28% of those polled stated that they would like to go back to the USSR and return to the path that the country was pursuing prior to the union's collapse. According to Pipiya, the public longing for the Soviet past is, above all, associated with the great power status and nostalgia for the sense of belonging to the grandeur of the empire rather than any ideological underpinning of the communist regime and socialist ideology as such.

Nostalgia as both a subconscious and deliberate denial of the present[6] began to surface and spread like a virus across the post-Soviet space in the mid-1990s, producing a binary of external (political and economic) and internal (moral[7]) uncertainties, which inevitably alienated the post-Soviet sphere from its post-socialist reality.[8] "The twentieth century began with utopia and ended with nostalgia,"[9] the late American scholar of Russian descent, Svetlana Boym wrote in 2007. Indeed, throughout the turbulent first decade after the collapse of the Soviet Union, the optimistic belief in the future and a sense of euphoria began to fade into the outdated past, swiftly replaced by nostalgia as both a phenomenon and a conceptual category for unifying, albeit disparate, remnants of the post-revolutionary void.[10]

The very definition of the word "nos-talgia" translated from Greek—nostos meaning "return" and algos "pain"—viewed in the post-Soviet context is a metaphorical "longing for a home that no longer exists"[11] or, worse yet, one that never even existed. This displaces the mythologized "living past"[12] into a new, unknown space by occupying an already familiar form that is, nonetheless, devoid of its original meaning and "retrofitting" it to suit the present environment, in turn creating an illusion of continuity with the Soviet past in the new post-Soviet reality. So vivid and persistent is the sentiment of longing for this imaginary but nonetheless very present and frequently entirely ahistorical "living past" that nostalgia evolves into what prominent Russian cultural critic, Natalia Ivanova coins "носталящее,"[13] translated into English as "nowstalgia."[14] Simultaneously a sentiment of loss and displacement, "nowstalgia" is further idealized and even romanticized within one's own, personal fantasy and the broader fantasy once offered by utopia.[15]

Exploring nostalgia as a tool denying the present in the name of the past produces a void between the sanitized nostalgic reproductions and the actual traumatic history.[16] Historically, nostalgia has numerously resurfaced in the societal psyche and public narratives after periods of revolution or political upheaval when individuals are forced to deal with the chaos and pain stemming from instability and an overwhelming diversity of cultural experiences.[17] This observation, alongside the disappointment following the failure of the fantasy and loss of societal innocence, further fuels the melancholic longing for the past seen in hindsight through rose-colored glasses.[18] Nostalgia thus becomes a subconscious mechanism of retrospective longing aimed at keeping together aspects of a past life dislocated and disbanded by external changes. Furthermore, it facilitates the very act of coming to terms with the upheaval that, in turn, allows reconciling of the restructured, if not entirely reimagined, past with the inevitability of the failed, tumultuous present.[19]

Svetlana Boym writes that "the spread of nostalgia had to do not only with dislocation in space but also with the changing conception of time."[20] Moreover, she notes that modern nostalgia in the post-Soviet space is not merely lamenting but to a degree also "mourning for the impossibility of mythical return, for the loss of an 'enchanted world' with clear borders and values."[21] This viewpoint could apply to the rebirth of nostalgia for the Soviet past, and the longing for the communal past of communally shared living as one of the primary elements. "It could be a secular expression of a spiritual longing, a nostalgia for an absolute, for a home that is both physical and spiritual, for the Edenic unity of time and space before entry into history."[22]

Through the seventeenth and eighteenth centuries, nostalgia was regarded and treated as a medical disease that was, curiously, "strictly confined to the Swiss." It was not until the early twentieth century that nostalgia began to be regarded as a psychiatric disorder with symptoms that included anxiety, sadness, and insomnia. "By the mid-twentieth century, psychodynamic approaches considered nostalgia a subconscious desire to return to an earlier life stage, and it was labeled as a repressive compulsive disorder. Soon thereafter, nostalgia was downgraded to a variant of depression, marked by loss and grief, though still equated with homesickness."[23]

However, in the modern interpretation of the phenomenon, according to Zala Volčič, "Nostalgia offers an idealized version of an unattainable past that can stunt the cultural imagination by discounting and excluding real viable options for social change."[24] Volčič's understanding of nostalgia can be directly linked with that of Fredric Jameson, who remarks on the precise period of the demise of the Soviet Union and the role of nostalgia in the moment of the regime's collapse within the society as an "embarrassing . . . cultural fantasy" and a "costume-party self-deception."[25]

Viewed through the lens of longing as pain and suffering for the lost homeland, the pain and suffering can, in turn, be linked to a matching bittersweet feeling of romanticized melancholia of simply "being away."[26] It has been historically traced that nostalgia appears most notably after periods of revolution or political upheaval when "individuals have to deal with the pain of instability" and an overwhelming "diversity of cultural experiences."[27] Hence, the appearance and an immediate rise of nostalgic sentiments among the Russian and broader post-Soviet society of the mid-1990s was a phenomenon that could have been anticipated due to the sudden shift of the regime and a sense of comfort in the not-so-distant past found in stability and the shared community that lacked privacy but instead eradicated all traces of loneliness that came with the novelty of the dawn of post-revolutionary Russia of the 1990s. With the demise of the familiar came the collective identity crisis and cultural trauma as one of its side effects, despite some visibly positive changes and not merely negative chaos and upheaval, which were also undeniably part of the immediate aftermath of the post-Soviet experiment.[28]

How does the conceptual theory of nostalgia explain Stalin's lingering and even increased popularity,[29] specifically among the older generation of pensioners, who were too young to be politically active at the time of the Great Dictator's reign? According to a sociological poll conducted four years after the August War of 2008, a total of 45% of respondents across Georgia held a favorable view of the prodigal autocrat, with 68% of them describing Stalin as a "wise leader." Meanwhile, a staggering 72% of pensioners harbored "positive" feelings toward the Georgian-born Soviet leader.[30] This phenomenon is ascribed by Russian sociologist Lev Gudkov and the director of the Georgian Museum of Literature, Lasha Bakradze, to a symptomatic "doublethink," whereby the same historical figure is viewed by the same group of respondents as simultaneously a "cruel tyrant" and a "wise leader" who brought the Soviet Union might and prosperity.[31]

In discussing what he admits were surprisingly positive sentiments vis-à-vis Stalin in modern Georgia, Lasha Bakradze does not believe that this demonstrates the South Caucasus country's nostalgia for totalitarianism and a firm "dictatorial" hand per se. "Nostalgia for the late Soviet past may be tied to the country's numerous freedoms and liberties in comparison with other countries under the Soviet umbrella, including Russia,"[32] the historian says. To this end, the phenomenon of nostalgia that dominates the Stalin question on the Georgian side signals a sense of longing for relative stability and prosperity of Soviet Georgia under the early-mid period of Leonid Brezhnev's rule.

However, there is also an alternative explanation to the soaring popularity of Stalin following the August War of 2008, which Bakradze predicts was either consciously or subconsciously fueled by the Georgian public's reaction to Mikheil Saakashvili's anti-Stalin policy paired with the anti-Russian propaganda campaign following the Georgian-Russian War of 2008. "In exploring the surprisingly high number of positive sentiments vis-à-vis Stalin, I also do not rule out the possibility that criticism and even outrage following Saakashvili's campaign, including the public toppling of the Stalin monument in Gori and other Soviet vestiges throughout Georgia in the aftermath of the August War, was a reflection of the Georgian majority's rejection of this policy,"[33] Bakradze observes. In pairing the two possible hypotheses, we can further argue that nostalgia in this context is not necessarily about fondly recalling the olden days but, rather, it is mainly born out of the crisis of the new, and the inability or entire rejection of absorbing and fully coping with the present.

The Third Stalin is equally made up of legacies of the era—cult of personality, trauma, nationalism, and nostalgia—the broken, often disjointed fragments of the past that construct identities in the present that will continue to build and grow upon the ashes of a ruptured past, constantly and inevitably returning to their roots like circles wrapped in a mysterious spiral, possessing no concept of an ending or a beginning, spinning endlessly, trapped inside the perpetual wheel of time.

NOTES

1. According to a Levada Center poll referenced here conducted in March 2019, over 51% of the respondents admitted that they "respect, like, or admire" Joseph Stalin. See more: "Dynamics of Attitudes towards Stalin," Levada Center.

2. "Joseph Stalin: Why So Many Russians Like the Soviet Dictator," BBC, April 18, 2019. Web. https://www.bbc.com/news/world-europe-47975704.

3. Ibid.

4. Elena Mukhametshina, "Tri chetverti rossiyan schitayut sovetskuyu epokhu luchshey v istorii strany," *Vedomosti*, March 24, 2020. Web. https://www.vedomosti.ru/society/articles/2020/03/23/825985-tri-chetverti.

5. Ibid.

6. Serguei Oushakine, "'We're Nostalgic But We're Not Crazy': Retrofitting the Past in Russia," *Russian Review* 66, no. 3 (July 2007): 452.

7. Maya Nadkarni and Olga Shevchenko, "The Politics of Nostalgia," *Ab Imperio* 2 (2004): 487–519.

8. Ibid., 508.

9. Svetlana Boym, "Nostalgia and Its Discontents," *Hedgehog Review* 9, no. 2 (Summer 2007): 1.

10. Nadkarni and Shevchenko, "The Politics of Nostalgia," 488.

11. Boym, "Nostalgia and Its Discontents."

12. Oushakine, "'We're Nostalgic But We're Not Crazy,'" 455.

13. A combination of "ностальгия" (in English: "nostalgia") and "настоящее" (in English: "present/real".)

14. Natalia Ivanova, "No(w)stalgia: Retro on the (Post)-Soviet Television Screen," *Harriman Review* 12, nos. 2–3 (1999): 25–32.

15. Ibid.

16. Oushakine, "'We're Nostalgic But We're Not Crazy,'" 452.

17. Timothy Barney, "When We Was Red: *Good Bye Lenin!* and Nostalgia for the 'Everyday GDR,'" *Communication and Critical/Cultural Studies* 6, no. 2 (2009): 132–51.

18. Nadkarni and Shevchenko, "The Politics of Nostalgia," 495–96.

19. Oushakine, "'We're Nostalgic But We're Not Crazy,'" 482, 473.

20. Svetlana Boym, *The Future of Nostalgia* (New York: Basic, 2002), 7.

21. Ibid., 8.

22. Boym, "Nostalgia and Its Discontents," 12.

23. Constantine Sedikides, Tim Wildschut, Jamie Arndt, and Clay Routledge, "Nostalgia: Past, Present, and Future," *Current Directions in Psychological Science* 17, no. 5 (2008): 304–307. For a review of historical conceptions of nostalgia and speculations about nostalgia's functions, see: Constantine Sedikides, Tim Wildschut, and Denise Baden, "Nostalgia: Conceptual Issues and Existential Functions" in Jeff Greenberg, Sander L. Koole, and Tom Pyszczynski, eds., *Handbook of Experimental Existential Psychology* (New York: Guilford, 2004): 200–214.

24. Zala Volčič, "Yugo-Nostalgia: Cultural Memory and Media in the Former Yugoslavia," *Critical Studies in Media Communication* 24, no. 1 (March 2007): 25.

25. Fredric Jameson, "Nostalgia for the Present," *South Atlantic Quarterly* 88, no. 2 (1989): 536; Jameson, *Postmodernism, or, the Cultural Logic of Late Capitalism* (Durham, NC: Duke University Press, 1991), 170.

26. Fred Davis, "Nostalgia, Identity, and the Current Nostalgia Wave," *Journal of Popular Culture* 11, no. 2 (Fall 1977): 418.

27. Barney, "When We Was Red: *Good Bye Lenin!* and Nostalgia for the 'Everyday GDR.'"

28. For more on trauma as a direct result of deep social changes, with specific focus on the collapse of communism in Eastern Europe, see: Pyotr Shtompka, "Sotsialnoye izmeneniye kak travma," *Sotsiologicheskiye issledovaniya* 1, no. 1 (2001): 6–16.

29. The author observes that this statement may be especially true for Georgia and Russia—two of the case studies presented in this work. The phenomenon does not, by default, hold for all of the other post-Soviet countries. The results of a survey conducted by Carnegie Endowment in November of 2012 showed that in Azerbaijan, a South Caucasian country bordering Stalin's birthplace, Georgia, 22% of the overall surveyed population and 39% of young respondents in particular do not know who Stalin is. In neighboring Armenia, 38% of respondents affirmed that Stalin was, indeed, a "wise leader." See more: Thomas de Waal, ed., "The Stalin Puzzle: Deciphering Post-Soviet Public Opinion" (Washington, DC: Carnegie Endowment for International Peace, 2013), 2–3.

30. Ibid., 1.

31. Ibid., 2.

32. Bakradze, interview with author.

33. Ibid.

Conclusion
Back to Gori

As I am scribbling these words by hand in a small Harriman Institute notebook, I am once again driving back from Gori to Tbilisi. Four years following the first trip to Gori depicted in the opening pages of the book, this feels like a déjà vu—same script, but a different taxi ... The driver's name is, ironically, Soso. He laments that he has not visited the Stalin Museum and adds that if Georgia is to survive this turbulent period in its current history, "the country will need another Stalin."

This day trip to Ioseb Jughashvili's hometown is different from my prior journeys to Gori. Normally, I would frequent the museum twice a year and, each time, most family friends and relatives would smirk whenever, upon visiting Tbilisi from my main base in New York, I would share my plans for a "traditional visit to Gori." "Are you going to visit Koba again?", they would ask me, teasingly.

Unlike my previous visits, this time around, as I walked into the building hand in hand with my mother, whose aunt, Nina Chichua-Bedia, was repressed during Stalin's Red Terror, I felt a perplexing sense of serenity. There I was, standing in the imposing entrance to the museum celebrating the life of one of the most revered and most feared tyrants of the twentieth century. A man whose rule, to this day, fills us with a variety of complicated, deeply personal, and complex sensations. A legacy that we have not and sadly, for the foreseeable generations, will likely fail to come to terms with. And yet, if the past and current attempts to erase our Soviet history persist in Georgia, while, in the meantime, Russian state authorities insist on glorifying the Stalin years, with particular emphasis on the Great Patriotic War, glossing over the tragic impact of the Great Purges, the generations to come will have few facts to rely on. Instead, these forthcoming generations will be left to their own devices to reach conclusions based on limited reliable information.

Conclusion

As stated in the opening chapter, the aim of this book is not to justify or judge Stalin's regime—for historians and biographers have already made numerous attempts, some with greater success than others. Every year, previously unavailable and newly declassified documents emerge from historical archives, and volumes of remarkable work on Stalin and his era grace the shelves of bookstores and academic journals, many of which were indispensable and truly invaluable in completing this work. The world may not need another book on Stalin; however, what we, the post-Soviet generation, remain in dire need of is the opportunity to fully embrace our past and the history of our ancestors, with all of its tragedies and glorious victories. We are in dire need of reconciling our past with our present with an ambitious hope of achieving a clearer future that always, inevitably, comes back in a full circle.

In the final analysis, through some inexplicable but prominent thread, Stalin—and in particular, the Third Stalin, the simultaneous hero and villain of this monograph—is ultimately a reflection of us—the generation that found itself in the midst of a void, forced to reinvent and rebuild itself upon the rubble of an abruptly interrupted past. This past remains vivid in the living memory and through the surviving, albeit slowly fading, remnants of vestiges and memorabilia, narratives and contradicting recollections of our predecessors and political talking-heads. We are the generation that was born and raised upon the ashes of his legacies, constantly wrestling with the numerous scars of that era and the greatness of our history, unable to reconcile the good and the evil, and in order to avoid the constant cognitive dissonance in our appraisal of history through the prism of Stalin, we frequently either demonize or glorify the Great Dictator. At times, and increasingly more so, we also entirely shut him out of our individual and collective memory, choosing to ignore that which is constantly staring at us through the reflection of our own selves in the mirror of our national, political, and personal history. The mysterious, often invisible link between the world that made Stalin and the world made *by* Stalin continues to haunt us well into the new millennium.

The burden of walking into the childhood home of the Red Tsar whose policies and politics changed the course of the twentieth and, to many degrees, also our current twenty-first century, all the while impacting the personal lives and serving as the root and the cause of countless tragedies for so many, including my very own family, is an unbearable burden to carry. Yet, paradoxically, being in the presence of his personal belongings—some authentic and others embellished and recreated as relics that serve a mythological purpose—is oddly therapeutic and offers the ancestral victims of his regime the ability to grieve and allows us to face our family's history undisguised, without shying away from the painful details, constantly hiding the scars instead of healing them through knowledge and awareness.

The paradox of the Third Stalin lies in the fact that both in justifying and criticizing Stalin, we are also justifying our own role in our country's history. Admiring or detesting an individual is always more feasible to fathom and process as a sentiment, rather than accepting the contradictions that one figure is capable of producing inside of us. To this end, the constant curiosity, fascination, and interest in the Stalin question by no means minimizes, let alone cancels out, the utter evil of the policies that brought pain and suffering and not merely glory, greatness, and "superpower" status to the Soviet Union and its remnants. There is clearly a good reason as to why, three decades following the collapse of the USSR and after regaining independence, Georgians as well as Russians—the inevitable heroes, both victors and victims of this book—are still struggling to reach a consensus on the Stalin question and the public sentiment per se, as demonstrated by surveys and polls which remain largely inconclusive.

In reaching a consensus on Stalin, we are also forced to reach a consensus on ourselves, our complicity, our own role and responsibility, no matter how miniscule or great, be it direct or indirect—an impossible task that we are either unwilling or unable to undertake, and so we remain on the merry-go-round never reaching an endpoint. As I gaze at the portrait of the Third Stalin, whose very image reignites and brings out deep anger, admiration, nostalgia, and terror all at once, I realize that at some point, I am no longer looking at Stalin—we are facing the familiar reflection, the mirror image of ourselves, our deepest, most sacred fears, wounds, secrets, and desires staring back at us, smirking, judging, fearing, and admiring that which we have produced. Stalin, thus, becomes us. And that realization, pregnant with boundless depths, doubts, and the heaviness of historical knowledge and the all-binding collective memory, is a bittersweet pill we will likely continue to reject for generations to come but will eventually have to swallow. In the end, this third Stalin, paired with his ultimate creation—the *sistema*—will outlive the other two Stalins who now belong to history. The Third Stalin, however, remains entrenched in the here and now—a timeless monument that cannot be toppled no matter how many monuments and vestiges we eradicate and replace, and one that will continue to stand strong as we stare at its mirror reflection, staring back at us.

© Tinatin Japaridze
En route from Gori to Tbilisi, April 2021

Bibliography

Aarons, Victoria, and Alan L. Berger. *Third-Generation Holocaust Representation: Trauma, History, and Memory*. Evanston, IL: Northwestern University Press, 2017.
Abesadze, Nino, and Otar Abesadze. "European Values and Georgia: Historical Aspects." *International Journal of Economic Theory and Application* 5, no. 2 (Spring 2018): 33–37.
Amosava, Tatsiana. "Nostalgia for the Soviet Past in the Post-Soviet Countries." Carleton University, Ottawa, Canada, July 10, 2015. https://carleton.ca/jewishstudies/wp-content/uploads/Zelikovitz-Centre-July-10-2015.pdf.
Anders, Jaroslaw. "Dead Souls." *New Republic Online*, February 13, 2005. https://newrepublic.com/authors/jaroslaw-anders.
Anderson, Benedict. *Imagined Communities: Reflections on the Origin and Spread of Nationalism*. London: Verso, 1991.
Apor, Balázs. "National Traditions and the Leader Cult in Communist Hungary in the Early Cold War Years." *Twentieth Century Communism* 1, no. 1 (June 2009): 50–71.
"Aqcia kulturis saministrostan." Ministry of Culture. Myvideo.ge, November 16, 2012. https://www.myvideo.ge/?video_id=1852094.
Arkhipova, Aleksandra. "Stalin bez Stalinizma." *InLiberty*, June 29, 2017. https://old.inliberty.ru/blog/2616-Stalin-bez-stalinizma.
———. "Strakh, kontrol' i velikaya pamyat': Komu u zachem nuzhen Stalin?" Recording of the oral presentation at the conference *Aktsiya: Anti-Stalin*. Sakharov Center, Moscow, Russia. June 23, 2017. YouTube video, 18:37. https://www.youtube.com/watch?v=x5Dz0mX40Zk.
Asatiani, Salome. "The Great Terror: In Stalin's Birthplace, Forgiving and Forgetting." Radio Free Europe, August 14, 2007. https://www.rferl.org/a/1078153.html.
Ashmore, Richard, Lee Jussim, and David Wilder, eds. *Social Identity, Intergroup Conflict, and Conflict Reduction*. Rutgers Series on Self and Social Identity 3. Oxford University Press, 2001.

Azrael, Jeremy. "Varieties of De-Stalinization." In Chalmers Johnson, ed., *Change in Communist Systems*. Palo Alto, CA: Stanford University Press, 1970.

Babaeva, Svetlana, i Georgiy Bovt. "Prezidentom Rossiyskoy Federatsii snova izbran V. V. Putin." *Izvestiya*, March 15, 2004. Web.

Bakradze, Lasha. "Georgia and Stalin: Still Living with the Great Son of the Nation." Washington, DC: Carnegie Endowment for International Peace, 2013.

———. "Past and Future of the Stalin Museum in Gori." *De Gruyter Oldenbourg* 103 (December 2020): 9–15.

Bakradze, Lasha, and Giga Zedania. "Stalinis muzeumshi." *Liberali*, no. 7 (August 11, 2009).

Balcer, Adam. "Long Live Stalin! Putin's Politics of Memory." *Heinrich Böll Stiftung*, July 2, 2018. https://eu.boell.org/en/2018/07/02/long-live-stalin-putins-politics-memory.

Barnard, Anne. "Georgia and Russia Nearing All-Out War." *New York Times*, August 9, 2008. https://www.nytimes.com/2008/08/10/world/europe/10georgia.html.

Barney, Timothy. "When We Was Red: *Good Bye Lenin!* and Nostalgia for the 'Everyday GDR.'" *Communication and Critical/Cultural Studies* 6, no. 2 (2009): 132–51.

Batiashvili, Nutsa. "Sites of Memory, Sites of Contestation: the Tbilisi Museum of Soviet Occupation and Visions of the Past in Georgia." *Cultures of History Forum*, June 1, 2017. https://www.cultures-of-history.uni-jena.de/exhibitions/georgia/sites-of-memory-sites-of-contestation-the-tbilisi-museum-of-soviet-occupation-and-visions-of-the-past-in-georgia/#fn-text8.

Baumann, Eveline. "Post-Soviet Georgia: It's a Long, Long Way to 'Modern' Social Protection." *Économies et Sociétés. Série F, Développement, croissance et progrès* 46, no. 1 (February 2012): 259–85.

Beatley, Meaghan. "Stalin Museum: The Creepy Attraction in Georgia That Still Worships the Communist Leader Like a God." *Independent*, November 21, 2017. https://www.independent.co.uk/travel/europe/stalin-museum-gori-georgia-open-joseph-communist-leader-dictator-death-mask-a8065256.html.

Bendtsen Gotfredsen, Katrine. "Void Pasts and Marginal Presents: On Nostalgia and Obsolete Features in the Republic of Georgia." *Slavic Review* 73, no. 2 (Summer 2014): 246–64.

Bennett, Kirk. "Georgia's Dilemma." *American Interest*, July 10, 2017. https://www.the-american-interest.com/2017/07/10/georgias-dilemma/.

Bilefsky, Dan. "In Georgia, a Reverence for Stalin." *New York Times*, September 30, 2008. https://www.nytimes.com/2008/10/01/world/europe/01stalin.html.

Blauvelt, Timothy. "Status Shift and Ethnic Mobilisation in the March 1956 Events in Georgia." *Europe-Asia Studies* 61, no. 4 (June 2009): 651–68.

Bloch, Marc. *The Historian's Craft: Reflections on the Nature and Uses of History and the Techniques and Methods of Those Who Write It*. New York: Vintage, 1964.

Bodaveli, Elene. "The Reflection of Communist Ideology in the Street Naming Policy in Soviet Tbilisi (1922–1939)." *Analytical Bulletin* 8 (2015): 156–78.

Bourke-White, Margaret. *Shooting the Russian War*. New York: Simon & Schuster, 1942.

Boym, Svetlana. *The Future of Nostalgia*. New York: Basic, 2002.

———. "Nostalgia and Its Discontents." *Hedgehog Review* 9, no. 2 (Summer 2007).
Buachidze, Tengiz. "Martovskaya tragediia 1956 goda v Tbilisi." *Literaturnaia Gazeta* 7 (1988): p. 111.
Cassiday, Julie A., and Emily D. Johnson. "Putin, Putiniana and the Question of a Post-Soviet Cult of Personality." *Slavonic and East European Review* 88, no. 4 (October 2010): 681–707.
Cattaruzza, Marina. "Introduction to the Special Issue of *Totalitarian Movements and Political Religions*: Political Religions as a Characteristic of the 20th Century." *Politics, Religion & Ideology* 6, no. 1 (2005): 1–18.
Chakhaia, Lela. "Who Misses the Soviet Union?" *Netgazeti*, July 3, 2017. Web.
Chechelashvili, Valeri. "Dugin Has Come Out as a Supporter of Georgia: How Did This Happen?" Georgian Foundation for Strategic and International Studies, June 20, 2019. https://www.gfsis.org/blog/view/956.
Cheremushkin, Pyotr. "Destalinizatsiya Rossii: Tret'ya Volna." *Golos Ameriki*, October 20, 2010. https://www.golosameriki.com/a/russia-stain-2010-10-20-105341173/189506.html.
Chikovani, Nino. "The Georgian Historical Narrative: From Pre-Soviet to Post-Soviet Nationalism." *Dynamics of Asymmetric Conflict* 5, no. 2 (July 2012): 107–115.
Chitanava, Ekaterine. "Salome Jashi Shows and Talks about Young Generation Raised in Patriotic Camps." *Georgia Today*, February 12, 2010. Web.
Chkhaidze, Irakli. "Post-Soviet Georgia: New Perspectives in Historical Research?" *Civilization Researches* 9, no. 1. UNESCO, 2012. http://www.culturedialogue.com/resources/library/civilresearches/journals/9.pdf.
Christensen, Julie. "Tengiz Abuladze's Repentance and the Georgian Nationalist Cause." *Slavic Review* 50, no. 1 (Spring 1991): 163–75.
"Chto, uzhe ukhodite? Kak rossiyane otnosyatsya k otstavke Putina v 2024 godu." Levada Center, March 5, 2020. https://www.levada.ru/2020/03/05/chto-uzhe-uhodite-kak-rossiyane-otnosyatsya-k-otstavke-putina-v-2024-godu/.
Clines, Francis X. "Upheaval in the East; Moscow McDonald's Opens: Milkshakes and Human Kindness." *New York Times*, February 1, 1990. https://www.nytimes.com/1990/02/01/world/upheaval-east-moscow-mcdonald-s-opens-milkshakes-human-kindness-reuters.html.
Conterio, Martyn. "Perm 36: The Soviet-era Gulag Museum Where Putin is Rewriting History." *History Answers*, March 7, 2017. https://www.historyanswers.co.uk/people-politics/perm-36-the-soviet-era-gulag-museum-where-putin-is-rewriting-history/.
Coynash, Halya. "'Perm-36' Labelled 'Foreign Agent' as Moscow Seeks to Expunge Memory of the Gulag." *Kharkiv Human Rights Protection Group*, May 8, 2015. http://khpg.org/en/index.php?id=1430909081.
Dadalauri, Nina, and Lars Johannsen. "Shevardnadze's Political Strategies: The Rise and Fall of the Incumbent." In Karin Hilmer Pedersen and Lars Johannsen, eds., *Pathways: A Study of Six Post-Communist Countries*. Aarhus, Denmark: Aarhus University Press, 2009.

Dalaqishvili, Nino. "Georgia's Soviet Nostalgia Proven by NDI Poll." *VOA Georgian Service*, May 12, 2017. https://www.amerikiskhma.com/a/ndi-research-in-georgia/3849689.html.

Daughtry, J. Martin. "Russia's New Anthem and the Negotiation of National Identity." *Ethnomusicology* 47, no. 1 (Winter 2003): 42–67.

Davis, Fred. "Nostalgia, Identity, and the Current Nostalgia Wave." *Journal of Popular Culture* 11, no. 2 (Fall 1977): 414–24.

De Waal, Thomas, ed. "The Stalin Puzzle: Deciphering Post-Soviet Public Opinion." Washington, DC: Carnegie Endowment for International Peace, 2013.

Dobbs, Michael. "Moscow Plays Ketch-Up; Fast Food Comes to Slow Food Capital." *Washington Post*, February 1, 1990. https://www.washingtonpost.com/archive/politics/1990/02/01/moscow-plays-ketch-up/2addbab1-da1c-4101-a2f3-3131a3a97035/.

Domańska, Maria. "The Myth of the Great Patriotic War as a Tool of the Kremlin's Great Power Policy." *Centre for Eastern Studies* 316, no. 1 (December 2019): 1–10.

———. "The Myth of the Great Patriotic War as a Tool of the Kremlin's Great Power Policy." Ośrodek Studiów Wschodnich/Centre for Eastern Studies, December 31, 2019. https://www.osw.waw.pl/en/publikacje/osw-commentary/2019-12-31/myth-great-patriotic-war-a-tool-kremlins-great-power-policy#_ftn25.

"Doveriye politikam." Levada Center, May 29, 2020. https://www.levada.ru/2020/05/29/doverie-k-politikam/.

Dugin, Alexander. "Iosif Stalin: Velikoye 'Da' Bytiya." *Ulpressa*, March 5, 2013. https://ulpressa.ru/2013/03/05/aleksandr-dugin-iosif-stalin-velikoe%DAbyitiya/.

———. "Manifest o prisoyedeneniiy Gruzii k Rossii." Dugin.ru via Tsargrad.tv., n.d. http://dugin.ru/video/manifest-o-prisoedinenii-gruzii-k-rossii.

Dunbar, William. "What Georgians Make of 'The Death of Stalin.'" *Economist*, February 16, 2018. https://www.1843magazine.com/culture/the-daily/what-georgians-make-of-the-death-of-stalin.

"Dynamics of Attitudes towards Stalin." Levada Center, April 16, 2019. https://www.levada.ru/2019/04/16/dinamika-otnosheniya-k-stalinu/.

Efimov, Vladimir. "O Politicheskom Zaveshyanii Stalina." *Journal of Economic Regulation* 11, no. 1 (2020): 6–35. https://hjournal.ru/en/journals/journal-of-economic-regulation/2020/236-no-1.html.

Erikson, Erik H. *Identity and the Life Cycle*. New York: W. W. Norton, 1980.

———. *Identity: Youth and Crisis*. New York: W. W. Norton, 1968.

Etkind, Alexander. *Warped Mourning: Stories of the Undead in the Land of the Unburied*. Stanford, CA: Stanford University Press, 2013.

Fein, Esther B. "At Least 16 Killed as Protesters Battle the Police in Soviet Georgia." *New York Times*, April 10, 1989. https://www.nytimes.com/1989/04/10/world/at-least-16-killed-as-protesters-battle-the-police-in-soviet-georgia.html.

Felman, Shoshana, and Dori Laub. *Testimony: Crises of Witnessing in Literature, Psychoanalysis, and History*. New York: Routledge, 1991.

"Figura Stalina v obshestvennom mnenii Rossii." Levada Center, March 3, 2016. https://www.levada.ru/2016/03/25/figura-stalina-v-obshhestvennom-mnenii-rossii/.

Filler, André, and Dimitry Filimonov. "Vladimir Putin: A Geopolitical Representation? From the Image to Usage." *Hérodote* 166, no. 3 (2017): 51–67.
Foy, Henry. "The Brutal Third Act of Vladimir Putin." *Financial Times*, March 11, 2021. https://www.ft.com/content/59498c92-799f-4c61-ac2e-77e7e302cc32.
Gachava, Nana. "Georgian President Blasted over Monument's Demolition." Radio Free Europe/Radio Liberty, December 21, 2009. https://www.rferl.org/a/Georgian_President_Blasted_Over_Monuments_Demolition/1910056.html.
Gel'man, Vladimir. "The Politics of Fear." *Russian Politics and Law* 53, nos. 5–6 (September–December 2015): 6–26.
Gessen, Masha. "'The Death of Stalin' Captures the Terrifying Absurdity of a Tyrant." *New Yorker*, March 6, 2018. https://www.newyorker.com/news/our-columnists/the-death-of-stalin-captures-the-terrifying-absurdity-of-a-tyrant.
Gogolashvili, Kakha. "The EU and Georgia: The Choice Is in the Context." *Europe in Dialogue* 1, no. 1 (2009): 92–129.
Golubkova, Mariya. "Obyavit' vsemirnym naslediyem." *Rossiyskaya Gazeta*, November 21, 2019. https://rg.ru/2019/11/21/rossiia-potrebuet-priniatiia-specialnoj-rezoliucii-oon-ko-dniu-pobedy.html.
Goscilo, Helena. *Putin as Celebrity and Cultural Icon.* New York: Routledge, 2013.
Gozalishvili, Nino. "The Late Cold War and Cracks in the Iron Curtain for Georgian Youth in the 1980s: The Subcultural Nature of the 'Jeans Generation.'" *Corvinus Journal of International Affairs* 3, no. 2 (October 2018): 42–54.
Graham, David A. "Where Will the Removal of Confederate Monuments Stop?" *Atlantic*, June 28, 2017. https://www.theatlantic.com/politics/archive/2017/06/where-will-the-removal-of-confederate-monuments-stop/532125/.
Gudkov, Lev. The Archetype of the Leader: Analyzing a Totalitarian Symbol." Washington, DC: Carnegie Endowment for International Peace, 2013.
———. "Stalin—eto mif." Lenta.ru, June 12, 2019. https://lenta.ru/articles/2019/06/12/stalin/.
Gugushvili, Alexi, and Peter Kabachnik. "Stalin Is Dead, Long Live Stalin? Testing Socialization, Structural, Ideological, Nationalist, and Gender Hypotheses." *Post-Soviet Affairs* 31, no. 1 (September 2015): 1–36.
Gugushvili, Alexi, Giorgi Babunashvili, Peter Kabachnik, Ana Kirvalidze, and Nino Rcheulishvili. "Collective Memory, National Identity, and Contemporary Georgian Perspectives on Stalin and the Soviet Past." Caucasus Research Resource Center, Tbilisi, Georgia, September 2015. https://www.researchgate.net/profile/Peter-Kabachnik/publication/282072355_Collective_Memory_National_Identity_and_Contemporary_Georgian_Perspectives_on_Stalin_and_the_Soviet_Past/links/56022e8d08ae42bbd541f78a/Collective-Memory-National-Identity-and-Contemporary-Georgian-Perspectives-on-Stalin-and-the-Soviet-Past.pdf.
Gvosdev, Nikolas K. *Imperial Policies and Perspectives towards Georgia: 1760–1819.* Basingstoke: Macmillan, 2000.
Hartog, Eva. "Is Stalin Making a Comeback in Russia?" *Atlantic*, May 28, 2019. https://www.theatlantic.com/international/archive/2019/05/russia-stalin-statue/590140/.
Hirsch, Marianne, and Leo Spitzer. "The Witness in the Archive: Holocaust Studies/Memory Studies." *Memory Studies* 2, no. 2 (2009): 151–70.

Hochschild, Adam. *The Unquiet Ghost: Russians Remember Stalin*. New York: Viking, 1994.
Hu, Caitlin. "Why Georgians Fight to Keep Statues of Stalin, as the Rest of the Former USSR Tears Them Down." *Quartz*, November 7, 2014. https://qz.com/292901/historical-statues-illegal-stalin-statues-keep-popping-up-in-gori-georgia/.
Ibragimowa, Elina. "Kak Rozkomnadzor vmeshalsya v pedagogicheskiy konflikt." *Deutsche Welle*, July 26, 2017. https://www.dw.com/ru/как-роскомнадзор-вмешался-в-педагогический-конфликт/a-39825535.
———. "Why Stalin is Causing a Classroom Storm in Russia." *Deutsche Welle*, July 29, 2017. https://www.dw.com/en/why-stalin-is-causing-a-classroom-storm-in-russia/a-39866244.
Ilyin, Vladimir, i Mikhail Morev. "Chto ostavit V. Putin svoemu priyemniku v 2024 godu?" *Ekonomicheskiye i sotsialniye peremeny: fakty, tendentsii, prognoz* 11, no. 1 (2018): 9–30.
"Information about the Patriotic Camps." Official Portal of Ministry of Diasporan Affairs of Georgia, 2008. http://civiclab.narod.ru/civic/c1_info/2008inf/patri-camps08.htm.
"Interview with Zviad Gamsakhurdia." *Sakartvelos Respublika* 36:56, February 22, 1991.
"Interview with Zviad Gamsakhurdia." *Sakartvelos Respublika* 39:59, February 27, 1991.
Iremashvili, Ioseb. *Stalin and the Tragedy of the Georgians*. Berlin: Selbstverl, 1932.
Ivanova, Natalia. "No(w)stalgia: Retro on the (Post)-Soviet Television Screen." *Harriman Review* 12, nos. 2–3 (1999): 25–32.
Ivanushkin, Georgiy. "Iz muzeya istorii politicheskikh repressiy ubrali upominaniya o Staline." Agency of Social Information, March 3, 2015. https://www.asi.org.ru/news/2015/03/05/iz-muzeya-istorii-politicheskih-repressij-ubrali-upominaniya-o-staline/.
"Izmeneniya i peremeny." Levada Center, June 19, 2018. https://www.levada.ru/2018/06/19/izmeneniya-i-peremeny/.
Jacobsen, Katherine. "New Museums in Russia are Airbrushing Stalin's Legacy." *Business Insider*, December 18, 2015. https://www.businessinsider.com/new-museums-in-russia-are-airbrushing-stalins-legacy-2015-12.
———. "Russia Opens New Stalin Museums, Grapples with His Legacy." *Times of Israel*, December 19, 2015. https://www.timesofisrael.com/russia-opens-new-stalin-museums-grapples-with-his-legacy/.
Jameson, Fredric. "Nostalgia for the Present." *South Atlantic Quarterly* 88, no. 2 (1989): 517–37.
———. *Postmodernism, or, the Cultural Logic of Late Capitalism*. Durham, NC: Duke University Press, 1991.
Japaridze, Tinatin. "Press Play for Politics: The Weapon of a Eurovision Song." *Inquiries Journal* 7, no. 10 (2015): 1–5.
Jones, Stephen. "The Role of Cultural Paradigms in Georgian Foreign Policy." In Rick Fawn, ed., *Ideology and National Identity in Post-Communist Foreign Policy*. New York: Routledge, 2003.

Kablukov, Evgeniy. "Iosif Stalin i Vladimir Putin: praktiki konstruktirovaniya obraza politicheskogo lidera v diskurse sovetskikh i rossiyskikh media." *Przegląd Wschodnioeuropejski* 11, no. 2 (2020): 73–84.

Kekelia, Tatia. "Building Georgian National Identity: A Comparison of Two Turning Points." In Alexander Agadjanian, Ansgar Jodicke, and Evert var der Zweerde, eds., *Religion, Nation and Democracy in the South Caucasus.* New York: Routledge, 2015.

Kennan, George F. "The Legacy of Stalinism." *Proceedings of the Massachusetts Historical Society*, Third Series 79 (1967).

Kirchick, James. "Statute of Limitations." *New Republic*, August 11, 2010. https://newrepublic.com/article/76970/russia-georgia-conflict-putin-stalin.

Kochieva, Inga, and Alexi Margiev. *Georgia: Ethnic Cleansing of Ossetians 1989–1992*. Moscow, Russia: Europe Publishing House, 2005.

Kolstø, Pål, and Aleksander Rusetskii. "Power Differentials and Identity Formation: Images of Self and Other on the Russian-Georgian Boundary." *National Identities* 14, no. 2 (2012): 139–55.

"Kolyma: Birthplace of Our Fear." vDud', April 23, 2019. YouTube video, 2h17m. https://www.youtube.com/watch?v=oo1Woul38rQ&t=1s.

Kotkin, Stephen. "Russia's Perpetual Geopolitics: Putin Returns to the Historical Pattern." *Foreign Affairs* 95, no. 3 (May–June 2016): 2–9. https://www.foreignaffairs.com/articles/ukraine/2016-04-18/russias-perpetual-geopolitics.

———. *Stalin: Paradoxes of Power, 1878–1928.* New York: Penguin, 2015.

Kovtiak, Elisabeth. "A Bridge to the Past: Public Memory and Nostalgia for the Communist Times in Modern Georgia." *Journal of Nationalism, Memory and Language Politics* 12, no. 1 (July 2018): 31–51.

Kravchenko, Stepan, and Andrey Biryukov. "Putin Doesn't Like Cult of Personality of Putin, Kremlin Says." *Bloomberg*, March 13, 2020. https://www.bloomberg.com/news/articles/2020-03-13/putin-doesn-t-like-cult-of-personality-of-putin-kremlin-says.

Kronenberg, Volker. *Patriotismus in Deutschland: Perspektiven für eine weltoffene Nation*. Wiesbaden: VS Verlag für Sozialwissenschaften, 2006.

Kun, Miklós. *Stalin: An Unknown Portrait*. Budapest, Hungary: Central European University Press, 2003.

Kushelevich, Mitya. "Taste of Freedom: What the Closure of the First Moscow McDonald's Means for Russia Today." *Calvert Journal*, September 1, 2014. https://www.calvertjournal.com/articles/show/3046/mcdonalds-moscow-closure-russia-martin-parr.

Lang, David M. *The Last Years of the Georgian Monarchy: 1658–1832*. New York: Columbia University Press, 1957.

László, János. *Historical Tales and National Identity: An Introduction to Narrative Social Psychology*. New York: Routledge, 2013.

Laurence, Peter. "Stalin Wiped from Soviet Gulag Museum." BBC, March 3, 2015. https://www.bbc.com/news/world-europe-31711287.

Lebow, Richard Ned. "The Future of Memory." *The Annals of the American Academy of Political and Social Science* 617 (May 2008): 25–41.

Ledeneva, Alena V. *Can Russia Modernise? Sistema, Power Networks and Informal Governance*. London: University College London, 2013.

———. "Cronies, Economic Crime and Capitalism in Putin's Sistema." *International Affairs* 88, no. 1 (January 2012): 149–57.

Lee, Yoonmi. *Modern Education, Textbooks, and the Image of the Nation: Politics and Modernization and Nationalism in Korean Education*. New York: Routledge, 2012.

"Letter of Nina Bedia's Mother to Stalin." Soviet Policy. The Archive of the Ministry of Internal Affairs of Georgia. Web.

Levering, Ralph. *American Opinion and the Russian Alliance, 1939–1945*. Chapel Hill: University of North Carolina Press, 1976.

Lipman, Maria. "Stalin Is Not Dead: A Legacy that Holds Back Russia." Washington, DC: Carnegie Endowment for International Peace, 2013), 17–18.

Lomsadze, Giorgi. "Missing the USSR, Even in Georgia." *Eurasianet*, November 7, 2017. https://eurasianet.org/missing-the-ussr-even-in-georgia.

Luxmoore, Matthew. "In Russia, 'The Death of Stalin' Is No Laughing Matter." New York Times, January 24, 2018. https://www.nytimes.com/2018/01/24/movies/death-of-stalin-banned-russia.html.

Macdonald, Sharon, and Gordon Fyfe, eds. *Theorizing Museums: Representing Identity and Diversity in a Changing World*. Cambridge, MA: Wiley-Blackwell, 1996.

Mankovskaya, Elizaveta. "Mythologizing the Past to Survive the Present: Trauma and Cultural Memory in Timur Bekmambetov's Imperial Bank Commercials (1992–1997)." *Ulbandus Review* 17, no. 1 (2016): 86–107.

Márquez, Xavier. "The Mechanisms of Cult Production: An Overview." In Kirill Postoutenko and Darin Stephanov, eds., *Ruler Personality Cults from Empires to Nation-States and Beyond: Symbolic Patterns and Interactional Dynamics*. New York: Routledge, 2021.

Martinez, Francisco. "To Whom Does History Belong? The Theatre of Memory in Post-Soviet Russia, Estonia and Georgia." *Anthropological Journal of European Cultures* 26, no. 1 (Spring 2017): 98–127.

McCall, Mac. "Georgia's Love-Hate Relationship with Joseph Stalin." *Atlas Obscura*, November 19, 2020. https://www.atlasobscura.com/articles/gori-georgia-joseph-stalin.

Medvedev, Roy. *Let History Judge: The Origins and Consequences of Stalinism*. New York: Knopf, 1971.

Medvedev, Sergei. "Jughaphilia." Radio Svoboda, March 29, 2020. https://www.svoboda.org/a/30511648.html.

Mekhuzla, Salome, and Aideen Roche. "National Minorities and Educational Reform in Georgia." European Centre for Minority Issues (ECMI), September 2009. https://www.files.ethz.ch/isn/106681/working_paper_46_en.pdf.

Mestvirishvili, Natia, and Maia Mestvirishvili. "'I am Georgian and Therefore I am European': Re-searching the Europeanness of Georgia." *Central European Journal of International and Security Studies* 8, no. 1 (May 2014): 52–65.

Metreveli, Tornike. "The Evolution of Totalitarianism: From Stalin to Putin." *Atlantic Community* (November 2013): 1–5.

Mitchell, Lincoln. "In Stalin's Hometown, Absent Statues and Lingering Legacies." *Observer,* July 31, 2015. http://observer.com/2015/07/in-stalins-hometown-absent-statues-and-lingering-legacies.

Monaghan, Andrew. "The Russian *Vertikal*: The Tandem, Power, and the Elections." Russia and Eurasia Programme Paper REP 2011/01. Chatham House, June 2011. https://www.chathamhouse.org/sites/default/files/19412_0511ppmonaghan.pdf.

Montefiore, Simon Sebag. *Stalin: The Court of a Red Tsar*. London: Weidenfeld and Nicolson, 2003.

———. *Young Stalin*. London: Vintage, 2009.

Morev, Konstantin. "Stalin i Stalinizm v Replikakh Vladimira Putina." *Istoricheskaya Ekspertiza* 4, no. 1 (2017): 134–41.

Mosier, John. *Deathride: Hitler vs. Stalin. The Eastern Front, 1941–1945*. New York: Simon & Schuster, 2010.

Mozokhin, Oleg. *Delo Lavrentiya Berii. Sbornik Dokumentov*. Kuchkovo Pole, 2015.

Mukhametshina, Elena. "Tri chetverti rossiyan schitayut sovetskuyu epokhu luchshey v istorii strany." *Vedomosti*, March 24, 2020. https://www.vedomosti.ru/society/articles/2020/03/23/825985-tri-chetverti.

Mukhina, Galina. *Lenin o Glasnosti*. Moscow, Russia: n.p. 1989.

N.a. "27 Years On from April 9 Tragedy: Georgia Remembers Heroes Who Died for the Country's Independence." Agenda.ge, April 9, 2016. https://agenda.ge/en/news/2016/843.

N.a. "At Least Seven Die in Shootout After Hijacking of a Soviet Plane." *New York Times*, November 23, 1983. https://www.nytimes.com/1983/11/23/world/at-least-seven-die-in-shootout-after-hijacking-of-a-soviet-plane.html.

N.a. "Bidzina Ivanishvili politikidan 'sabolood' midis." Civil.ge, January 11, 2021. https://civil.ge/ka/archives/390513.

N.a. "Boris Gryzlov schitayet Stalina 'nezauryadnym chelovekom.'" RIA Novosti, June 6, 2008. https://ria.ru/20041221/766724.html.

N.a. "Conversation with Vladimir Putin: Full Transcript." RBC, December 3, 2009. https://www.rbc.ru/politics/03/12/2009/5703d80a9a7947733180cf19.

N.a. "Culture Ministry: Stalin Statue, Removed Three Years Ago, Planned to Be Put in His Museum." Civil.ge, July 30, 2013. https://civil.ge/archives/123060.

N.a. "Dmitry Medvedev: Stalin vyol voynu s sobstvennym narodom." Interfax, October 30, 2012. https://www.interfax.ru/russia/273531.

N.a. "Gauqmdeba tu ara sabtchota okupatsiis muzeumi?" Netgazeti, November 12, 2012. https://netgazeti.ge/news/17425/.

N.a. "George Washington Statue Toppled by Protesters in Portland, Oregon." CBS News, June 19, 2020. https://www.cbsnews.com/news/protesters-portland-oregon-topple-george-washington-statue/.

N.a. *Georgia Mineral & Mining Sector Investment and Business Guide: Strategic Information and Regulations*. Washington, DC: International Business Publications, 2013.

N.a. "Gosduma obvinila Stalina." Interfax, November 26, 2010. https://www.interfax.ru/russia/166628.

N.a. "Great Patriotic War, Again." *Economist*, May 2, 2015. https://www.economist.com/europe/2015/05/02/great-patriotic-war-again.

N.a. "Gulag Museum to Reopen But Proof of Stalin Crimes Removed, Director Says." *Moscow Times*, March 5, 2015. https://www.themoscowtimes.com/2015/03/05/gulag-museum-to-reopen-but-proof-of-stalin-crimes-removed-director-says-a44496.

N.a. "Is Georgia Europe?" *Intermedia Georgia*, August 20, 2019. http://intermedia.ge/სტატია/117737-არის-თუ-არა-საქართველო-ევროპა/21/.

N.a. "Iuri mechitovi: okupatsiis muzeumis dasakheleba da arsi absurdia." *Tabula*, November 23, 2012. http://www.tabula.ge/ge/story/62773-iuri-mechitovi-okupaciis-muzeumis-dasaxeleba-da-arsi-absurdia.

N.a. "Joseph Stalin: Why So Many Russians Like the Soviet Dictator." BBC, April 18, 2019. https://www.bbc.com/news/world-europe-47975704.

N.a. "Kaluga Expert: De-Stalinization is a Provocation Aimed at Splitting Society." Regnum News Agency, April 11, 2011. www.regnum.ru/news/1392889.html.

N.a. "Khrushchev's Secret Speech, 'On the Cult of Personality and Its Consequences,' Delivered at the Twentieth Party Congress of the Communist Party of the Soviet Union." February 25, 1956, History and Public Policy Program Digital Archive, From the Congressional Record: Proceedings and Debates of the 84th Congress, 2nd Session (May 22, 1956–June 11, 1956), C11, Part 7 (June 4, 1956), 9389–9403. http://digitalarchive.wilsoncenter.org/document/115995.

N.a. "Khrushchev's Secret Speech, 'On the Cult of Personality and Its Consequences,' Delivered at the Twentieth Party Congress of the Communist Party of the Soviet Union." February 25, 1956, Russian State Archive of Contemporary History, stock 1, inventory 2, document 3, Russian Federal Archives, Moscow, Russia.

N.a. "Kosh'unstvo i glumleniye: fil'm 'Smert' Stalina' ne pustili v prokat." RIA Novosti, January 23, 2018. https://ria.ru/20180123/1513179176.html.

N.a. "M. S. Gorbachev." *Moskovskii Komsomolets*, March 12, 1985.

N.a. "March Riot Dead in Tiflis Set at 100." *New York Times*, April 22, 1956.

N.a. "More of Europe in Georgia and More of Georgia in Europe." Georgian News Agency, May 5, 2019. https://www.ghn.ge/news/225607-meti-evropa-sakartveloshi-da-meti-sakartvelo-evropashi-salome-zurabishvili.

N.a. "'Perm-36' Soviet Political Repression Camp (GULAG) & Chusovaya History Museum Excursion." Travel Agency Krasnov, 2014. http://www.uraltourism.com/perm36.php.

N.a. "Putin Declares Patriotism Russia's Only National Idea." *Moscow Times*, February 4, 2016. https://www.themoscowtimes.com/2016/02/04/putin-declares-patriotism-russias-only-national-idea-a51705.

N.a. "Putin Keeps Stalin's Crimes Under Wraps in WWII Battle With West." *Moscow Times*, February 13, 2020. https://www.themoscowtimes.com/2020/02/13/putin-keeps-stalins-crimes-under-wraps-in-wwii-battle-with-west-a69274.

N.a. "Putin soglasilsya s Medinskim po paktu Molotova-Ribbentropa." Interfax, May 10, 2015. https://www.interfax.ru/russia/440996.

N.a. "Rogor gaarides stalinis muzeumis eqsponatebi rusebs." Kvira.ge, August 7, 2020. http://kvira.ge/586780.

N.a. "Rossiiskiye BBC razbombili pozitsii gruzinskoy artillerii bliz Gori." Lenta.ru, August 9, 2008. https://lenta.ru/news/2008/08/09/gori/.

N.a. "Russia Unveils New National Anthem Joining the Old Soviet Tune to the Older, Unsoviet God." *New York Times*, December 31, 2000. https://www.nytimes.com/2000/12/31/world/russia-unveils-new-national-anthem-joining-old-soviet-tune-older-unsoviet-god.html.

N.a. "Russia's Putin Signs Law Banning Fake News, Insulting the State Online." Reuters, March 18, 2019. https://www.reuters.com/article/us-russia-politics-fake news-idUSKCN1QZ1TZ.

N.a. "Russian Jets Attack Georgian Town." BBC, August 9, 2008. http://news.bbc.co.uk/2/hi/europe/7550804.stm.

N.a. *Sak'artvelos istoriisa da kulturis żeglta ağceriloba*, vol. 5 (Tbilisi, 1990), 40–45.

N.a. "Saprotesto aqcia muzeumis gauqmebis cinaaghmdeg." Palitratv.ge, November 15, 2012. https://www.palitravideo.ge//yvela-video/akhali-ambebi/23513-saprotesto-aqcia-okupaciis-muzeumis-gauqmebis-tsinaaghmdeg.html.

N.a. "Sibiryaku, napisavshemu pro nizkuyu zarplatu i nazvavshemu Putina na bukvu 'P,' naznachili shtraf za oskorbleniye vdvoye vyshe zarobotka." News.ru, August 13, 2019. https://www.newsru.com/russia/13aug2019/noskov.html.

N.a. "Soviet Nostalgia on the Path to Euro-Atlantic Integration through Anti-Western Media Influence." Qartli.ge, January 20, 2018. https://www.qartli.ge/ge/akhali-ambebi/article/7447-sabtcothanostalgiaevroatlantikurgzazeantidasavlurimediis gavlenith.

N.a. "Stalin Center Opens in Central Russia." *Moscow Times*, December 22, 2015. https://www.themoscowtimes.com/2015/12/22/stalin-center-opens-in-central-russia-a51301.

N.a. "Stalin's Approval Rating Among Russians Hits Record High." RBC News, April 16, 2019. https://www.rbc.ru/politics/16/04/2019/5cb0bb979a794780a4592d0c.

N.a. "Stalina mogila ispravila: 125-letiye vozhdya otmetili u Kremlyovskoy steny." *Kommersant*, December 22, 2004. https://www.kommersant.ru/doc/535369.

N.a. "Statue of Queen Victoria Defaced in Hyde Park, Leeds." BBC, June 9, 2020. https://www.bbc.com/news/uk-england-leeds-52985627.

N.a. "V Kutaisi vzorvan Memorial slavy: pogibli dva cheloveka." RBC, December 19, 2009. https://www.rbc.ru/society/19/12/2009/5703d8729a7947733180d544.

N.a. "V Novosibirske ustanovili pamyatnik Stalinu." RIA Novosti, May 8, 2019. https://ria.ru/20190508/1553341814.html.

N.a. "V SPCH opasayutsya, chto Iosif Stalin raskolet obshestvo." *Kommersant*, March 30, 2015. https://www.kommersant.ru/doc/2698033.

N.a. "V Surgute aktivisty ustanovili banner s blagodarnost'yu Stalinu." Znak, May 8, 2019. https://www.znak.com/2019-05-07/v_surgute_aktivisty_ustanovili_banner_s_blagodarnostyu_stalinu.

N.a. "Vid Leninizmu do leninopadu." Radio Svoboda, December 12, 2014. https://www.radiosvoboda.org/a/26770232.html.

N.a. "Vladimir Putin at Seliger 2014 National Youth Forum." Kremlin.ru, August 29, 2014. http://en.kremlin.ru/events/president/news/46507.

N.a. "Why Are Georgians Nostalgic for the Soviet Union?" Ambebi.ge, May 21, 2019. Web.
N.a. "Zhitelya Krasnoyarskogo kraya otshtrafovali na 30 tysyach rubley za slova o Putine." *Svoboda*, August 13, 2019. https://www.svoboda.org/a/30107224.html.
Nadkarni, Maya, and Olga Shevchenko. "The Politics of Nostalgia," *Ab Imperio* 2 (2004): 487–519.
Nakhimova, Elena. "Ideologema Stalina v sovremennoy massovoy kommunikatsii." *Politicheskaya Lingvistika* 2, no. 36 (2011): 152–56.
Nelson, Todd H. "History as Ideology: The Portrayal of Stalinism and the Great Patriotic War in Contemporary Russian High School Textbooks." *Post-Soviet Affairs* 31, no. 1 (Summer 2014): 37–65.
"News Conference of Vladimir Putin." Kremlin.ru, December 19, 2013. http://en.kremlin.ru/events/president/news/19859.
Nodia, Ghia. "Georgia and Europe and the Geopolitics of Values." *Forbes Georgia*, January 9, 2014. https://forbes.ge/evropa-da-saqarthvelo-ghir/.
———. "Political Turmoil in Georgia and the Ethnic Policies of Zviad Gamsakhurdia." In Bruno Coppieters, ed., *Contested Borders in the Caucasus*. Brussels: VUB University Press, 1996.
Notadze, Nodar. "Siskhliani paraskevi." In G. Vepkhvadze, ed., *9 marti, 1956: kadrshi da kadrgaret.* Tbilisi: Garchi, n.d.
Oktyabr'skaya, Nadezhda. "Putin sozdal problemy, a komu ikh reshat'?" *Zdorovye—osnova chelovecheskogo potentsiala: problem i puti ikh resheniya* (2020): 1227–30.
Oreshkin, Dmitry. *Jughaphilia and the Soviet Statistical Epic Poetry*. Moscow, Russia: Mysl', 2019.
Orwell, George. *1984*. New York: New American Library, 1983.
Orzoff, Andrea. "The Husbandman: Tomáš Masaryk's Leader Cult in Interwar Czechoslovakia." *Austrian History Yearbook* 39, no. 1 (April 2008): 121–37.
Osborn, Andrew, and Polina Ivanova. "Sixteen More Years? Russian Parliament Backs Move to Keep Putin in Power." Reuters, March 11, 2020. https://www.reuters.com/article/us-russia-putin/sixteen-more-years-russian-parliament-backs-move-to-keep-putin-in-power-idUSKBN20Y0VC.
Oushakine, Serguei. "'We're Nostalgic But We're Not Crazy': Retrofitting the Past in Russia." *Russian Review* 66, no. 3 (July 2007): 451–82.
Overy, R. J. *The Dictators: Hitler's Germany and Stalin's Russia*. New York: W.W. Norton, 2004.
Ozhegov, Sergei I., and Nataliia Iu. Shvedova, eds. *Tolkovyi slovar' russkogo iazyka: 72,500 slov i 7,500 frazeologicheskikh vyrazhenii*. Moscow, Russia: Az, 1995.
Panov, Pyotr. "Poleticheskiy poryadok i problema proizvodstva vlasti: institut preemnika." *Politicheskaya ekspertiza: Politeks* 6, no. 3 (2010): 19–33.
Parfitt, Tom. "Vladimir Putin 'Backs Russian Fast-Food Rival to McDonald's'." *Daily Telegraph*, April 9, 2015. https://www.telegraph.co.uk/news/worldnews/europe/russia/11524817/Vladimir-Putin-backs-Russian-fast-food-rival-to-McDonalds.html.

Partsvaniya, Helen. "Georgia: 20 Years of Independence." Institute of World Policy, February 28, 2001. http://georgia.iwp.org.ua/eng/public/133.html.

Pavlovsky, Gleb. "Russian Politics Under Putin: The System Will Outlast the Master." *Foreign Affairs* 95, no. 3 (May–June 2016): 10–17.

Pinchuk, Denis, and Andrew Osborn. "Russia Cancels Release of 'Insulting' Film about Stalin's Death." Reuters, January 23, 2018. https://www.reuters.com/article/us-russia-film-stalin/russia-cancels-release-of-insulting-film-about-stalins-death-idUSKBN1FC1X6Pisch, Anita. *The Personality Cult of Stalin in Soviet Posters, 1929–1953: Archetypes, Inventions and Fabrications*. Canberra, Australia: ANU Press, 2016.

Pkhakadze, Nikoloz, and Eric Livny. "Georgia between Two Fires: Russia or Europe?" ISET Policy Institute, June 6, 2014. Web.

Platt, Kevin M. F. "Secret Speech: Wounding, Disavowal, and Social Belonging in the USSR." *Critical Inquiry* 42, no. 3 (Spring 2016): 647–76.

———. *Terror and Greatness: Ivan and Peter as Russian Myths*. Ithaca, NY: Cornell University Press, 2011.

"The Plenary Sitting of the Parliament of Georgia." Parliament of Georgia, December 10, 2010. http://www.parliament.ge/en/media/axali-ambebi/the-plenary-sitting-of-the-parliament-to-of-georgia-26511.page.

Pocheptsov, Georgiy. "Ot mifa revolyutsiy k mifu Pobedy, ot mifa Stalina k mifu Putina." Mariupol State University, July 18, 2018.

Polese, Abel, and Slavomir Horák. "A Tale of Two Presidents: Personality Cult and Symbolic Nation-Building in Turkmenistan." *Journal of Nationalism and Ethnicity* 43, no. 3 (May 2015): 457–78.

"The President of Georgia Met the Representatives of EU Countries." Official Website of President of Georgia, Mikheil Saakashvili, May 12, 2008. www.president.gov.ge/en/PressOffice/News/SpeechesAndStatements?p=2337&i=1.

Pukareva, Elena, and Svetlana Pukareva. "Tipy Politicheskikh Liderov: Sravneniye I. V. Stalina i V. V. Putina." *Nauka bez granits* 12, no. 17 (2017): 79–83.

Putin, Vladimir. "It is impossible to move forward without spiritual, cultural and national self- determination." Russia Today, September 20, 2013. https://www.rt.com/russia/official-word/putin-valdai-national-idea-142/.

Putkaradze, Iakob. "Ar unda dagvrches 'tetri lakebi': sakartvelos gasabchoebis samartlebrivi shepaseba." *Komunisti*, August 25, 1989.

Putzier, Konrad. "Putin and Stalin: Mirror Reflections." World Policy, December 23, 2014. http://worldpolicy.org/2014/12/23/putin-and-stalin-mirror-reflections/

Radzinsky, Edvard. *Stalin*. New York: Doubleday, 1996.

Randall, Francis B. *Diary and Journal of Francis B. Randall*. Guide to the Gay Humphrey Matthaei and Francis B. Randall collection of Photographs, Films, and Clippings. 1954–2010. 1954. The Matthaei/Randall Collection of Photographs, Films, and Clippings. Box 1, Folder 1, Rare Book and Manuscript Library, Columbia University Library.

Rees, E. A. "Introduction: Leader Cults: Varieties, Preconditions and Functions." In Balāzs Apor, Jan C. Behrends, Polly Jones, and E. A. Rees, *The Leader Cult in*

Communist Dictatorships: Stalin and the Eastern Bloc. Hampshire, UK: Palgrave Macmillan, 2004.

Reisner, Oliver. *Die Schule der Georgischen Nation: Eine Sozialhistorische Untersuchung der Nationalen Bewegung in Georgien am Beispiel der 'Gesellschaft zur Vorbereitung der Lese-und Scheibkunde unter den Georgiern' (1850–1917)*. Wiesbaden, 2004.

———. "Georgia: The Making of a National Culture." International Conference at the University of Michigan, Ann Arbor, May 18, 2008.

"Report to Washington on Montgomery's Conversation with Stalin." January 17, 1947. History and Public Policy Program Digital Archive, National Archives of the UK. http://digitalarchive.wilsoncenter.org/document/134377.

"Represii XX veka: pamyat' o blizkikh." VTsIOM, October 5, 2018. https://wciom.ru/index.php?id=236&uid=9344.

Rieber, Alfred J. "Stalin, Man of the Borderlands." *American Historical Review* 106, no. 5 (December 2001): 1651–91.

Ritzer, George. *The McDonaldization of Society*, 3rd ed. Thousand Oaks, CA: Pine Forge, 2000.

Rubin, Julia. "Meditations on Russia: Yeltsin Calls for a New National Idea." Associated Press, August 2, 1996. http://www.apnewsarchive.com/1996/Meditations-on-Russia-Yeltsin-Calls-for-New-National-Idea-/id-122cd732a8cf8b35989afeec4db69dcd.

Rukhadze, Vasili. "Kolektiuri Mekhsiereba." Pirvelebi, n.d. 2010. https://iberiana.wordpress.com/iberiana/rukhadze2/.

Russian Federation. Gosudarstvennaya programma "Patrioticheskoye vospitanie grazhdan RF na 2006–2010 gody." Kremlin.ru, 2010. http://www.ed.gov.ru/junior/new_version/gragd_patr_vospit_molod/gosprog/.

Russian Federation. "Ukaz Prezidenta Rossiyskoy Federatsii ot 29.12.2012 g. № 1710." Kremlin.ru, December 29, 2012. http://www.kremlin.ru/acts/bank/36611.

Russian Federation. "Zakonoproekt № 102766-6 O vnesenii izmeneniy v otdel'nye zakonodatel'niye akty Rossiyskoy Federatsii v chasti regulirovaniya deyatel'nosti nekommercheskikh organizatsiy, vypolnyayush'ikh funktsii inostrannogo agenta." State Duma of the Russian Federation, 2013. http://asozd2.duma.gov.ru/main.nsf/%28SpravkaNew%29?OpenAgent&RN=102766-6&02.

Ryan, Karen L. *Stalin: In Russian Satire, 1917–1991*. Madison, WI: University of Wisconsin Press, 2009.

Sabbagh, Dan, and Vikram Dodd. "BLM Organisers Call Off London Event to Avoid Clashes with Far Right." *Guardian*, June 11, 2020. https://www.theguardian.com/uk-news/2020/jun/11/blm-organisers-call-off-london-event-to-prevent-clashes-with-far-right.

Safire, William. "Essay; Putinism Looms." *New York Times*, January 31, 2000. https://www.nytimes.com/2000/01/31/opinion/essay-putinism-looms.html.

"Sakartvelos umaghlesi sabchos tavmjdomaris Zviad Gamsakhurdias saakhaltslo mimartva televiziit." *Sakartvelos Respublika* 1, no. 12 (January 1, 1991): n.p.

Sakwa, Richard. *Gorbachev and His Reforms, 1985–1990*. Deddington, Oxon: Philip Allan, 1990.

Saluashvili, Mikheil. *Otkhmotsdatertmeti: sakartvelos prezidenti Zviad Gamsakhurdia*. Tbilisi, Georgia: Khma Erisa, 1995.
Santner, Eric. "History Beyond the Pleasure Principle." In Saul Friedlander, ed., *Probing the Limits of Representation: Nazism and the "Final Solution."* Cambridge, MA: Harvard University Press, 1992.
Sasse, Gwendolyn, and Félix Krawatzek. "Young Russians Want Putin to Step Back from Power." Carnegie Europe, June 24, 2020. https://carnegieeurope.eu/2020/06/24/young-russians-want-putin-to-step-back-from-power-pub-82357.
Scott, Erik. *Familiar Strangers: The Georgian Diaspora and the Evolution of the Soviet Empire*. London: Oxford University Press, 2016.
Sedikides, Constantine, Tim Wildschut, and Denise Baden. "Nostalgia: Conceptual Issues and Existential Functions." In Jeff Greenberg, Sander L. Koole, and Tom Pyszczynski, eds., *Handbook of Experimental Existential Psychology*. New York: Guilford, 2004.
Sedikides, Constantine, Tim Wildschut, Jamie Arndt, and Clay Routledge. "Nostalgia: Past, Present, and Future." *Current Directions in Psychological Science* 17, no. 5 (2008): 304–7.
Seleznyova, Antonina V. "Obraz prezidenta Rossii V.V. Putina v soznanii rossiyskikh grazhdan." *Russkaya Politologiya* (2018): 4–11.
Shantall, Hester Maria. "A Heuristic Study of the Meaning of Suffering Among Holocaust Survivors." University of South Africa. June 1, 1996. https://uir.unisa.ac.za/handle/10500/16020.
Sharpe, Matthew. "Alexander Dugin, Eurasianism, and the American Election." *Conversation*, November 13, 2017. https://theconversation.com/alexander-dugin-eurasianism-and-the-american-election-87367.
Shebelist, Serhii. "Leninfall: The Lack of Adequate Commemoration Policy in Ukraine Provokes the New Tide of the War of Monuments." *Day.Kyiv.ua*, September 30, 2013. https://day.kyiv.ua/en/article/society/leninfall.
Sherlock, Thomas. "Confronting the Stalinist Past: The Politics of Memory in Russia." *Washington Quarterly* 34, no. 2 (October 2009): 93–109.
Shlapentokh, Vladimir. "Putin as a Flexible Politician. Does He Imitate Stalin?" *Communist and Post-Communist Studies* 41, no. 2 (June 2008): 205–16.
Shogren, Elizabeth. "Soviets Pursue an American Dream: Trends: Once Cursed in the Soviet Union, U.S. Pop Culture—from 'Tarzan' to Rap—Is Where It's At." *Los Angeles Times*, August 1, 1991. https://www.newspapers.com/newspage/175295533/.
Shokarev, Sergey. "Prezident V. V. Putin ob 'izvrasheniyakh' nashey istorii." *Istoricheskaya Ekspertiza* 4, no. 1 (2017): 142–44.
Shulman, Ekaterina. "Navyazannaya Lyubov': Zachem gospropaganda risuyet reiting Stalinu." Recording of the oral presentation at the conference *Aktsiya: Anti-Stalin*. Sakharov Center, Moscow, Russia. June 23, 2017. YouTube video, 24:52. https://www.youtube.com/watch?v=O4WKYgWY-CM.
Smith, Kathleen E. *Mythmaking in the New Russia: Politics and Memory in the Yeltsin Era*. Ithaca, NY: Cornell University Press, 2002.

Smith, Trevor J. "The Collapse of the Lenin Personality Cult in Soviet Russia, 1985–1995." *Historian* 60, no. 2 (Winter 1998): 325–43.

———. "Lenin for Sale: The Rise and Fall of the Personality Cult of V. I. Lenin in Soviet Russia, 1935–1995." Master's thesis, University of Ottawa, 1995: 34–96.

Snyder, Timothy. *Bloodlands: Europe Between Hitler and Stalin*. New York: Basic, 2010.

———. "Hitler vs. Stalin: Who Killed More?" *New York Review of Books*, March 10, 2011. https://www.nybooks.com/articles/2011/03/10/hitler-vs-stalin-who-killed-more/.

"Speech by President Dmitry Medvedev: Pamyat' o natsional'nykh tragediyakh tak zhe svyashchenna, kak pamyat' o pobedakh." Kremlin.ru, October 30, 2009. http://kremlin.ru/video/256.

Staub, Ervin. "Blind versus Constructive Patriotism: Moving from Embeddedness in the Group to Critical Loyalty and Action." In Daniel Bar-Tal and Ervin Staub, eds., *Patriotism: In the Lives of Individuals and Nations*. Nelson-Hall, 1997.

Stone, Oliver. *The Full Transcripts of the Putin Interviews: Oliver Stone Interviews Vladimir Putin*. New York: Hot Books, an Imprint of Skyhorse Publishing, 2017.

Strunk, Mildred. *Public Opinion, 1935–1946*. Princeton: Princeton University Press, 1951.

Suny, Ronald. "Rethinking Social Identities: Class and Nationality." In *The Revenge of the Past: Nationalism, Revolution and the Collapse of the Former Soviet Union*. Stanford, CA: Stanford University Press, 1993.

Surmanidze, Lali, and Lia Tsuladze. "The Formation of Nation-State and Cultural Identity: A Georgian Perspective." *IBSU Scientific Journal* 2, no. 2 (2008): 87–102.

Sutcliffe, Carol Maurine. "The Role of Teachers in the Identity Formation of Adolescents Restrained in Their Becoming." University of South Africa, November 1996. https://core.ac.uk/download/pdf/43175455.pdf.

Sztompka, Piotr. "Sotsialnoye izmeneniye kak travma," *Sotsiologicheskiye issledovaniya* 1, no. 1 (2001): 6–16.

Tabarovsky, Izabella. "The Price of Silence: Family Memory of Stalin's Repressions." *Wilson Quarterly* (Fall 2016). https://www.wilsonquarterly.com/quarterly/the-lasting-legacy-of-the-cold-war/the-price-of-silence-family-memory-of-stalins-repressions/.

Taylor, Adam. "How McDonald's Went from Hero to Zero in Russia." *Washington Post*, April 16, 2014. https://www.washingtonpost.com/news/worldviews/wp/2014/04/16/how-mcdonalds-went-from-hero-to-zero-in-russia/.

Tevzadze, Gigi. "The Birth of the Georgian Nation: Identity and Ideology, Political and Societal Identities, Nationality and Religiosity." *Identity Studies* 1, no. 1 (January 2009): 5–21.

———. "Georgia at the Crossroads of European and Asian Cultures." Speech at Symposium, Harriman Institute at Columbia University," May 4, 2009.

Toidze, Levan. *Interventsiats, okupatsiats, dzaldatanebiti gasabchoebats, paktobrivi anektsiats*. Tbilisi, Georgia: Metsniereba, 1991.

Toria, Malkhaz. "The Soviet Occupation of Georgia in 1921 and the Russian-Georgian War of August 2008: Historical Analogy as a Memory Project." In S.

F. Jones, ed., *The Making of Modern Georgia, 1918–2012: The First Georgian Republic and its Successors.* London: Routledge, 2014.
Trevelyan, Mark. "Curator Hides Stalin Mementoes from Russian Bombs." Reuters, August 31, 2008. https://www.reuters.com/article/idINIndia-35253120080831.
Trotsky, Leon. *Stalin: An Appraisal of the Man and His Influence.* New York: Harper & Brothers, 1941.
Tsuladze, Lia. "Georgian Dilemma: Concerns for National Identity and Quests for Europeanness." *European Studies* 12, no. 1 (2018): 37–62.
Tucker, Robert C. "A Case of Mistaken Identity: Djughashvili-Stalin." *Biography* 5, no. 1 (Winter 1982): 18.
———. *Stalin as Revolutionary, 1879–1929: A Study in History and Personality.* New York: Norton, 1973.
Turchenkp, Sergey. "Krovaviy reys #6883." *Trud*, February 8, 2000. https://archive.is/20130416214702/www.fsb.ru/fsb/history/author/single.htm!id%3D10318151@fsbPublication.html#selection-281.14-281.16.
Turovsky, Daniil. "Russian City Opens Cultural Centre Celebrating Stalin." *Guardian*, January 11, 2016. https://www.theguardian.com/world/2016/jan/11/stalin-russia-penza-cultural-centre-meduza.
Vekua, Marine, and Ramaz Lominadze. "The Long Way of Georgia to Europe." *Politické Vedy* 4, no. 1 (2017): 134–52.
"Vladimir Putin, Press Conference after Visiting the Butovo Memorial Site." Kremlin.ru, October 30, 2007. http://archive.kremlin.ru/eng/speeches/2007/10/30/1918_type82912type82915_149844.s html.
Volčič, Zala. "Yugo-Nostalgia: Cultural Memory and Media in the Former Yugoslavia." *Critical Studies in Media Communication* 24, no. 1 (March 2007): 21–38.
Volkan, Vamık D. "Chosen Trauma: The Political Ideology of Entitlement and Violence." Paper presented at Berlin Meeting, June 10, 2004.
———. "Large Group Identity and Chosen Trauma." *Psyche* 54, no. 9 (2000): 931–53.
———. "Le trauma massif: l'idéologie politique du droit et de la violence." *Revue française de psychoanalyse* 71, no. 4 (2007): 1047–59.
Volkov, Denis. "Podberut cheloveka: chto dumayut rossiiskiye izberateli o probleme-2024." RBC, May 14, 2019. https://www.rbc.ru/opinions/politics/14/05/2019/5cda6f089a794770fbfb5ec9.
"Vozmozhniy preemnik V. Putin na postu prezidenta Rossii." Levada Center, January 20, 2014. Web.
Wakamiya, Lisa Ryoko. "Post-Soviet Contexts and Trauma Studies." *Slavonica* 17, no. 2 (November 2011): 134–44.
Weiss, Phillip W. *Comparing Hitler and Stalin: Certain Cultural Considerations.* Graduate Center, City University of New York, 2014.
"Welcome to the Council of Europe in Georgia." Council of Europe, accessed on March 23, 2021. https://www.coe.int/en/web/tbilisi/field-office/overview.
Wheeler, Angela. "Restored: Architectural and Territorial Integrity in the Republic of Georgia." *Aesthetics of Decay*, unpublished (April 4, 2015).

Winning, Alexander. "Communists Mark Anniversary of Stalin's Death." *Moscow Times*, March 5, 2013. https://www.themoscowtimes.com/2013/03/05/communists-mark-anniversary-of-stalins-death-a22089.

Yurchak, Alexei. *Everything Was Forever, Until It Was No More: The Last Soviet Generation*. Princeton, NJ: Princeton University Press, 2005.

Zerubavel, Eviatar. *Time Maps, Collective Memory and the Social Shape of the Past*. Chicago: University of Chicago Press, 2003.

Zimmerman, William. *Ruling Russia: Authoritarianism from the Revolution to Putin*. Princeton, NJ: Princeton University Press, 2014.

"Zurab Zhvania addressed the Council of Europe." Uploaded on February 10, 2010, YouTube. Web.

"Zviad Gamsakhurdia's Speech of May 26, 1990." July 2, 2010.

Index

Abkhazia, 38, 40, 117, 121
Abuladze, Tengiz, 29, 100–101
Academy of Arts in Tbilisi, 47
Aeroflot flight 6833 hijacking, 110n14
April 9, 1989 event, 40, 51, 116
Arab Spring, 107
August War of 2008. *See* Georgia-Russia War of 2008

Bagrati Cathedral, 37
bank robbery in 1907, 30, 53, 62n88
Battle of Stalingrad, 98
Bedia, Erik, 7–9;
   The Communist, 7.
   See also Chichua-Bedia, Nina
Berdzenishvili, Merab, 38
Beria, Lavrenti, 7–8, 37, 52, 100
Bolshevik Revolution. *See* October Revolution of 1917
Bourke-White, Margaret, 1, 5, 23
Boym, Svetlana, 128–29
Brezhnev, Leonid, 27, 74, 90, 130

Chavchavadze, Ilia, 54
Chichua, Ekaterine, 8
Chichua-Bedia, Nina, 7–9, 133
Cold War, 20, 69
Columbia University, 1–2, 23;
   Harriman Institute, 1–2, 12n4, 133

Cromwell, Oliver, 87

de-Nazification, 15.
   See also Nazi Germany
de-Sovietization, 24, 42
de-Stalinization, 3, 15–16, 24–28, 38–48, 57, 65, 74–75, 87–90, 115, 121, 127
The Death of Stalin, 29, 97–100.
   See also Armando Iannucci
Demonstrations in 2011–2012, anti-Putin, 107
Dud', Yury, 81n13
Dugin, Alexander, 90–91, 102–5

Euromaidan, 92, 120
European Broadcasting Union, 21
Eurovision Song Contest, 21

Filippov, Alexander, 69
The Foreign Agent Law, 77, 83n43

Gamsakhurdia, Zviad, 11, 48, 117, 121
Georgia-Russia War of 2008, 3, 4, 20–21, 26, 36–38, 40, 50, 56, 100, 130–31
Georgian Democratic Republic, 6, 41, 50, 116
Georgian Dream, 3, 26, 42–44, 57

Georgian identity, 38–43, 47–48.
  See also national identity
Georgian Ministry of Culture, 37,
  42, 44
Georgian Museum of Literature, 130
Georgian National Museum, 35
Georgian Orthodox Church, 116
Georgian Public Broadcaster, 21
Gessen, Masha, 99
glasnost', 1, 50, 54, 65, 88–89, 100,
  105, 122
Glinka, Mikhail, 1, 74, 81n28
Gorbachev, Mikhail, 15–16, 27, 66, 75,
  88, 95, 105, 121
Great Patriotic War, 5, 8, 28, 52–56,
  70–75, 86–87, 90, 98–102, 118–27,
  130, 133
Great Terror, 5, 15–16, 47, 54, 86,
  94n1, 119.
  See also Stalin's purges and
  repressions
Gryzlov, Boris, 74
Gulag History Museum, 88

hierarchy of suffering, 119, 125n19
historical propaganda, 93
Hitler, Adolf, 15, 17
Hitler-Stalin Pact, 4, 100, 105
Holocaust, 10, 53
House of Terror. See "Italian Villa"
House of Tolerance, 44

Iannucci, Armando, 29, 97–100.
  See also de-Nazification
Ikhlov, Eugene, 22–23
  Stalinshchina, 22–23
Iron Curtain, 24, 52, 65
"Italian Villa," 6–7.
  See also House of Terror
Ivanishvili, Bidzina, 3, 45, 55, 57

Jefferson, Thomas, 93

Katyn Massacre, 4, 69, 71, 81n22,
  89–90

Kennan, George F., 17
Khrushchev, Nikita, 3, 15, 27, 38,
  44–48, 74, 88, 103.
  See also "Secret Speech"
Kostava, Merab, 48, 50

Lenin, Vladimir, 38–39, 54, 66, 73, 75,
  92, 105–6.
  See also Lenin Mausoleum
Lenin Mausoleum, 3, 38
"Leninfall," 92–93

Maglakelidze, Robert, 37
Makharadze, Philipe, 6
  See also "Italian Villa"
McDonald's, 65–67
Medinsky, Vladimir, 76, 98–99
Medvedev, Dmitry, 76–77, 89–90
Merkel, Angela, 120
Metchitov, Yuri, 44
Mikhalkov, Sergei, 73–74
Millennial Generation, 23–24, 68, 85
Ministry of Culture of the Russian
  Federation, 76, 97–98.
  See also Vladimir Medinsky
Mkhedrioni Movement, 51
Molotov-Ribbentrop Pact, 69, 120
Montefiore, Simon Sebag, 1, 5, 10,
  25, 85
Museum of Soviet Occupation, 26,
  35–37, 43–45

national anthem, 73–74
national identity, 20–25, 55–56, 70, 79,
  85, 116, 123–27
  See also Georgian identity
  See also post-Soviet identity
  See also Russian identity
National Liberation Movement, 116
Nazism. See Nazi Germany
Nazi Germany, 5, 9, 15–16, 27, 36–38,
  65, 69–72, 76–78, 86, 98, 119–20
neofascism, 71
NKVD, 7, 8, 36
nomenklatura, 99, 122

October Revolution of 1917, 6, 46, 105
Orakhelashvili, Mamia, 6
Orjonikidze, Sergo, 52
Orwell, George 72

"Patriots' Camps," 41
perestroika, 1, 54, 65, 75, 105, 122
Perm-36 Memorial Museum, 77, 82n42
Peskov, Dmitry, 103
Peter the Great, 66, 78
post-Soviet identity, 28, 71, 74, 116, 120, 122
Putin, Vladimir, 11, 18, 21, 27, 55, 65–70, 75, 79, 86–89, 98, 101–8, 119–34

Randall, Francis B., 2, 5
re-Stalinization, 28, 57, 65–67. *See also* de-Stalinization
Red Army, 8, 26, 28, 50, 66, 71, 76, 117
Repentance, 29, 100, 110n14
Rose Revolution, 25
Roskomnadzor, 69
Rurua, Nikoloz, 36
Russian Military History Society, 76
Russian national identity, 87
Russian Orthodox Church, 105, 123
Rossiyskaya Gazeta, 122
"Russkiy mir" (Russian world), 71, 103

Saakashvili, Mikheil, 3, 11, 24–26, 35–37, 40–45, 57, 120, 130
sanctions, 66–67
"Secret Speech," 3–4, 27, 45–48, 53, 95nn11–12
Seliger National Youth Forum, 87

Shevardnadze, Eduard, 24, 121, 125n25
sistema, 15, 45, 108–9, 113n52
South Ossetia, 38, 40, 117, 121
SovLab, 47
Stalin Center in Penza, 77–78
Stalin Museum, 2–12, 36–43, 52, 55, 76, 100, 127, 133
Stalin's purges and repressions, 3, 6–9, 68, 72, 78, 88–89, 118–119, 133
State Archives of the Russian Federation, 120
Student demonstrations in 1956, 47

Tsereteli, Akaky, 54

United National Movement, 3, 35–36, 40–44, 50, 57
United Nations, 16, 18;
  General Assembly, 16
  Security Council, 16
United Russia, 74

Valdai International Discussion Club, 122
Voroshilov, Kliment, 101

Washington, George, 93

Yalta Conference, 16, 72
Yeltsin, Boris, 65, 74–75, 99, 116, 121–23

Zhvania, Zurab, 24, 33n31
Zourabichvili, Salome, 38
Zyuganov, Gennady, 75

About the Author

Tinatin Japaridze serves as the Director of Policy and Strategy at The Critical Mass and brings over fifteen years of international relations, media, communications, and security experience. She previously worked for the City of New York, first as the Field and Digital Community Engagement Specialist at the NYC Census, a Mayoral initiative, and later as the Press Secretary for New York's COVID-19 Response at NYC Health & Hospitals. Previously, she was the United Nations Bureau Chief for Eastern European media outlets and a UN Radio host and producer of her own radio show on current affairs and security in the international arena. She is an accomplished journalist and is fluent in four languages including English, Russian, Georgian, and French, and is proficient in Ukrainian. Her work on US-Russian relations and Eurasian security has been widely published by various media outlets, including the *Moscow Times*, the *Washington Post*, and the *Atlantic*. In 2019, she became a Carnegie Council for Ethics in International Affairs student ambassador on cyber ethics and digital leadership. Tinatin also serves as a mentor at Girl Security, a nonprofit that aims to close the gender gap in the security sector, focusing on both national and information security-related matters. Over this past year, she worked as a "Go Big" officer at the European Leadership Network (ELN), crafting a digital campaign to extend the New START Treaty between Russia and the United States. In 2021, she became a member of the ELN's Younger Generation Leaders Network and a fellow of the National Endowment for Democracy-funded Eurasia Democratic Security Network. Tinatin Japaridze holds a bachelor's degree from Columbia University's School of General Studies, and a master's degree in Russian Regional Studies with focus on cybersecurity and digital diplomacy from Columbia University's Harriman Institute. *Stalin's Millennials: Nostalgia, Trauma, and Nationalism* is Japaridze's debut monograph, and she is currently working on her second manuscript.

www.ingramcontent.com/pod-product-compliance
Lightning Source LLC
Chambersburg PA
CBHW020124010526
44115CB00008B/960